BASEBALL TOWN

ALSO BY BOB WHITTEMORE:
All We Had Was Us (1992)

BASEBALL TOWN

A Place Where

Yankees Grow

By Bob Whittemore

Marshall Jones Company
Publishers Since 1902
Manchester Center, Vermont

©Robert Whittemore, 1995
Library of Congress Catalog Card Number 95-075080

I.S.B.N. 0-8338-0218-6 (Hardcover)
I.S.B.N. 0-8338-0219-4 (Paperback)

Printed in the United States of America

DEDICATION

To Brad, a son and a pal, who passed away in 1979.
He was a part of the baseball scene and would enjoy this book.

ACKNOWLEDGEMENT

D uring the two years of work which went into the preparation of this book, I was blessed along the way by family and friends who willingly volunteered to lend a hand in many ways.

This is a sincere note of thanks to all and an apology to those I might have inadvertently missed.

A special note of thanks to my devoted wife Betty who spent hours at the computer compiling lists and rewriting chapters; and to daughter Beth who logged even more hours working out computer technicalities. Beth and her husband Terry who made room for us in their home and gave us full use of computer facilities. Daughter Barbara and her husband Joe accepted my crazy hours and opened their home to my frequent and often unscheduled visits. I am grateful to them and our son Brian and his wife Jan for the hours they spent perusing the book and discussing all phases of the project.

My gratitude to Frank Hart, a lifelong friend who proved every bit as good an editor as he is a friend.

To the New York Yankees, who graciously granted permission for use of their logo, a note of thanks. Over the years they have been warm and friendly hosts at Yankee Stadium and at their Spring Training facilities in Florida.

A special thanks to my friend Artie Richman in the Yankee front office who always answered my calls.

The Nader family contributed mightily to this effort and are important to the story and to its development.

Thanks to the players, coaches and managers who have passed our way, without whom there would be no story.

I cannot forget Ed and Joan Dorr for their patience and understanding in the early days and for their professional handling of an often difficult job. Nor can I forget Merilyn Sargent, an old and true friend whose help down the stretch was invaluable.

The staff at Huntington Library in Oneonta were most pleasant and cooperative in making files and records available at a moment's notice.

My gratitude to Bill Guilfoile, a very special friend, and his colleague Jeff Idelson at the National Baseball Hall of Fame and to Tom Heitz, former researcher and librarian at the national shrine for their patience, support and cooperation over a very long period.

A warm thanks to Dick Cavanagh, the best public address man the NY-P League ever knew and one of the best friends I will ever have. His knowledge of baseball is astounding, his recall of events and people incredible. He pushed me to get going on this project and I will always be grateful.

A note of gratitude to Andrew Gross, young writer who covered the O-Yanks for the *Daily Star* in the early nineties. He was also a willing and helpful accomplice. A gratitude to photographer Julie Lewis and librarian Barbara Allison of the *Daily Star* for their help in ferreting out pictures and Editor Ken Hall for his help and encouragement.

The research is a long and exhausting process and results often depend upon the work of those who have gone before. I therefore offer my gratitude to those who make up what will pass for my bibliography. They include:

Baseball's Canadian-American League by David Peitrusza; *Diamonds in the Rough* by Ken Rappaport; the *Canadian-American League Orange Book*; *The New York-Penn League Record Book*; *The Sporting Eye*, a weekly paper written and edited by Mike Brown; the *Daily Star* in Oneonta; the old *Oneonta Herald*; the *Evening-Sunday Press* in Binghamton; the *Rome Daily Sentinel*; the *Amsterdam Recorder* and the *Utica Newspapers*.

—*Bob Whittemore*

PROLOGUE

A train, more than 100 cars long, crept through Oneonta, New York on the Delaware and Hudson Railroad carrying freight toward the Port of Albany and New England destinations. It was a cool morning in late April, 1966.

On one side of the tracks was Neahwa Park (in which was located the ballpark in later years renamed Damaschke Field). It was home for the Oneonta Red Sox where Manager Matt Sczesny was getting ready for batting practice.

On the other side of the long freight was Harry Greenfield, an outfielder struggling with a .103 batting average. Greenfield knew it would cost him if he was late for practice. For one thing, he would be fined but, more important, he might lose his outfield job and like all of the athletes which made up that team, he desperately wanted to be in the lineup every day.

The train seemed endless. What to do?

Harry Greenfield did what any red-blooded American boy would do in a spot like that. He jumped onto one of the slowly moving freight cars, clambered over the roof and down the ladder on the other side of the car.

He made it safely, was on time for practice, his hitting began to improve and he made the lineup every day. When the feisty little manager found out days later what Greenfield had done, he gave his outfielder the required chewing-out and then patted him on the butt. Sczesny liked that kind of competitive spirit in his athletes.

Greenfield typified that 1966 New York-Penn League team, last to play the full-season schedule of 125 games. They were a free-wheeling bunch, featuring guys like Jack Mountain, Joe Sylvonic, Fred Wolcott, Cat Shitanishi, and a kid named Amos Otis on his way to major league stardom. The club roster was dominated by the last of a dying breed— the career minor leaguer—and they played with a dash and a fury never seen again at Damaschke.

The fans loved them and attendance was good despite terrible weather most of the summer.

Also, the 1966 team brought organized baseball back to Oneonta after a 15 year absence and the fans enjoyed just being back at the ballpark to watch the pros.

The Oneonta club stayed with the Boston organization through the

1966 season but became a New York Yankee farm club in the winter of 1966-67. The rest is history—in the ensuing quarter century, the Oneonta Yankees proceeded to ring up the best won-lost record in all organized baseball.

No team, in the majors or the minors, won more consistently than have the O-Yanks. In the process of compiling that record, the Oneonta club captured 13 regular season titles and 11 playoff championships! When you add the fact that, when the 1994 major league season began, 25 of the 28 clubs listed a former O-Yank player, coach or manager on the roster it is easy to see why club officials and the entire community developed a sense of pride which remains strong to this day.

This is the story of the Oneonta Yankees. This is the story of players like Andy Bottin whose war-scarred legs couldn't meet the challenge of his magnificent heart.

It is the story of players like Don Mattingly and Willie McGee—each went on to be named the major leagues' most Valuable Player in the same year, 1985—Mattingly in the American League and McGee in the National League.

It is the story of scores of players who went on to realize their ambition to play in "the bigs" and hundreds who didn't make it.

It is the story of lovable characters like pitcher Wayne "Boom-Boom" Crowder, whose E.R.A. once soared to the 37.51 mark and infielder Brian Engle who hit a ball over the fence in Auburn and stood watching at the plate. When O-Yank manager Jerry Walker yelled, "Run, Brian, run," Engle—still standing at the plate—answered, "But Skip, I don't have a home run trot. I never hit one before."

It is the story of managers like Walker, George Case, Mike Ferraro, Art Mazmanian, Ken Berry, Buck Showalter, Gary Allenson and Trey Hillman who led their young charges to NY-P League championships and etched their names indelibly into Oneonta sports records not only as managers but of teachers and leaders of young men.

And it is the story of Albert S. Nader, the son of immigrant parents, whose great love for his family, his city and for baseball (in that order) has produced this story of victory on and off the field, of immense camaraderie among fans and players, of success almost unmatched anywhere the grand old game is played.

This a book about kids playing the game on grass fields in tiny ballparks where the fans are close enough to see the agony on the face of an athlete who has just struck out with the winning run on base.

It is about rookies who make incredible plays and moments later, equally unbelievable mistakes, each the result of intense effort—something you see a lot in the minors.

It is about an owner who takes no salary but whose love of the game and his ballclub enables him to work year 'round, 10 to 15 hours a day in season sitting at an aged typewriter in a tiny office steamy hot in summer and icy cold in fall and spring.

It is about the New York Yankees who have treated their farm team in rural New York with warmth and genuine concern. This, incidentally, is a big reason for the club's success.

But mostly it is the story of a community and its love affair with the game of baseball, a love affair which has endured for more than 130 years.

There are many reasons for selecting Oneonta, New York as the scene for this book—a winning record which stands almost unmatched in baseball annals; a ball park which is the oldest consecutively used park in the country; family ownership stretching back more than a quarter century.

Also in many respects the Oneonta story is the story of minor league baseball throughout the land where thousands of little people have stood by their game for a century or more.

This is a look at some of those little people; the owners who struggled to make ends meet; the players who gave so much in their effort to get to The Show; the umpires who live an incredible life at the Class A level and the fans (once called "cranks") who were there on cold, rainy nights and on nights when it was so hot you could fry an egg on the sidewalk.

It should be remembered that, in most cases, Oneonta was the site of the young player's first season as a professional athlete or a young manager's debut. There are many things to learn other than baseball fundamentals...many adjustments to be made in a young man's personal life (frequently, there is a severe battle against homesickness). A player may remain in baseball for years at all levels but the memory of the first year remains strong. It is made even better by the memory of a pennant and the championship ring given by an appreciative Oneonta Yankee management.

It is the total atmosphere, the charisma, which breeds success and causes men like Buck Showalter to say "the good Lord blessed us by letting us start out in Oneonta."

Or George Steinbrenner to remark "I know of no better place for a young athlete to start his professional baseball career than Oneonta, New York."

Somewhere along the line it occurred to me and to alert editors that there didn't seem to be any "bad guys" in the story. And you know what? There have been very few.

Oh sure, there were players and managers and coaches who had their bad moments; there were those with whom I had private and personal conversations over a few beers when on the road. Those were confidential moments resulting in trusts I cannot break.

Serious dissension in the clubhouse has been rare; there just isn't time in the minors to get involved to that extent. When such a problem did appear it was usually nipped in the bud by an astute manager. And finally, the possibility of a fine and a blot on the record would stop a career-minded player.

More than 850 young men have passed through Oneonta with dreams of reaching The Show. In all the years there have been just three minor incidents involving the local police...all were minor. Those episodes were dismissed.

I have not broken confidences in telling this story nor have I embellished. This is simply the way it happened.

—*Bob Whittemore*

TABLE OF CONTENTS

Appendix

" One of the sweet rewards of being baseball commissioner is that you see the country, the cities of the majors and the minors. If you want to enjoy baseball at its best, go see the Oneonta (New York) Yankees where the little family that owns the franchise also cooks the hot dogs. Don Mattingly broke in there. "

Former Baseball Commissioner Peter Ueberroth in his book, "Made in America."

" I know of no better place for a young athlete to start his baseball career than Oneonta, New York. "

George Steinbrenner, Principal Owner, New York Yankees

" I've met and been exposed to some quality people along the way, but none as sincere as the people and leaders of the Oneonta community and baseball operations. "

Buck Showalter, 1985-86 Oneonta Yankees Manager and 1994 American League Manager of the Year with the New York Yankees

1 SAM

T he debut of the Oneonta Yankees in 1967 was no spur of the moment decision by baseball officials sitting around some smoke-filled room tossing darts at a board which listed several cities anxious to get into organized baseball.

Baseball returned to the *"City of Hills"* largely because of the dedication and unceasing efforts of one man. There were other men of good will, men who loved their city and the game of baseball and who were willing to put time and money into the effort. But it was Albert S. "Sam" Nader who was, and still is, the prime mover of professional baseball in Oneonta.

Sam Nader gets things done. Always has. Now in his seventies, he puts in a full day at his non-paying job as general manager of the Oneonta Yankees. Actually he is chairman of the board, CEO and whatever other title one wishes to bestow.

Tuffets of grey hair jut out from his Yankee cap and his eyes peer out from under the brim as he bustles about the tiny office which is Oneonta Yankee headquarters. As he sits in front of his aging typewriter he adjusts his Yankee sweater and checks the time on his Yankee watch.

Nobody has ever asked but it is quite possible that he is wearing Yankee shorts. He is a Yankee man for the duration and that's for sure.

Asked at the close of the 1994 season, which was not one of the best in the O-Yank annals from the standpoint of wins and losses as well as attendance, whether he would be back in 1995, he replied, "What do you want me to do, die? Of course I'll be back; we have an agreement with the big club and a rejuvenated ballpark. This is no time to step down.

"Besides, I want to go out a winner."

That sums up Sam Nader. A loyal Yankee man to the hilt, a hard worker for whom a 16-hour day is nothing special. He wants to win; he wants his Yanks to win; he wants pinstripe pride to return to Oneonta.

Winning is something to which he has become accustomed. He has won personally with a loving family strong enough to survive deep personal tragedy. He has won professionally, rising to a high position in his company. And he has won in the community, capturing public office by winning tough elections against heavy odds.

Winning is no accident. Nader is a strong man; you realize that as soon as you shake his hand. He has a pleasant grin and a friendly manner. He can a best friend or a tough enemy, but if you play square with Sam Nader he'll play square with you.

But he has had time to relax, too. He loves to play golf and his foursomes with Buck Showalter, Monk Meyer and Bill Hughes were legendary at Oneonta Country Club. He has been a New York Giant football fan for years and still holds season tickets.

He is proud of his Lebanese heritage, handling jokes about the Lebanese with good humor, and coming back with an Italian or an Irish joke - whatever fits the occasion.

His career with the O-Yanks hasn't been all roses. There are those who criticize the way he runs the ballclub and those who say he regards it as his own private domain and will tolerate no interference. Not long ago a group showed interest in buying his team. It's not for sale.

"I know about the critics," says Nader. "To them I say come forward, share your ideas and let's talk. Until they do and until they show me a better way, we'll go on the way we have been going.

"And for those who constantly push me to sell beer at the ballpark I can only say that I will not change my position against it."

Sam Nader learned many of the rules by which he lives from his hard-working, deeply religious immigrant parents.

Elias Nader and his wife arrived in America from Lebanon in 1911 and, with assistance from a cousin who preceded him, found his way to Oneonta. Sam's father landed a job as a laborer with the Delaware and Hudson Railroad (D&H) at a time when it seemed as if everyone worked for the railroad. Life centered around the D&H; anyone from Oneonta was quick to tell you the D&H roundhouse was the biggest in the world.

The Naders took up residence in Oneonta's low-lying area between the Susquehanna River and the Delaware and Hudson Railroad, an area once known as "the Lower Deck", and began to raise a family.

Sometimes life could be difficult as the family adjusted to life in their new homeland. A large colony of Lebanese Catholics lived in The Lower Deck, along with other immigrant families of many nationalities, and there were times when they felt prejudice. Sam Nader can remember seeing Klu Klux Klan crosses burning on the hillsides overlooking the Sixth Ward, but it did not cool his love for the area and city and he remains a resident of the Sixth Ward.

One of six Nader children, young Sam worked, as did the entire family, sometimes handling three jobs. He found time to play baseball having fallen in love with the game as a youngster. He proved quite good at it and after a successful high school career, he went on to Bates College where he became a varsity pitcher. Despite his success, Sam insists to this day that his older brother Naussif, who died several years ago, was a better player.

But there was little time for the brothers to pursue the baseball dream and they went to work. Sam went back to college for one term, but never graduated; the family came first.

He carved out a career in industry, spending 43 of his working years at a plant in Sidney, known locally to this day as "Bendix" even though the corporate name has changed many times over the years. He rose to upper level management with the firm and did so well he became a consultant after retiring from Bendix.

When World War II came along it was only natural for Sam Nader to answer the call. He served in the Army and saw action in the European Theater with a heavy machine gun company of the 28th Infantry Division.

After returning home, he married Alice House, daughter of a respected Oneonta doctor and a member of the family which first settled Oneonta. She became a prominent community figure in her own right and is well remembered for her civic activities and as "house mother" to a lot of young ballplayers and, sometimes, their managers. Sam and Alice, with son John and daughters Alice and Suzanne, teamed to give the O-Yank organization the family aura it maintains to this day.

They succeeded in making everyone feel at home, from visiting officials, guest speakers for the annual banquet, wandering journalists or sometimes scouts. The lights at 95 River Street often burned into the wee hours.

Son John, who has a doctorate in economics, continues to serve as business manager and is constantly busy with a multitude of chores. He oversees the field work, handles matters concerning arriving and departing ballplayers, gets each night's program ready and so on. John is a bundle of nervous energy and seldom sits down for any length of time during baseball season. His wife Ellen and son Mark have adapted to John's whirlwind schedule, which recently included working as a county legislator, carrying a full teaching load at nearby Delhi Tech and successfully pursuing his doctorate in economics.

Daughter Suzanne (now Suzanne Longo and a mom) has helped out around Damaschke Field for years. She even ran the club one year as general manager and was honored for her work in that capacity. Older daughter Alice (affectionately known as "little Alice" by the ball park

Sam Nader is General Manager of the Oneonta Yankees.
—The Daily Star

faithful) served in a number of capacities, including working in the concession stand and office, running errands - whatever was needed. She left Oneonta for a job with the Atlanta Braves. Now married, she and her young family still live in Atlanta, but Alice remains close to her dad and the Oneonta Yankee decision-making process. Sports writer Roger Angell, in his marvelous piece in the *New Yorker* magazine, likened the family operation at Damaschke Field to a small-time traveling circus where the pretty ticket taker turns up in the show as one of the star trapeze artists.

And, since the beginning, there was "big Alice," Sam's wife and mom to the busy family. Like the rest of the brood, her duties (all volunteer work) were many and varied. You might see her come on the field with a wheelbarrow full of sand to be spread on a rain-soaked base path, or walking the offspring of a young manager like Buck Showalter, or tending to a very ill young player like Brian Butterfield.

She was always looking after the young ballplayers, coming up with a remedy for acute homesickness or case of "the blahs." There were jokes about "Mother Superior" or "den mother" but she was revered by all who were touched by her warmth and genuine concern at the ball park or in the community.

While en route to see a doctor in Atlanta for an allergy problem in March, 1991, the car in which Alice and Sam were riding was rammed by another vehicle. Alice died a few hours after the crash and Sam was hospitalized for severe injuries. As 1992 got under way, he was still undergoing surgery in a continuing effort to repair his damaged legs. And today he still feels the effects of the terrible injuries.

The Nader family, showing a courage of which Alice would have been proud, buckled down and continued to work with the ballclub as she would have wanted them to do but her death was a severe blow to everyone connected with the Yankees and to baseball generally.

An indication of how the New York-Pennsylvania (NY-P) League felt about her came in late 1991 when the league championship trophy was named in honor of this fine lady.

The family picture was completed by LeRoy "Sonny" House, Alice's brother and Uncle Sonny to the Nader children. He was a special man, remembered by players and fans alike for his gravelly voice and special night pronouncement "laze and gennemun, heerz anutherluckynumber" as he gave away prizes.

Somewhat of a character (he quit his O-Yank job, by his own admission, "738 times"), Sonny was a pillar of the organization from the beginning. Nobody could sell scoreboard advertising, season tickets or program ads, better than LeRoy S. House, Jr.

After a heated discussion with Sonny one day, an exasperated Sam Nader mopped his brow and exclaimed, "Wow, what a guy!" Then, after pausing a moment to calm down, he said, "The O-Yanks would be lost without him."

The Oneonta community also benefitted from LeRoy House's activity. He became involved with nearly every worthwhile community endeavor for years, particularly if fund raising was involved.

If you were to use the word "revered" in front of Sonny House, he would give you a deprecating wave of the hand and, embarrassed, turn the conversation to another subject.

But the truth is when he died in the fall of 1992, he was one of the most revered men in Oneonta. And, when the 1993 O-Yank season began, many fans said, "The ball park just won't be the same without Sonny."

The Nader family influence, one of the big reasons for the club's success, has brought a great deal of comment from the national media over the years. Many writers and sportscasters have commented on the fact that Oneonta does not sell beer in its stadium even though doing so could mean the difference between a marginal fiscal operation and a highly profitable one.

Nader has stubbornly refused to go along with those who urge him to sell beer.

"We want a family atmosphere in our park where folks can bring their children to a game," he firmly states. "If I have to sell beer to sell baseball, then I will get out of baseball. Period!"

After World War II and while he was carving out a career in industry, Sam Nader launched his political career in 1949, strongly motivated by a desire to get some things done he felt needed doing and to repay his city for all that it meant to him and his family.

Running on the Republican ticket, he won a seat on the Common Council representing his Sixth Ward by a margin of 408-325.

He remained on the Common Council, and as the years passed by, his role increased. Sam Nader was a strong voice and not one to be ignored. Ready for bigger and better things, he sought the GOP backing for a run at the mayor's chair in 1961. The Republican leadership turned away from Nader in favor of a young and active attorney named John Dunn.

Not to be denied, Nader formed the Good Government party, ran against Dunn and, keyed by a strong show of support from his own Sixth Ward, won a close election.

On January 1, 1962 Sam Nader, son of immigrant parents and a man intent on serving the community he loves, was sworn in as mayor of Oneonta while his parents looked on with pride. "It was a great day for them," Sam later said.

Less than 60 days after the inauguration, he called the first meeting to launch the campaign to bring about the return of professional baseball to Oneonta.

He gathered "Dutch" Damaschke, Louis Laskaris, Wes Coddington, Sidney Levine and Henry Bunn at the mayor's office on February 25, 1962 to discuss the possibility of bringing in two Eastern League clubs for an exhibition game at Neahwa Park.

Damaschke, by this time, was heading up the city's Recreation Commission with Laskaris as his assistant. Coddington, a successful florist, was an active member of that commission and a baseball fan. Levine and Bunn had been involved with organized baseball in Oneonta since the Can-Am League days.

Nader called the meeting to discuss the game plan which had a dual purpose: it was to be a charity game to benefit children's wading pools for the city's parks and it was a way to test the waters to determine whether Oneonta's fans were still interested in pro ball. The Canadian-American (Can-Am) League had folded 10 years earlier after a successful stand in Oneonta which, by the way, was the only Can-Am club ready for the 1952 season.

Mayor Nader got the green light at that meeting in February, 1962 and a flurry of letters, telegrams, phone calls and meetings over the next 12 months or so got under way. Finally a regular season game between the Binghamton Triplets and Reading, Pennsylvania, managed by former Oneonta manager Eddie Popowski, was arranged in July, 1963.

The event was a success and Nader's hopes were buoyed by the almost 2,000 fans who were on hand. Money was raised for the kids, and the ball park for the most part drew good ratings from league officials, the competing clubs and the players.

Everyone went away happy even though there had been some ruffled feathers during the spring when Binghamton abruptly cancelled original plans for the game. Strongly worded protests from several people, including officials of the National Baseball Hall of Fame in Cooperstown and the National Association front office, caused the Binghamton people to reconsider.

Nader and Binghamton Club President Lou Rappaport became good friends during that period. Rappaport and Triplet Business Manager Jerry Toman were to prove most helpful in the events of the mid-Sixties.

Don't get the impression baseball was the only subject which occupied Mayor Nader during his terms in office. He can proudly point to substantial flood control measures, a high rise building for the elderly which carries his name, an airport capable of serving commuter aircraft, a lovely downtown shopping area and many other positive results of his administrations which produced one of the most progressive eras in the city's history.

But, even as he battled his way through issue after complex issue, Sam Nader never lost track of his deep desire to return baseball to Oneonta.

2 YANKS!

T his was not an easy time for Sam Nader. It was early 1967 and his baseball world had been shattered by a call from Boston Red Sox farm director Neil Mahoney who told him the Sox would not be coming back to Oneonta.

"It wasn't the best of times," said the O-Yank owner. "We had a good 1966 and we were all set for 1967. After all the work which went before 1966, it was unbearable to think we had lost baseball."

Like the Lone Ranger riding to the rescue, along came Johnny Johnson to save the day.

A genial man with a love of the game which matched his vast knowledge, Johnson was farm director for the New York Yankees. Through Joe Buzas, who brought the Red Sox into Oneonta from Wellsville, Johnson had learned of Nader's plight.

He realized that Oneonta was in the market for a minor league franchise and Johnson was looking for a Class A league opening.

It didn't take long for the capable Johnson, the dedicated Nader and the free-swinging Buzas to get together. The Oneonta Yankees became a reality.

Sam Nader and "The Boss," NY Yankee owner George Steinbrenner, enjoy a ballgame at Damaschke Field.

Johnson was a great friend to Oneonta and he started a warm relationship which lasts to this day. Through all the changes at Yankee Stadium and the transition from one ownership to the other, the Oneonta-New York ties have remained strong. The parent club's interest sometimes borders on paternalism.

Like the incident of the batting cage.

In 1973, Nader got a call from George Pfister in the New York player development office. Pfister, now in the office of the commissioner of baseball, had developed a personnel file for Johnson in the Yankee office which was considered the best ever devised. He was a friend of Oneonta's from the beginning and his daughter attended the State University there.

On this day in 1973, Pfister, aware of the rusty, creaking batting cage in use at Damaschke Field, asked Nader if the O-Yanks could use the one from Yankee Stadium. At that time, the New York club was going to use Shea Stadium while Yankee Stadium was being refurbished and the batting cage had no home.

"Are you interested in buying it?" asked Pfister.

"You bet your life," responded the O-Yank owner. "Name your price."

"I'll get back to you," said the Yankee executive.

Later that day, the phone in the O-Yank office rang. It only rang once before an excited Nader grabbed it.

George Pfister was on the line. "I've got some news, Sam," said Pfister. "You can't buy the batting cage."

Nader's heart sank. He had been like a kid anticipating a new toy thinking about that batting cage.

"I've just talked with Mr. McPhail and he says you can't buy the cage," said Pfister. Then, figuring he had teased the O-Yank boss enough, he added, "He says you can borrow it."

Pfister added a condition. The cage must be picked up within 48 hours.

"I'll have a truck on the road within the hour," said the elated Nader. And he did.

The cage is still in use at Damaschke Field and fans enjoy looking at it as they would a museum piece. And they allow themselves to think about all the great baseball players who have taken their practice swings in that cage during the years at Yankee Stadium.

That was only one of many things McPhail and others have done for the O-Yanks over the years.

McPhail was a hands-on general manager who kept track of his farm hands and their summer home in Oneonta, New York.

Once in Auburn he opened a conversation with a sportswriter covering the O-Yanks. He asked for some honest suggestions regarding the Yankees' Oneonta operation.

The sportswriter suggested something might be done to replace the old and worn road uniforms. And he told the general manager of the Yankee scout he had heard promise a contract to a young local ballplayer. He added that the player and his family had waited and waited but had heard nothing since. The June draft had come and gone...no word.

"I don't think the Yankees do business that way," he told McPhail.

"We don't," said the general manager. The young man was signed less than a week later and new uniforms arrived within 10 days.

One day, when a writer and his wife and son visited the Stadium they quietly rode up to the office level on the freight elevator. When the doors opened, McPhail was there to greet them, smiling and congenial. A tour of the farm system office was followed by lunch. After lunch, the visitors watched that day's game from the owner's box. Throughout the day, they were treated like special people; memories of days like that never fade.

Although things have changed at the Stadium, much congeniality and good fellowship remains in the relationship between New York and Oneonta.

George Steinbrenner has visited Damaschke Field on several occasions. General Manager Gene Michael has been at Damaschke and Bill Livesey, now a vice president heading up the Player Development office at the Stadium, is on hand several nights each summer.

"Oneonta is important to us." he says. "It is the right atmosphere for these young players. We like it, too, because it is not too far from New York."

Steinbrenner, talking one night to the O-Yank beat writer, said, "I know of no better place for these young players to start their baseball careers than Oneonta."

Even though the intimacy slackened somewhat after the departure of Johnson and McPhail, there remains an atmosphere of congeniality.

Once when Steinbrenner planned to visit Oneonta, he called Nader and asked him to arrange a rental car for his use.

Nader replied, "No problem, I'll handle it."

When Steinbrenner checked into Oneonta and contacted the O-Yank boss, he was told that a "Rent-a-Wreck" vehicle was at his disposal. He was startled.

"Rent-a-Wreck?" grumbled The Boss, "What kind of a deal is that? What's going on? I want a car, not a wreck!"

When he saw the vehicle arranged for him and realized "Rent-a-Wreck" was a catchy name for a substantial auto rental business, Steinbrenner chuckled and was pleased.

General Manager Michael revealed the Yankee brass's feeling regarding Oneonta when he said, "We feel very fortunate about our long and friendly relationship with Oneonta. Our young athletes are true beneficiaries of this situation."

Mitch Lukevics, director of minor league operations for the parent club, said, "The New York Yankees appreciate the community support given our young players and the local club for so many years. Oneonta has a very fine reputation in professional baseball circles and has proven to be a great place to indoctrinate young players into professional baseball and the Yankees' approach to playing the game."

Over the years people like Whitey Ford and Mickey Mantle have come to Oneonta to help teach the young players and the Yankees have sent men like Clyde Klutts, Bobby Hoffman, Mickey Vernon and Hoyt Wilhelm as instructors.

Gene Tenace, Tony Cloninger, Albie Pearson are among those who have had instructional roles and the New York organization always sent top people, officials and/or players, to the Oneonta Hot Stove dinner in January each year.

More than a quarter century has gone by and the New York people remain steadfast in their support of the little farm club 200 miles from The Stadium. They have supported the Oneonta faction at difficult major-minor league meetings; they have sent in some of their best talent, including first round draft picks; they have helped with Damaschke Field refurbishing and with lobbying efforts when the City of Oneonta considered a much stiffer rental program for the O-Yanks at Damaschke Field.

Sam Nader is listened to in New York. Once, when the parent club was considering naming a manager who Nader preferred not to have, he stated his case at The Stadium. The manager was reassigned. It was the only time Nader made such a request; usually he is more than satisfied with the people sent to Damaschke Field to work with the young players.

The Oneonta-New York connection has been a happy and productive one, one that has benefitted both participants and the loyal Damaschke Field faithful.

But time marches on. The future is uncertain as people and physical facilities grow older. But the Yankees will be back in Oneonta for 1995 and, right now, that knowledge is good enough.

3 BUCK

On a cold morning in mid-December of 1984, Sam Nader hung up the telephone and sat down in front of his old typewriter. It was one of the times he liked best, the time when he announced appointment of the Oneonta Yankee manager for the coming season.

The voice on the phone from Yankee Stadium told him that William Nathaniel "Buck" Showalter would pilot the O-Yank team in the 1985 NY-P League campaign.

"Who?" was the first response from the veteran Oneonta executive who never heard the name. Information on the man was scarce but with help from the front office, Nader was able to put together a decent article on the new manager.

Thus was launched a managerial career which led to Buck Showalter being named 1994 American League Manager of the Year.

Once finished with his typing, Nader drove over to his friend Sid Levine's place of business and made copies of the news release. Then it was on to the various media outlets in Oneonta and to the post office to mail out the remaining copies. It was a labor of love and the Oneonta Yankee General Manager thoroughly enjoyed his day.

It was the first of many happy days that year. In his news release, Nader said Showalter "comes highly recommended by knowledgeable baseball people and is labelled as a winner. Our fans should be in for a very exciting season and I am confident that Buck Showalter will lead us back to our glory days."

Former O-Yank Manager Buck Showalter was 1994 American League Manager of the Year.

The great prophet Nostradamus couldn't have done much better than the Oneonta general manager did in that prophesy. Oneonta won 55 games in the regular season, eclipsing the old NY-P mark for victories in a short season set by Mike Ferraro's 1974 Oneonta club. Showalter's 1985 team won the pennant by a whopping 19 1/2 games.

And in 1986, Showalter's O-Yanks came back to set a new mark by winning 59.

The glory days were indeed back.

When reporters turned up at Damaschke Field for the first workout of the 1985 O-Yanks, they started looking for the new manager. Looking out over the field they could see a group of young men starting their drills—there was no sign of a grizzled older man in uniform.

Finally they figured out the short, firmly built young man with the blond hair showing from beneath his cap was the new manager. At 28 when he joined the club, Showalter looked very much like his players.

It didn't take long for even the most seasoned sportswriter to realize this man was special.

Looking like one of the players, being young enough to identify with them and understand their problems has put many minor league managers in a difficult position.

But not Buck Showalter. He walked the fine line between buddy and taskmaster without difficulty, getting his lessons across. He could be tough, he could praise, he could dispense baseball knowledge day and night. He was always genuine - no tricks, no gimmicks, no games.

His managerial tactics have changed little through the years from the short-season Class A O-Yanks to Yankee Stadium. He is a player's manager, not because he coddles his charges but because he treats them like professionals.

"I get to deliver more bad news than good in this job," he says, "I have to release people and make other changes which affect their lives and their careers."

But he gives it to them straight, man-to-man, eyeball-to-eyeball. A Yankee player will never learn of his fate on the back page of a tabloid or on a radio talk show as long as Buck Showalter is manager.

The New York manager named the American League's best in 1994 is the same manager who was named the New York-Pennsylvania League's best nine years earlier and that's his "secret": consistency.

He was pleased he had been overwhelmingly named best manager in the AL and he treated the announcement gracefully and with gratitude. Tanned and rested from a prolonged stay in Florida, dividing time between the Yankee Tampa headquarters and his home in Pensacola, Buck wore a brighter smile than normal while talking about the award.

But he lamented the fact the season was shortened by the strike. His ballclub was leading by six and a half games at the time of the walkout, had been in the division lead since mid-May and was on the way to its first title since 1981. Ahead lay the possibility of a playoff and World Series appearance.

He gazed wistfully out over the quiet and empty Yankee Stadium in October, 1994 and said, "You look out there and realize what could have happened here today.

"You have to think about what should be happening on that field."

Showalter, true to form, called the Manager of the Year award an "organizational honor... a reflection of what our team accomplished."

Unlike many who would predictably utter such words, William Nathaniel Showalter means it. There never has been anything phony about him.

From the red-eyed weary manager wearing his game face to the young man who, with a twinkle in his eye enjoys fencing with media people, he is the genuine article.

And, while there are people who question the way he manages, they are relatively few in number because his system works and it has for nine productive years.

But he is now and always has been his own man, learning every day, and believing in consistency.

"I think the one thing players want from the manager is consistency," he states. "They have to know every day what reaction they are going to get out of given situations."

But don't get the idea that there is no sense of humor in the young manager's makeup. Lurking just behind the serious manner, the stern visage and intensity which are Buck's trademarks, is a quiet sense of humor which is a delight to those who get to know and understand this man. He can be laughing inside at a private little joke while the person to whom he might be talking isn't even aware of what is happening.

Family history has had a lot to do with the making of a major league manager in the matter of William Nathaniel Showalter III, known as "Buck" since a minor league manager once commented on his tendency to walk around a locker room "buck naked."

The family, William Nathaniel II, wife Lina, three daughters and a son moved to Century, Florida in the early 1950's where Buck's dad became high school principal. Century, a town in the Florida panhandle much more "Bible Belt South" than Florida Northerners know, was deeply segregated but young Nat Showalter was an athlete and he played his sports on both sides of the tracks.

History caught up with Buck's dad when desegregation came, by federal decree, to Century. His father, who had been tough enough and good enough to play pro football in the NFL's rough and tumble days, was rough enough and tough enough to proceed with desegregation as mandated.

This was not easy for the elder Showalter and his family but he stuck to his guns and earned the deep and lasting respect of many people, friend or foe. Buck remembers those days vividly and frequently calls upon things he learned from his dad in those difficult times.

Buck's dad died in November, 1991 during surgery he risked rather than live as an invalid.

The younger Showalter continued his athletic career through the sandlot, Little League, high school and college. He went into pro baseball after graduating from Mississippi State University where he had been an All-American. He was drafted by the Yankees and assigned to Fort Lauderdale where he played first base and the outfield and hit .362.

He continued his great hitting through a minor league career which spanned seven seasons and produced a lifetime batting average of .294 in 793 games. But a nagging injury ended his playing career.

He served as a coach at Fort Lauderdale before launching his managerial career in 1985. It was a career eventually led him to the organization's top job at Yankee Stadium.

"I picked him out when he was a player," says Yankee boss George Steinbrenner. "I saw him in camp and he ran every sprint at 110 percent. He is very determined and baseball is his life away from his family."

Among those greeting Buck when he arrived in Oneonta was a returnee from the coaching ranks of the 1984 O-Yanks, a gruff baseball veteran named Russ "Monk" Meyer. The old pro wasn't too sure of "this young guy with yellow hair sticking out of his cap" at first but it didn't take Buck long to win over the outspoken pitching coach. And out of mutual respect began a relationship which lasted through the 1992 season when Meyer realized his long, long dream of returning to the big leagues.

Theirs is a special relationship. There is a deep personal feeling, certainly, but above all there is a genuine respect for the other as a professional.

Of Meyer, Buck said, "I only rent pitchers from Monk. He works with them, tells me who is ready for a given situation and who isn't. He's seldom wrong."

Of Showalter, Monk said, "He has the best baseball mind I've ever been in contact with. At any level of this game, I have never known a guy who could grasp a situation and act quicker than Buck Showalter. He's seldom wrong."

These men won in short season Class A, in full season Class A and in Class AA. Ill health forced Monk Meyer out of the Stadium dugout after the 1992 season and the curtain came down on the "Monk and Buck Show."

They are special people and their time in Oneonta was special to fan and player alike.

4 MAZ

He came from California and Oneonta baseball struck it rich. Slightly bow-legged, short of stature with a shock of white hair and a sunburned face, Art Mazmanian arrived from the West Coast to take charge of the fortunes of the Oneonta Yankees in the New York-Pennsylvania League in June, 1977. His lovely wife, Shirley, came along and added much to the very special aura which prevailed during the Mazmanian years at Damaschke Field.

When Mazmanian left at the end of the 1981 season he expected to return to Oneonta for the following campaign. He and Shirley loved Oneonta and they were very much a part of the community beyond the ball park during their stay in the City of the Hills.

Highlight of the Art Mazmanian era: Winning 17 of 18...O-Yanks on a tear.

But he wasn't re-hired. When he returned to Damaschke Field, he was managing another ball club in the NY-P League and about to write an incredible finish to his long personal association with Oneonta. Reasons for the change of heart in New York regarding Mazmanian remain a puzzle. It is known, however, there were people among the New York decision makers who didn't agree with Maz's methods, saying he was, "Too much of a cheerleader." They said this despite the fact he produced five consecutive pennants and four playoff championships in the five years he managed in Oneonta.

Mazmanian's methods? They revolved around his basic philosophy which governed him through all the years of coaching at Mt. San Antonio College in California and at various minor league stops in places like Twin Falls, Idaho and Great Falls, Montana and the Appalachian League in Virginia.

He believes in never pushing an athlete to do more than the athlete's natural abilities allow him to do.

"I tell my players that I never expect them to make great plays, just make the routine plays and make them every time," says Maz. "Games are lost by failure to make the routine play."

Mazmanian, who played in nearby Binghamton at one point in his career, knows about being pushed beyond his natural abilities. As a player, he said, "they wanted me to be a home run hitter. I never hit a home run in my life. They made me a shortstop but second base was always my position.

"It seems I was always expected to do more than my abilities would allow me to do."

Not a physically large man, he was always intense on the field. Mazmanian literally bounced from place to place while in Oneonta, moving with those short little choppy strides which got him to the outfield quickly from the dugout area when he had an urgent message for an erring player.

Looking beyond the Mazmanian years in Oneonta and looking back over the years which preceded his arrival, one quickly realizes the basic strength of the bouncy little Californian lay in his affinity with the young charges under his control. He gained their respect early on and he kept it until the end of each season and beyond. The things he told them made sense, the way he told them was firm yet acceptable and above all, they worked.

Long before he came to Oneonta, he had a pitcher named Jack Clark. Mazmanian realized early on that Clark had far more potential as a hitter than as a pitcher and convinced the athlete to become an outfielder. Jack Clark has made a decent living for several season by hitting the ball out of the park for major league clubs including the New York Yankees.

"He's a blankety-blank cheerleader," some baseball men would say about Mazmanian. "That stuff doesn't go anymore."

But it does and that's the story of Art Mazmanian. His value is great at the Class A level because that's where his personality and his tactics are so successful. He is the first to state those tactics might not work in The Show and that doesn't bother him.

He is philosophical about never having managed above Class A. A deeply religious man, Art Mazmanian said, "I believe I am where the Lord wants me to be. If He meant for me to be in the big leagues, that's where I would be."

Art really believed his services were most needed at the lower minor league level when the careers, sometimes even the future lives off the field, of young players hang in the balance.

And, while he could be accused sometimes of being a "Mother Hen" to his players, he was, and is, a stern taskmaster.

"I treat my players the same way I treat my kids," he said one night during one of his long bull sessions with a sportswriter acquaintance and friend. "I'm not going to baby them. It's the kids who have not been babied who survive."

This is another area of disagreement among pro coaches and managers. He believes in going over something again and again until the players get it right - even to the point of embarrassment. "If a player misses first base, I will make him do it over and over until he remembers - 4,000 times if necessary.

"I'm thinking of the player's future. Better he be embarrassed down here than by making the error in Yankee Stadium.

"I know I'm not easy to play for at times. But I'm not necessarily trying to be their friend, I'm interested in teaching them baseball."

Mazmanian proved his point one night early in his Oneonta stay when the ball club arrived home early in the morning after a long road trip. They were playing only 500 ball at that point and things were looking pretty grim.

The players got to bed around 6 a.m. and then reported at the ball park around 3 that same afternoon to play a doubleheader. The O-Yanks were a tired ball club and played that way during the doubleheader, making errors, not hitting, playing listlessly.

But they hadn't seen anything yet. The players were told not to leave after the games had ended. After all the spectators left the ball park, Mazmanian took the team into the outfield area and ran them and ran them and ran them.

"It was drastic treatment and I know they hated me for a while (I could hear the words `Captain Bligh' coming from disgruntled players)," he said, "but they had to learn."

He told them they played like they were tired and he said, "I will give you a reason to be tired.

"I told them this is what will happen every time they played the way they did that night. I wasn't going to be embarrassed that way again and I know they didn't want to look that bad," he said.

The result? The O-Yanks went on a tear which became a hallmark of the Mazmanian era, winning 17 of their next 18 games.

5 'Skip'

O neonta Yankee General Manager Sam Nader sat down in front of his aging typewriter for his annual ritual of preparing a news release regarding the Oneonta Yankee manager for the upcoming season. This was only the third occasion of such announcement for Nader but, as a baseball fan, he already felt a stir of excitement.

This release announced George Washington Case would manage the Oneonta NY-P League entry in 1969. "George Washington who?" asked younger sports writers and announcers.

But the veterans dove for the record book well aware of George Case's major league reputation, particularly as a base stealer.

Case was a winner in his four Oneonta years, just as he had been a winner every place. But it was the man who left the mark in Oneonta more than the .640 percent baseball played by his teams.

Players, officials, fans, umpires, citizens not even connected directly with the ball club agreed he was the most respected, well-liked man ever to wear the O-Yank uniform.

"We have had great managers over the years," said Sam Nader, "but to everyone connected with the ball club over all years there has been only one 'Skip' and that was George Case."

Case played most of his 11-year major league career in relative obscurity for the Washington Senators, but his skills were obvious nonetheless. He set the American League base stealing record five consecutive years. He made an art form out of stealing bases by using his great speed and an uncanny ability to study opposing pitchers and their delivery as a key to when to go.

This latter ability he used as a minor league manager. Before an O-Yank game, he would watch a young pitcher warm up and then say something like, "We should steal four tonight." It usually turned out he was right on the money.

Bowie Kuhn, who went on to become Commissioner of Baseball, was a law student in Washington, D.C. when Case was with the Senators.

"I'd arrange my schedule around Senator games," he said during a visit to Oneonta as commissioner. "I just wanted to see the man play."

"As a matter of fact, if I couldn't arrange my schedule, I would duck out and go to the ballpark anyway. George Case was always worth it."

Case tied a major league record when he collected nine hits in a doubleheader in 1940, hit over .300 three times during his career and became an expert in the art of drag bunting.

Case was clocked consistently in the 10 second time for the 100 yard dash, running in uniform on a grass surface.

Once, as a publicity stunt, they matched him against Olympic champion Jesse Owens.

"I got off to a good start," Case was to recall in later years, "and actually thought I was going to beat him. But, suddenly, I heard him coming and he was past me so quick, I couldn't catch him."

After his major league career was over, he returned to his hometown of Trenton, New Jersey to run his sporting goods business and was out of baseball four years. He returned to the game as a coach at Rutgers University and then went with the Washington Senators as a coach and a scout. He managed the Senators' top farm club in Hawaii, became first base coach for the Minnesota Twins in 1968 and joined the New York Yankee organization in 1969. George Case died in 1989 but the spirit remains among Oneonta fans and former O-Yank players who will always recall him as "the Skip."

The fans loved the man. There was a team farewell party at the close of the 1971 season after another pennant had been secured. Joyce Allard, a ceramics specialist who never missed a Yankee game, fashioned dolls for each player, including "Skip." Each one had the correct number and personal characteristics such as red hair for Randy Robbins or glasses for "Skip" Raschke. The players gave Case an expensive hunting rifle complete with inlaid wood stock.

George Washington Case...the manager known as "the Skip" joined the Yankee organization in 1969.

It was that kind of feeling which prevailed around Case ball clubs the four years he managed the Oneonta team.

It troubled Case he was working without the help of coaches, as is the practice today. It wasn't the work, for he was a bear for work and loved the game deeply. He was concerned he couldn't give his young players the attention he felt they should have.

This attention began with basics such as eating right.

"How can a kid eat potato chips and soda for breakfast?" he would ask. "They need better than that if they are to maintain their health while playing the kind of schedule the minors play, what with the long bus trips and night games.

"They have a lot of guys in The Bigs getting decent money for part time jobs. Why not send a few down here where the help is really needed?"

Case once said, "What the people upstairs don't see is that these youngsters are not professionals even though they are being paid. They are here trying to learn how to become professionals and how to cope with life in a game which is played competitively every day. They fight homesickness and some don't really know how to care for themselves."

As far as curfews or "night patrol" to catch those who were inclined to party into the wee hours, Case would only say: "Hey, that's up to the players. It won't take me long on a given day to find out who was out carousing late the night before."

The Skip also believed there were reasons along these lines so few of these young players reach the big leagues.

"Some, although good enough to have caught a scout's eye, don't have big league talent. Others don't want to wait five or six years for their chance. But perhaps the biggest reason is most of these kids just don't want to pay the rather incredible price that must be paid to reach the big leagues. It's that simple."

Case's love for the game was genuine and deep. Although he was generally the quiet man, once in a while the deep feeling would emerge in surprising fashion. One night in Newark after Case endured a series of rhubarbs with the young umpires, he was eating with his sportswriter friend when a man who had obviously been indulging came to the table.

Trying to make friends with Case, the inebriated gentleman said, "That umpiring was rotten tonight," and he added a couple of obscenities to push his point.

That was a mistake.

George Washington Case moved his chair back, stood up, faced the man and said, "Why don't you wise up? It's OK to disagree with an umpire's call and to yell a bit. That's baseball. But the way you were going about it and the language you were using don't belong in the ball park.

"These are young umpires trying to learn one of the toughest jobs in the world. Jerks like you in the stands, yelling the kind of crap you were yelling doesn't help anybody.

"People like you aren't true baseball fans so why don't you just shut up and enjoy the game or, better yet, stay home. Now go away and let us eat."

Shocked, the man stumbled away to lick his wounds.

Case heaved a sigh, said, "Why do I bother" and returned to his spaghetti with chicken livers, one of his favorite dishes. And he asked his friend to put a couple of coins in the jukebox so he could hear his favorite tune "Bubbles in the Wine" and relax a bit.

George Washington Case is one of those people who remain with you as long as you live. Perhaps the greatest tribute to him is the number of people who every day, years after his death, remember him or respond to something they learned from him as an athlete or as a man.

6 Walker

A tall, rangy Oklahoman who looked as if he would be completely comfortable riding the range with Randolph Scott became the first Oneonta Yankee manager to win a NY-P League championship. His name was Jerry Walker and he was the opposite of 1967 O-Yank pilot Frank Verdi in his approach to managing a young ball club. Walker was low key, his message was delivered in a pleasant drawl. But he was every bit as intense as his predecessor. Aware that the prime goal at the short-season Class A level is to develop ballplayers, he was convinced that you could do that and win as well.

He proved his point by welding his 1968 team into a strong unit as August rolled around. The O-Yanks made a strong stretch drive, made the playoffs and won the flag.

Walker was deceivingly easy-going. He was a pleasant companion on the long bus rides and in the motel lobbies—conversation flowed easily. But there was a strong inner drive, a deep love for the game and a knowledge to match. And he really wanted to win.

He was not bitter, although badly disappointed over his shortened major league career. Walker had been a most promising pitcher for the Baltimore Orioles. He was big and strong and could throw heat. A long career in the bigs seemed a certainty. He was in the majors at 18, and won 11 for Baltimore while pitching to an era. of 2.92 at age 20.

But along the line a chronic sore shoulder developed and the arm couldn't meet the demands of the great competitive heart. The Orioles let him go and he subsequently pitched for Kansas City and Cleveland before finally giving in to the bum shoulder. Rather than leave the game he loved, "the only thing I really know," he once said to a sportswriter companion, he turned to coaching.

He worked in the minors and then the majors for several clubs before moving into the front office, eventually becoming general manager of the Detroit Tigers, a post he held until early 1994.

In the spring of 1993, as the Tigers struggled through a 1-15 schedule in Florida, Walker was hard at work trying to bolster the Detroit pitching staff for the coming American League campaign. A visitor to his office quickly sensed the mood of staff members each of whom was working hard and each of whom talked to and about their boss in a tone which showed the deepest respect and admiration.

Busy as he was, Walker took a moment to reflect on that summer 25 years earlier and recall Damaschke Field, Oneonta and the players who made up that O-Yank club.

"Those were great days," he said. "I was learning my job just as those kids were learning theirs. We had some wonderful days and some that weren't so wonderful."

He and his wife arrived in Oneonta in June of 1968 and left in September with the NY-P League playoff title - the first of many to fly over Damaschke Field - firmly in hand.

Walker, talked to his players in that lazy drawl which he had acquired in his hometown of Ada, Oklahoma, and enjoyed instant communication. He had the players' respect from day one and worked wonders with the diverse group of athletes the New York club sent into Oneonta.

As long as baseball is played in Oneonta, Jerry Walker will be remembered not only as a manager who brought home the first NY-P League flag, but as a real gentleman and an all-around good guy.

Jerry Walker's 1968 O-Yankees turned a strong stretch drive into a playoff title and the flag.

7 FERRARO

M ike Ferraro's stay in Oneonta as manager of the Oneonta Yankees was interesting to say the least. He went from managing
a big winner to piloting a struggling also-ran in two seasons.

The quiet young man was greeted as the 1974 camp opened in
early June by one of the finest arrays of talent ever assembled by a NY-
P League club.

His team waltzed to the pennant by 17 and a half games, set a
winning record of .768 which still stands and set the mark for wins in
the short season (53).

(Buck Showalter's 1986 Oneonta club broke the games won record
with 59 but missed the won-lost percentage record by just two points.)

In 1975, Ferraro welcomed a group of young athletes which was
largely Latin-American. Some of the youngsters could not speak English and many had never been to America before.

When he started North to assume control of that 1975 team, Ferraro
was handed a list of 10 orders written in Spanish. He was told to learn
those phrases well so that he could speak directly to his young players
and learn them he did.

"They were all pleasant baseball phrases," said the handsome young
manager. "But there were times early in that 1975 season when I thought
some good, solid cuss words might have been more effective."

That team struggled badly in the early going but came together as
the season wore along and finished above .500.

"There were moments when we thought that, if we were playing a
full season of 130 games or more, we might have caught the leaders,"
Ferraro said.

"Key thing about that team is that the kids never quit; as a matter
of fact they tried like hell all the time. But sometimes the instant communication wasn't there at a time when it was badly needed and an
opportunity slipped away."

Most of the Damaschke Field regulars agree that Mike Ferraro was
a better manager during that 1975 campaign than he was with the easy
winner of 1974.

The Kingston native's career continued upward after that as he became a coach with the parent New York Yankees and then managed the Cleveland Indians.

"Managing this club has been like a dream," Ferraro said of his 1974 winners. "With a Dave Bergman, Dennis Werth, Mike Heath, Marv Thompson or Pat Peterson available, managing became a matter of filling out the lineup card.

"And we had the pitching."

Those around the ballclub knew the talent was there but they also knew Mike Ferraro handled that talent deftly. His ability to reach the young ballplayers under his command made for a happy clubhouse, something so important with these young minor league ballplayers.

They also are aware that at least 15 players who learned their trade early under Mike Ferraro at Oneonta went on to become major leaguers.

One of the big reasons for the Oneonta community's warm and pleasant relationship with the Oneonta Yankees is the fact that nearly all of the managers have become well-known around town and away from the ballpark.

In spite of their frantic schedule— long days at the park when the team is home, drilling and/or counselling young players and the long, tiring bus rides, managers have found time to walk up and down Main Street, greeting people and passing a bit of time as is the custom in small-town America.

Mike Ferraro managed the O-Yanks to a big season one year and a losing year the next.

Mike Ferraro was no exception. It was said he looked a little like screen actor John Agar and he became easily recognizable as he walked Main Street.

Again this was a manager who will be remembered personally and professionally as the years go by and they continue to play ball in the old ball park.

8 MUGSY

His nickname, according to the *Encyclopedia of Baseball*, was "Hardrock" and he started his managerial career in Oneonta as if he wanted to live up to that name.

Gary Allenson put on what he called his "game face" as he approached Damaschke Field each day. He was stoic, often remote, hard to get to know. He seemed cool to folks he didn't know and was particularly stand-offish with reporters.

All of this puts together a picture of the 1987 Oneonta Yankee manager which is inaccurate. Allenson, in truth, was one of the most caring, dedicated and concerned managers ever to wear the pinstripes in Oneonta. Off the field, he was warm and pleasant and possessed a great sense of humor.

Later, he was to say, "I don't know where they picked up that name 'Hardrock.' I was never called that by anybody - teammates, friends, family - anybody. That's literary license, I guess."

Sometime during the second tour of duty in Oneonta, Allenson picked up the nickname "Mugsy," a name that was still being used by Boston Red Sox announcers in 1994 when Allenson was third base coach for the Sox. It seemed to fit in Oneonta and it seemed to fit Gary as he struggled through the season at Fenway.

In 1987, only months away from the major leagues where he had caught seven years (six for Boston), Allenson had to make the major adjustment to life in the minors and to the necessity of working with young and inexperienced ballplayers and umpires. And he had to work at making the adjustment to the New York Yankee way of doing things.

So, as he said himself with a chuckle later in the season, "Gary was wary at first " and that wariness was easy to misinterpret.

He got on well with the players who, young and inexperienced as they were, nonetheless recognized a professional when they saw one and Gary Allenson was indeed a professional.

The Gary Allenson who drove his Bronco into Oneonta in June, 1988 wasn't quite the same man as the one who drove away in September of the previous year.

By his own admission, a winter of introspection, a winter of discus-

Gary Allenson's 1988 O-Yanks celebrate the NY-P Playoff Championship.

—The Daily Star

sions with his loving and supportive wife Dorothy, a winter of decisions had set the stage for his return to the minor league baseball wars.

Nothing indicates the change in Gary Allenson than his action as he arrived in Oneonta, as the 1988 season got under way.

He felt confident but not overly so as he drove up to the familiar gates of Damaschke Field that sunny morning. He walked up to the front door of the little building which serves as the Oneonta Yankee office (when not in winter quarters at 95 River Street) and looked in to see exactly what he expected: Sam Nader at his desk talking to a potential ticket buyer.

Once the greetings were exchanged and Sam had been assured the Allensons were comfortably set up in their summer home, the manager said, "Sam, I understand you give championship rings to your teams that win a pennant. Is that true?"

"Yes, we have done that in the past," said Nader, proud of the fact the Oneonta Yankees were one of the few minor league clubs to have established such a tradition, perhaps the only one in Class A. "Why?"

"I think you should give some thought to ordering them," came the reply. "We plan to win it all this summer."

Nader was pleased at this quiet display of confidence. It was not said in a cocky way but from the sincere belief by the man sitting next to him he had learned from his 1987 experiences and, given the right people, he felt certain he could put that experience to positive use.

"I'll do that, Gary," said Sam, and he scribbled a note to himself on his cluttered pad.

On a sunny September morning some 12 weeks later, members of the 1988 Oneonta Yankee team proudly looked over their championship rings as they stood outside the old ball park and said their goodbyes. Bobby DeJardin, Skip Nelloms, Jay Makemson, Bruce Prybylinski and Pat Kelly stood around for a few minutes, shrugging off the effects of last night's celebration and, in the way of all young athletes, stalling a bit because they were afraid of showing any emotion. Other members of that team hurried by on their way to a waiting car or to a taxi which would take them to the airport.

In his tiny office, Manager Gary Allenson struggled unsuccessfully to wear his game face as he cleaned up his final reports and packed his gear. Pride and strong emotion showed through and the young skipper couldn't keep from smiling. This was not his game face, the stern visage which had carried him through the often tense NY-P league pennant race of 1988, the face that earned him the nickname "Mugsy" from his players. He became aware of the nickname late in the season and secretly he was very proud.

"It will be a long time before I forget this season," said Mugsy on this September morning. "What a group of kids this is!

"Let me say something else, too. Because Watertown upset Utica on the last night of the regular season and we lost doesn't mean we backed into this thing. I want the fans to remember this ball club won 14 of its last 17 games - that's why we won the pennant."

The 1988 Oneonta Yankee team stands alone as one of the most memorable of all the Damaschke Field clubs. Their all-for-one attitude and their sheer guts under pressure every day toward season's end was breathtaking to watch and served as a just tribute to the strong young man who was leading them.

"Hardrock" or "Mugsy," Gary Allenson was one helluva minor league manager. Damaschke Field folks believe he would be the same in The Bigs given the opportunity.

9 BERRY

K en Berry had 14 years in the big leagues behind him and a long record as a coach. But he had yet to try his hand at managing in the professional ranks. He got his shot in 1982 at Oneonta.

When he and Aleda, his wife who proved the old adage that baseball wives are among the most attractive women in all of sports, arrived in Oneonta for the 1982 season, Ken Berry was confronted with an interesting set of challenges.

First, he was following a legend. Art Mazmanian had won the regular season division flag every one of his five years in Oneonta and was revered by the fans who were disappointed that he had not returned for 1982 as expected.

Second, Berry found that he would be working for a female general manager, and a young girl at that. Third, he was to manage a super athlete whose every move was covered by the national electronic and print media.

Berry, who looked out at the world through sharp eyes hidden by the shadow from his baseball cap visor, handled all challenges well - well enough to bring a sixth consecutive division title to Damaschke Field and well enough to leave Oneonta knowing the fans had accepted him and his ball club fondly and with respect.

The issue of a young female manager was never an issue at all. Suzanne Nader had been brought up with the Oneonta Yankees. Since early childhood she had been at the ballpark with Mom Alice and Dad Sam, sister "Little Alice" and brother John. During the happy summers, and often in the wintertime, the Nader house on River Street was host to players, coaches, managers and Yankee officials. Baseball talk swirled around their home and Suzanne was comfortable with it.

The years moved on and Suzanne finished high school and then completed her studies at Ithaca College. By June 1982 she was ready and, when Sam Nader asked his daughter if she could run the ball club, she jumped at the chance.

"When Ken Berry reported," she recalls, "I could see he was taken back not only because I was a female, but because I was young.

"Ken was a gentleman and, when he realized I actually knew what I was doing, he warmed up and we got along just fine."

Suzanne was bouncy and bright, firm but fair and she soon gained the respect of the players, Yankee officials, other club officials, umpires and the Damaschke Field crew. Her Dad was around for the major decisions but, by and large, she ran the club all summer long and ran it well.

"It was a good experience for us all," Berry said. "A good job in the front office manifests itself in many ways on the baseball field and, in this case, was a large factor in our winning the division."

Following Mazmanian as manager of the Oneonta Yankees was a tough way to start. But right off the bat, Berry realized he had to do things his way and hope his way would be good enough.

"Coming here was tough for me, after Art. He had such an established winning situation and was a crowd favorite. But I think the fans accepted me and the style of my ball club," he said when the season ended.

He was correct. His style was different from the flashy little Californian and his club got off to a bad start (1-6 the first week.) But the athletes hustled and Berry kept a tight rein on things. Q.V. Lowe turned in another fine job as pitching coach and a winner emerged in September after a hair-raising race with Utica.

And, as a veteran major league player, Ken Berry commanded the respect due someone who had made it to the Bigs and stayed there 14 seasons. That helped him get his message across. He wasn't a screamer and wasn't dramatic, but he knew his game and got his knowledge across with conviction.

The super star who played for Berry in Oneonta was John Elway, a versatile athlete who starred in collegiate football and baseball at Stanford. Football recruiters salivated over him and Kansas City Royal baseball scouts liked him well enough to select him in the 18th round of the 1979 free agent draft. He opted for college, however, and he went on a highly publicized career quarterbacking Stanford University to three winning seasons.

Yankee West Coast scouts saw him perform in the less publicized arena of college baseball and liked him well enough to offer him a $150,000 deal. He agreed and was assigned to Oneonta, heading East that summer of 1982 still undecided between football and baseball.

It was an exciting and interesting summer for all concerned. Berry concentrated on making certain that Elway got no special treatment either way and it was never a problem. The players accepted John and got a vicarious pleasure out of the media attention he drew.

"The John Elway thing was good for me," Berry was to say at the close of the season. "It was good for the club and good for him. It was the kind of situation that you hear about and read about; it's different when you're involved.

"We were right in the middle of a big one. But John was a class person, a good guy and a great kid to work with, and the players respected him and accepted him."

The O-Yanks had a great race and reached the playoffs only to lose to Niagara Falls in an exciting championship series.

Berry, familiar with the vagaries of baseball, was philosophical when it was over. He looked up from packing his bag and said, "These players never gave up. Losing the playoffs is very tough but it doesn't take anything away from the season we've had. If the guys had quit, maybe I'd feel differently."

With that, he zipped up the bag and stuck out his hand. "Thanks for everything," he said. And he was gone.

One of Oneonta's most exciting baseball seasons was over.

10 PREACHER

N ow it was the young Texan's turn. Trey Hillman rode into town on his Bronco in June, 1990 and when he rode out of town in September, he rode out a winner.

The slim Texan with the piercing eyes and engaging smile produced a ball club which was second only to the great 1986 team in fielding. This 1990 team won 52 games and drew the greatest season attendance in club history - an impressive total of 58,625. By the way, the O-Yanks also won the 1990 NY-P League championship, taking their division title and then stopping Geneva and Erie in the playoffs.

Like all the managers who have gone through Damaschke Field, Trey Hillman spent countless hours at the ball park, showing up in mid-morning most days and leaving at night as the clock ticked past the midnight hour.

Part of the reason for the great attendance was Hillman himself. He was lively, animated, inquisitive. He wanted to know how people thought he was doing, he wanted to please the fans. His players called him "Preacher" at first, because of his professed Christian views. But they soon came to realize Hillman's religion was genuine. At the same time they learned his knowledge of baseball was broad and they came to realize he knew what it was like to be a rookie.

Hillman was strong on human relations and wanted to get along with everyone. Often, he would ask the opinion of older hands around the ballpark in matters involving personalities.

At one point he had a mild beef with a young sportswriter who misquoted him. He was advised to forget the matter because it was trivial and didn't matter much.

"But it was wrong," he insisted. "Besides, the kid is avoiding me and I don't like that. I've got a job to do and so does he and until we settle this, we both will be hampered."

And settle it he did. A couple of nights later he caught the writer alone and insisted on an eyeball-to-eyeball discussion of the issue. He was right, the writer apologized and the issue was history.

He managed the club adroitly and teamed with Pitching Coach Mark Shiflett to use that talented pitching staff just right. The team got off to a good start, had a good mid-season, and then tailed off toward the end as fatigue and a touch of homesickness set in.

But they had a solid cushion and beat out Watertown and Pittsfield by eight and a half games to capture the McNamara Division title.

They beat Geneva in the first playoff game and then left for Erie. The Yanks won there but were defeated at home to set up the title game.

"That loss tied the series," said Hillman, "and put us in a tough spot because we were a very tired ball club.

"I don't want to go out a loser after the season we've had and I don't believe you do, either," he told his players in a dramatic pre-game pep talk. "So let's get it together and give it our best shot for one more game."

They did.

Trey Hillman later said, "I thank God that I was able to start my managerial career in Oneonta. There is no place like it and I will never forget it."

And the Oneonta fans were to say they were better off for Trey Hillman having passed their way, if only for one summer.

11 GATHERING

S ince 1967, when the New York Yankees officially made Oneonta home for its first year players, nearly 1,000 young athletes buoyed by the hope they can make it all the way to The Bigs, have arrived at Oneonta's Damaschke Field.

Sad but true is the fact that a large percentage of them fail to make it. The latest, and unofficial, figures show that 118 players who made the Oneonta roster got to play in the major leagues.

Some, like Don Mattingly, Willie McGee, Hal Morris, Cesar Geronimo, Dave Bergman, Mike Heath, Mike Pagliarulo, Dan Pasqua, Pat Kelly, Bernie Williams, Jim Leyritz, Doc Medich, Rex Hudler, Pat Tabler, Roberto Kelly and Bob Tewksbury have solid major league careers. Others had brief careers and still others were up only long enough for the proverbial "cup of coffee."

The Class A NY-P League players, many still in their teens, come from every walk of American life and from every corner of the land. And anyone who has been around at all knows full well that life as a youngster in rural America can be light years removed from life as a youngster in the streets of one of the great cities.

Willie McGee, who became good enough to win National League MVP

Current NY Yankee star Jim Leyritz hangs up the "no admittance" sign for this sliding Newark baserunner during his O-Yank days.
                                                                    —The Daily Star

honors in 1985, the same year Mattingly was named MVP in the American League, is typical of a young rookie at the Class A level.

One night at Damaschke Field, he won a spaghetti dinner for hitting a home run. But he didn't claim his prize because this was his first time away from home and he never had spaghetti.

The blending of these young men from such diverse cultures into a ball club in the brief period from June to September is a minor miracle in itself. Truly, managers and coaches at this level must be very special people.

This experience has a telling effect on players and the first year experience is one players usually recall vividly.

Years after his active days as a major league player had ended, Willie Upshaw would say, when asked about Oneonta, "I will never forget it. I loved it."

In mid-June the camp opens for the Oneonta Yankees and the work begins. Pitchers incessantly work on the play in which they cover first base on an infield grounder to the right side. Infielders handle literally thousands of ground balls in drills that never really cease. Outfielders work on handling ground balls and hitting the cutoff man until they dream about the coach yelling "Hit the cutoff man, goddam it!"

Catchers have their own agony; they will practice blocking off the short-hop pitch over and over again as coaches toss the ball into the dirt while shouting, "Keep the ball in front of you - in front of you."

And the pitchers throw and throw. Coaches are ever mindful of the danger of tired arms, particularly in players so young, but they keep working to get a little more on the fast ball or more bite on the curve.

Sometimes it can be difficult for the young pitcher who has been taught one thing in college only to find himself as a pro trying to learn something completely different.

He, for instance, might work for Tony Cloninger, now pitching coach for the parent club, who spent years training minor league pitchers on their way up.

"I wish they had never invented the speed gun," he remarked one year during spring training drills. "We find young kids coming along whose main interest is to hit 95 plus on the gun.

"They throw hard but they don't pitch and there's a helluva big difference."

As pre-season training moves along, the pace picks up. In a short-season Class A league, players report the first week in June and have just about 10 days to get ready for the league season. The schedule goes from one-a-day practice sessions to a schedule calling for two drills each day. The work day runs from 10 a.m. until evening and, once they start practicing at night to become familiar with the lights, the day lasts even longer.

They get tired. It isn't too difficult to remember Gary Washington, the big first baseman from Paragould, Arkansas sitting in the dugout and drawling, as sweat dripped from his forehead, "I've been putting on the jock every day since I was 10 years old and ahm simply tahred."

Or Shane Turner, the talented infielder from California, sitting in the same dugout at Damaschke a few years later and asking, "What am I doing here? Right about now all of my friends are heading for Malibu and I would love to be a part of that. I miss it."

Then he answered himself by saying, "I am here because I love baseball and want to play it until I can't play anymore. I want to make The Bigs."

Turner made it to The Bigs but only for a brief time with the Philadelphia Phillies. He wound up his career in the minor leagues but he got his chance to play the game he sincerely loved.

Once the season gets under way, there is little time for socializing among the ballplayers. They report to the park around 3 p.m. when in Oneonta and leave somewhere around 11. Then there is the rush to find a place to eat, a little while to check out the local women and then time to rest. They usually indulge in a couple of beers but there isn't much serious drinking—there's too much at stake for these young players.

Minimum pay for Class A players is $1,200 per month, out of which, the athletes pay for their rooms and meals while at home.

Rooms can be a problem. The Oneonta ball club has a list of places ready for the players when they arrive and those places are checked out individually by the players. Some of them room together in dorm-like facilities used by the college students in Oneonta during the fall, winter and spring months.

Such a place in the Seventies was "Myrtle Manor"

Willie McGee began a career in Oneonta that took him to 1985 National League MVP honors.

run by the Stewart Bagg family. Named after the street on which it was located, it was like a dorm but it was home, too. Many a bull session went on long into the night in those years and, cynics may scoff at this, the subject was almost always baseball.

Just around the corner was Sargent's Market, a "mom and pop" grocery store run by Merilyn and Fred Sargent. "Momma Merilyn" cared for the players, counselling the homesick, advising those with a stomach ache, and offering solace for the young ballplayer who received a "Dear John" letter.

"O-Yank alumni" remember those episodes and some still contact the Sargents from time to time. Fred and Merilyn remain O-Yank fans and have a box seat at Damaschke Field where Merilyn keeps a box score every night, looking up at times to yell encouragement to the players or express her dissatisfaction over an umpire's call.

The Sargents loaned a Spanish book to Cheryl Bagg one time so she could work with one of the players who could not speak English. The lessons turned out well and by September the young athlete had become fluent and at ease in English and Cheryl was speaking Spanish.

Other players find individual rooms with families and a few stay in motels as long as they can afford it. Not many players have cars simply because they have little time to use them.

For the road trips, the players report to the ball park in the morning, early for the long trips such as the run to Jamestown, later for the "commuter" to Utica from which they return the same night.

Most sleep on the bus, some play cards, others just listen to the radio. A few, such as Lyle Mouton, the big slugger from Louisiana on the 1991 club, used every minute to read and study. The big guy, often thought rather distant by some play-

Hal Morris tips his cap to O-Yank fans passing through enroute to Big League stardom in Cincinnati. Happy batboy is Eddie Taylor.
—The Daily Star

ers, was simply pursuing his education and it was more important than small talk.

Some players use the opportunity to talk with the manager about his own hitting or that night's opponent or whatever. Baseball pretty much occupies the lives of these young athletes, leaving precious little time for anything else. Small wonder they are tired out when early September rolls around. This is short-season baseball in name only.

As for the manager, multiply that by at least 25. He is in charge of these young athletes who represent a lot of money to the big club. He must be friendly with them, yet remain a bit aloof. He is advisor, surrogate parent and healer as well as instructor in the art of baseball. His job at this level is not so much to win as to develop players for the future at Yankee Stadium or in the trade market.

He leads an incredibly busy life during the 12 weeks of the NY-P League season. Managers literally work about 12 hours a day, seven days a week during the season. Those who are married find some solace in being able to come home to a prepared meal, a tender word or touch, and an understanding wife.

Buck Showalter, who managed Oneonta for the 1985 and 1986 seasons, said it so well: "God bless the wives of baseball men. I don't know how they put up with it but we are fortunate that they do. Without them, life wouldn't be worth much and neither would we, no matter how much we love the game."

Baseball is a marvelous game, perhaps the best. But it demands much of the men involved, much more than most boys and men are willing to give.

12 MATTINGLY

The Oneonta Yankee team bus rolled through the summer night, a careful and skilled driver named Lynn Armstrong making certain he took the curves along New York State Route 20 as gently as possible. The team had just suffered a tough loss in Batavia, ahead lay a home game that night and the young athletes needed some sleep.

Most were nodding in their seats, some were slumbering in the overhead luggage racks.

One of the players on that 1979 O-Yank club wasn't sleeping. In a mood so typical of this athlete, he was thinking about that night's game and how it might have gone Oneonta's way.

Finally, he decided to talk about his thoughts. He was seated not too far from Skipper Art Mazmanian who was nodding in his customary seat right behind the driver.

"Skipper," said the player, "I think you could have used your left-handed hitters tonight."

Mazmanian stirred in his seat and turned to look down the darkened aisle. He knew who had spoken up; it was a young rookie named Don Mattingly who the manager even then was recognizing as a kid with a special attitude. He realized the youngster wasn't cocky or over-confident; he simply wanted to play and believed even then he could do the job.

Mattingly, up to that point, hadn't played much. He was being used as designated hitter and once in a while got the chance to play the outfield. He had played first base in high school and believed that to be his position, but the Yankees had a bonus baby named Todd Demeter stationed at first for the O-Yanks and Mattingly had to be satisfied with what chance he got.

"He got a lot more for signing than I did," said Mattingly, "so I knew he was going to play first. I just wanted to play so I took what they gave me."

Although a gambling, free-wheeling manager, Mazmanian was baseball man enough to play percentages and he usually went with righties against a left-handed pitcher.

But the 1979 O-Yank skipper was a student of psychology as well as baseball tactics and he was fully aware of the courage it took the young

Mattingly to speak up and the conviction which stood behind it.

He decided to challenge the rookie.

"You think you can hit left handers?" he asked.

"Yes, sir, I do," replied Mattingly.

"Okay," said Mazmanian. "Geneva will certainly use their top lefty against us tonight and you'll get the chance to prove it."

The skipper was as good as his word and Mattingly started that night. Never one to let opportunity slip away, the kid from Evansville responded with a three for five night at the plate. He was in the starting lineup the rest of that season and finished with a .349 average.

He was on his way to a career which was to make him a Yankee hero and a household name among baseball fans everywhere.

Later, Mazmanian was to warmly remember the 1979 bus episode as the start of something special.

A lot has happened to Mattingly since that night, but 15 years later he could recall the conversation with his manager.

"I was young," he said, "but even then I felt a sense of urgency, the feeling that time would pass me by. I wanted so badly to play."

He had arrived in Oneonta in June, a teenager just a bit homesick. He left in September after putting up solid numbers and

He's called "Hitman" and "Donnie Baseball" and is certain to become a NY Yankee immortal when he retires. After beginning his career in Oneonta, he became the 1985 American League MVP.
—Yankees Magazine

impressing everyone with his dedication. During the winter months he was assigned to Greensboro, next step up the organizational ladder.

His career was on the move. Playing primarily in the outfield with an occasional shot at first base, he posted a .358 year at Greensboro in the strong Carolina League in 1980, followed that with a solid 1981 season in Class AA Nashville and a great year at Columbus in 1982, at the end of which he went on to Yankee Stadium.

As 1983 got under way, New York Manager Billy Martin finally gave Mattingly a chance to play first base on a regular basis. Since then he has become a Yankee Stadium fixture, a Golden Glove first baseman, captain of the team and one of the most popular Yankees ever.

Few players got more attention in the 1994 major league season than did Don Mattingly. He had recovered from his injury-plagued season of 1993 and was solid at the plate, hitting well over .300 when the strike ended the season. He had captured baseball fans everywhere on a western swing by getting his 2,000th hit and hitting a late inning grand slam to win a game in California.

Mattingly's success came as a surprise to some baseball people. A three-sport letterman at Memorial High in Evansville, Indiana, he had not even been selected by the Yankees until the 19th round because the scouts who signed him, Jax Robertson and Gus Poulus, believed he would probably go on to college on a football scholarship.

The 18-year-old Mattingly was in luck right off the bat. He launched his career with a family-oriented Oneonta Yankee organization which is one of the most caring in all of baseball. And he was playing for Art Mazmanian, a manager whose greatest strength lie in his ability to understand young ballplayers and communicate with them.

The family approach in Oneonta came quite naturally to the Naders and manifested itself in many ways. Alice Nader, for example, found more comfortable lodgings for the young player when the place to which he originally was assigned was less than satisfactory. She eased him through a bout of homesickness as she had done with so many players before him and was to do with so many players still to come.

The 1979 squad got down to work under the critical eye of Mazmanian

Geneva catcher Mike Diaz chases Don Mattingly to record a putout after a missed third strike. Don struck out but six times all season long. —The Daily Star

who seemed to see everything, be everywhere. He had a good club to work with - nine of the 1979 O-Yank squad went on to play in the majors.

"At first, Don didn't stand out from the other players," Mazmanian was to say in later years. "But it wasn't long before we were to become aware that here was a kid with an outstanding attitude. He was first at the park each day and last to leave.

"He was in the batting cage at every opportunity and very few pitches got by him.

"One of the things that impressed me most was the way Don, although he really felt first base was his position, willingly tackled an outfield position or accepted assignment as designated hitter on a given night."

It took time but Mattingly began to make an impression. As he stood around the batting cage day after day, Mazmanian said he found himself watching Mattingly more and more. Gradually, he became aware of the young player's ability in selecting pitches.

"It was unusual for a kid his age. He's 18 years old; if he hits .260 in this league, we would have been pleased."

When the regular season was over, Mattingly hit .349 to put him third on the all-time O-Yank list. He had three homers, two triples and 10 doubles and 31 runs batted in. He was among the leaders in all categories despite playing in only 53 games. Demeter, in 66 games, hit .253 with eight homers, three doubles and 38 runs batted in.

Mazmanian respected Mattingly for the athlete's belief in himself, his certainty that he would make the big leagues and his ability to live up to his own expectations.

In his year-end report, the Oneonta pilot gave Mattingly a "6" in hitting potential, above average even for a major league player. He was the only player in the entire NY-P League to earn a 6 from Mazmanian.

Almost as an afterthought in his year-end report, the manager added, "Some day will hit with power."

That comment surprised even Mattingly when he learned of it years later. "I can't understand why he would have said that," he said.

"I don't understand either," Maz said, "but there was just something about Mattingly that made you believe."

The only rap on Mattingly was his lack of speed; he really didn't run well.

"But, don't forget, I was grading him as an outfielder, not a first baseman," Mazmanian said. "So it's even more to Don's credit that he made it all the way."

Mattingly was liked and respected by his mentors and by his team mates. Everyone seemed to realize he was on a mission and understood when, on some nights at Damaschke in his desire to get to the field, he didn't pause and mingle with fans like some of the players enjoyed doing.

Oneonta fans, although perhaps the quietest fandom in sports, know what's going on and they know baseball. So they were aware of Don

Mattingly and his unswerving dedication to his goal of playing major league baseball. While nobody could forecast what his future held, nobody was surprised that he made it big.

And to this day, Oneonta Yankee fans follow the athlete who, above all others, shows that dedication and devotion to an ideal do pay off.

Sam Nadar and his son, John, pause for a Florida spring training photo with two all-time favorite O-Yanks, Mike Paglliarulo (left) and Don Mattingly.

—The Daily Star

13 ELWAY

The John Elway face pro football fans usually see behind a mask during Denver Bronco games is remarkably just like the face Oneonta Yankee baseball fans saw peering out from under the baseball cap at Damaschke Field in the summer of 1982. Despite the years of pounding he has taken as one of the National Football League's premier quarterbacks, he retains the boyish expression and the shock of unruly blond hair that he brought to Oneonta.

He came to the Class A Yankee farm club as a much heralded athlete. He was here in an honest effort to make a decision as to his future career as a professional athlete. He had decided that six weeks of daily toil should be enough to give him an idea about his baseball potential. Dad Jack Elway, a top collegiate football coach, agreed.

Wanting to give Elway a realistic and fair chance, Oneonta Skipper Ken Berry treated him as he did the rest of the players, managing to find time for counselling and a few extra swings in the batting cage.

Elway started slowly, getting only one hit in his first 17 at bats as cleanup hitter. But he stuck with it and on July 4th had a four hit game, including two doubles. His Mom and Dad were on hand at Damaschke Field 10 days later when he hit his first home run.

"Ken Berry and all the Yankee people were most gracious and cooperative," said John. "They were patient with me and gave me the opportunity to try their game for the summer and see how things turned out. And my teammates helped out."

When Elway arrived in Oneonta in June, 1982, he was followed by an entourage of media people who were to surround him like flies at a Sunday school picnic all summer. To his credit, it might be said that Elway avoided the publicity when he could do so courteously but was always polite to media people when trapped. And he was wise enough to be careful about what he said. He must have been asked, "What's it going to be, John, baseball or football?" a thousand times.

As the season wore on, it gradually became obvious that football had the inside track. Most of the hype surrounding the young athlete came from the football people and, in August, ABC network crews showed up to do a special on Elway. Shortly after that, Elway left Oneonta because of football commitments and the die was cast.

He was drafted number one in the 1983 NFL draft by the Baltimore

Colts but he preferred not to play there and said so pointedly. Eventually, a deal was worked out that sent him to Denver and he was been thrilling fans at Mile High Stadium ever since.

The gridiron won the war, but Oneonta gave John Elway, a future NFL superstar quarterback with the Denver Broncos, a chance to make a decision on a baseball or football career.

—The Daily Star

It should be said that, despite the publicity and the unceasing glare of the media spotlight, John Elway did well as a baseball player. He appeared in 42 games for the O-Yanks and after the slow start, went on to hit a solid .318 for the season. He flashed that strong right arm of his frequently from the deep reaches of spacious Damaschke Field and is remembered for the strike he threw one night from the right field foul pole to home plate in the air to nail a runner trying to score. The fans loved it and the scouts drooled.

John Elway was a darned good baseball player but John Elway was an even better football player and that's the way it finally went.

How Elway's O-Yank teammates felt about him was obvious every day. And when he left, the players gave him a rousing and spontaneous sendoff party, an act which showed their genuine respect and admiration for John.

Elway recently said he recalled the Oneonta days in spite of all that's happened since his departure a decade ago.

"I remember the guys and Ken Berry and the Nader family. Most of all I remember the great fans.

"I'm glad that great old ball park hasn't changed much because it's a very special place."

14 BALLPARK

O n a beautiful July morning in 1992, the young man stood at home plate in Damaschke Field. He gazed out over the freshly cut infield grass and the manicured "skin" portion. He allowed his eyes to wander out over the vast reaches of the outfield where the grass glistened with the morning dew.

He looked out over the outfield fence to see trees leaning toward the barrier as if to watch what was going on. The blue hulk of Franklin Mountain loomed as a fitting backdrop, gazing over the verdant baseball scene as it had for almost 100 years.

The young man finally pulled his eyes from the scene and turned to the clipboard he had in his hand.

"I just never expected anything like this," he mused. He turned to the sportswriter who stood nearby and said "I wouldn't be surprised if some players in the old woolen uniforms and the tattered gloves appeared as if by magic to play a game.

"This is what small town baseball is all about."

The young man was from Kansas City, Missouri and he was in Oneonta representing the architectural firm which had been hired by major league baseball to study minor league parks with an eye toward eventually bringing those parks up to standards agreed upon in the major-minor league working agreement of 1991.

His firm was given the job of surveying every minor league park in the nation. He had been in more than 60 parks before arriving in Oneonta to study its ancient facility. He found some things that needed doing: better lighting, improved infrastructure such as toilets and player/umpire dressing facilities and he found some work that needed doing on the field itself. But he also found a baseball atmosphere which helped explain the long winning record established by the men and boys who played there for almost a century.

Many changes have taken place and improvements made since games first were played on the site in 1905. But the atmosphere surrounding the game as it was played there nearly a century ago remains. You only have to close your eyes for a moment to imagine rows of straw hats in the stands, the baggy uniforms of the players, the kids chasing foul balls, the freight cars on the nearby railroad covered with enthusiastic "cranks."

In the years when Oneonta was represented for the most part by strong semi-pro teams, work was done on the playing surface, a wooden grandstand was built and dugouts were put in place. At one point, a fence was constructed around the entire ball park.

Then, in the late thirties, as the Depression receded into memory and professional baseball loomed as a distinct possibility, vast renovations were undertaken at the ball park which already had become a landmark.

Wise and far-sighted men, representing the City of Oneonta as well as those who had actively pursued the baseball idea for years, put together a fiscal formula using money donated for that cause by William Eggleston, who had launched the Oneonta Grocery Company, and funds from the federal Works Progress Administration.

Then, they stirred in an appropriation from the city, which owned the ballpark and came up with a winning recipe for Neahwa Park. Lights were erected on six huge wooden poles, one by the first base dugout, one by the third base dugout, one by each bullpen and two outside the outfield fence.

Lighting was upgraded several times but the big poles remained in place until 1986 when they were replaced by steel poles outside the fence. Although the majestic wooden poles were in play, there never was a serious accident involving a player colliding with the heavily padded giants.

During the flurry of activity in 1939-1940, workmen also replaced the old wooden grandstand with the steel structure which is still in use today and built new bleachers.

Oneonta's playing field was notorious for its ability to absorb water. Many times heavy rains came along in late afternoon but a game has gone on as scheduled at 7:15 or so. According to legend, the reason for the excellent drainage was WPA workmen in the thirties dumped as many as 25 old cars into the area when they were rebuilding the field and covered them with tons of dirt, then topsoil. The legend has never been disputed. But complete renovation of the playing surface in the fall of 1993 ended Damaschke Field's unique ability to absorb water and the car theory has been questioned in recent months.

Damaschke Field remains one of the largest in the minors in terms of the playing field dimensions. When box seats were placed in the park in time for the Can-Am League season, the distances were reduced to their present marks of 410 to center field, 360 down the left field line and 350 to right. Home runs are not cheap in the Oneonta park and triples more frequent than in most stadiums because of the spacious power alleys.

In the late sixties, fire caused extensive damage to MacArthur Stadium in Syracuse, home of the International League Chiefs. The O-Yanks promptly offered the Damaschke Field facilities and the Chiefs accepted. They played a series with Toledo at the Oneonta park and it can be said very few homers were hit even by the heavy hitting Triple A players.

At the close of the season, Syracuse General Manager Tex Simone invited Sam Nader to Syracuse and presented a plaque in appreciation.

In recent NY-P League seasons, there have been summers in which as few as four home runs have been hit through the 39 games by both teams combined and, from time to time, there have been suggestions the dimensions be shortened. But debate on that issue has never been serious.

Interested local citizens have had a positive influence on the baseball facility. The clubhouse now used by the Oneonta Yankees was donated to the city by Angela Farone in memory of her husband, Albert, one of the men most influential in the return of organized baseball to Oneonta. The electric scoreboard and the sportsmobile used as an "aid station" for the trainers were gifts from Ian Smith, founder of the successful Medical Coaches corporation and an ardent fan of the O-Yanks. Smith's son Geoff now runs the successful business.

The lighting system was the key to the 1940 season. The minors, led by Judge William G. Bramham who was elected chief of the National Association in 1934 during the latter days of the Great Depression, had been born again. (It might be noted that Bramham, although he attended law school, never did sit on the bench. He got his nickname from fellow law students because of his dignified mien, something which stood him in good stead when he was pounding away at people to keep the minors alive.)

By the time 1940 arrived, growth was the pattern everywhere. Bramham and his promotional aide, Joseph F. Carr, had brought the minors through the Depression years and back to the point that 41 leagues were ready to play ball in 1940. The Shaughnessy playoff system and the launching of the farm system program by the major league clubs were two strong reasons for the minors' resurgence. But the big reason was night baseball which enabled the working family to get to the ball park to see the locals in action.

The friendly old ball park, now known as Damaschke Field.   —The Daily Star

15 FANS

B aseball fans driving into Oneonta for that night's game do so over trails blazed by Iroquois Indians, later traders and then Colonial soldiers, all trying to get to "the place where the rocks stick out" (a loose translation of the name Oneonta from the Iroquois).

As they drive toward the little city nestled in the foothills of the Catskill Mountains, they enjoy the beauty of the bucolic countryside. Dairy farms dot the hillsides and acres of corn wave their long green arms as if in greeting.

Tops of the surrounding hills are covered by trees of infinite variety. Occasionally there is a rich country home, surrounded by carefully trimmed hedges and reached by a long driveway curving through the trees and shrubs.

Fans familiar with Oneonta Yankee players chuckle as they recall young ballplayers who were surprised there was so much open country in New York. Many of them first thought of New York in terms of big buildings surrounded by parking lots..

O-Yank fan Lu Beers (left) and Suzanne Nader share a laugh with a player after a 1982 game.

As the fans drive down Main Street, they check out the banner hung across the main drag that reads, "Oneonta, home of the Yankees."

Like all communities, Oneonta has seen changes but there are still tree-lined streets of fine old homes. Memories linger under the maples and the elms.

The travellers arrive in Neahwa Park, a spacious area dotted with softball fields, a couple of basketball courts, picnic tables under magnificent old shade trees, a pond, a pavilion and soccer fields. People are everywhere enjoying the recreational facilities or getting ready for that evening's band concert.

As they take cushions and jackets from the car (seats get hard and the nights get cool in the little ball park 200 miles from Yankee Stadium) the fans hear the sound of a baseball being struck by a wooden bat....a sound which always thrills the true baseball fan.

Fans from miles around have followed the old Indian trails (now well maintained state highways) to the ball park. They come from villages around the area, villages which join the city of Oneonta in creating a population of 55,000. O-Yank officials proudly point out that figure is just about what the ball club draws every year.

Sometimes in those late innings, it can get a bit nippy in the old ball park.

—The Daily Star

The stadium itself is baseball history personified. The game was first played on this site in 1905 and games have gone on here every summer since. The grandstand, lights and bleachers have been renovated over the years.

The crowd on an average night include people from all over the country and occasionally from a foreign land. Scouts and writers, parents of the players, fans who have been visiting Cooperstown mingle comfortably with the regulars. The regulars have supported the team since the beginning, some have not missed a home game in 25 years and many have occupied the same seats every night for a decade or more.

Perhaps such things are not unusual but the steadfast loyalty of these fans, many of them related to trailblazers who first arrived here by way of those Indian trails, is something special. They are the reason baseball has flourished in Oneonta for more than 130 years.

Their unflagging support, plus the fiscal backing of several community-minded business and professional people, added to the dedication of the Nader family which owns the club, totals up to a winner.

Oneonta crowds are notoriously quiet and many young Oneonta players, nearly all in their first year of professional baseball, misinterpret the silence as indifference and get the feeling the spectators don't really care. Nothing could be further from the truth as most players find out before the summer ends.

Many people have formed lifelong friendships with players who pass through the City of the Hills and continue corresponding long after the athlete's season in Oneonta.

This warm relationship between fan and player is a very special phase of the O-Yank tradition and accounts in no small way for the fact the Oneonta team has won 13 division titles and 11 overall New York-Pennsylvania League pennants in the past 27 seasons. And, incidentally, won at a record pace in the pre and post World War II era of the Oneonta Red Sox in the old Can-Am League.

Accounting in part for this warmth is the O-Yank Boosters Club, headed up by Marion Aeppli who rarely misses a game. This group of diehard fans arranges bus trips for spectators, puts out a newsletter and arranges such things as the annual picnic (which players really enjoy). The club also puts together welcome packets which help the young athletes get acquainted with their new summer home. The O-Yank Boosters Club has become an integral part of each season.

Groups of fans might be on hand for one of the "special nights" at Damaschke Field, when as many as 5,000 people pushed into the old park as guests of firms like Allied Amphenol, Mirabito Fuel Group, Country Club Chevrolet or Wilber National Bank.

The big event of these nights is the egg toss which players still talk about long after Oneonta days. Selected O-Yank players are teamed with local kids to toss raw eggs back and forth until only one Yankee-kid team is left. The fans really get into it, cheering every successful toss and catch and laughing uproariously when an egg is missed and breaks all over a "receiver." The fact there always is a winner and that it is pretty difficult to "short hop" a raw egg, leads people to believe there is one hard-boiled egg in play. Oneonta management never comments on this speculation.

Once in a while a special event misfires. The Pony Night special ended when a little boy's parents couldn't handle the news that junior was coming home from the ball park with a pony. Jalopy Night was discarded when a young ballplayer named Rafael Santana won a car and couldn't drive it away because he was too young to have a driver's license.

A nightly gem which is still going on and always draws laughter from the fans comes when the public address man, in serious tones, reads an auto license number. He pauses for theatrical effect and then says, "You have the dirtiest car in the parking lot." They hear it every night, but the spectators still get a kick out of it and the driver who wins gets a free wash and wax at a neighboring establishment.

Off the field activity also helps create the camaraderie between player and townsmen. Pitcher "Doc" Medich, for example, loved to fish and was delighted when a local guided him to the Ouleout, a semi-private trout stream in nearby Delaware County. Ken Patterson and Dean

Wilkins loved Delaware County for its rugged terrain and its enchanting golf course in Delhi, the county seat.

Many residents opened their homes to players, some of them room with city folk, others might be invited for an early afternoon backyard picnic before reporting for their eight hour day at the ball park. The Baseball Hall of Fame in Cooperstown is a half hour away and nearly every player gets there at least once during his summer in Oneonta.

There are restaurants and night spots in the city and the players manage to find these rather quickly. But these young men have a goal and at this point are primarily dedicated to their baseball careers. They are smart enough to be sensible about their nocturnal activities.

Over the years several players married Oneonta women and most of them spent their lives in the area.

In the community they found a city which has supported the game of baseball since pre-Civil War days. Oneonta traces its history back to Colonial times when Indians held their councils on the site and later white men set up a trading post along the banks of the Susquehanna, a main artery of travel in early America.

The community grew slowly through its early history but took off in 1865 with the arrival of the Iron Horse. When the railroad established shops here, population grew rapidly. At one time the city was served by the Delaware and Hudson, the Ulster and Delaware and a couple of other roads. Twenty-four passenger trains a day served the city and its businesses. Every family had a member who worked for the D&H in the first half of the Twentieth Century.

Autograph hounds always get their man at Damaschke Field.

—The Daily Star

Oneonta is located halfway between Binghamton and Albany in the northernmost reaches of the Catskill Mountains and it was a natural site for shops serving a railroad which linked the coal fields of Pennsylvania with the Northeastern industrial cities.

Since World War II, the importance of the railroad has diminished and Oneonta has become a center for education, commercial enterprise and professional services. The State University of New York and privately-endowed Hartwick College have replaced the railroad as principal employers. But the D&H is still going strong under its most recent management (The Canadian Pacific) and long freight trains still thunder past the old park, their whistles sometimes drowning out the voice of the public address announcer.

Damaschke Field, now in its 89th year of service, is one of the most spacious in the NY-P League. Signs on the fences down the foul lines indicate the distance from home plate is 338 feet and at straightaway center 404 feet. Ball park denizens will argue the field is bigger than that and theorize many balls caught in this stadium would be out of most league parks. Over the left field wall and beyond the spacious Neahwa Park looms Franklin Mountain at the northwesterly edge of the Catskills. Over the right field fence twinkle the lights of the city. The buildings of Hartwick College, perched precariously on steep Oyaron Hill, keep watch on the old stadium where that college's baseball, soccer and (once upon a time football) teams have played.

The venerable park is aging but is not neglected. Work has continued over the years on improving the facility and, under a recent grant from the State of New York and with help from the always supportive City of Oneonta (which owns the facility), more work is scheduled. It appears the old girl will be around for her 100th birthday party when the year 2005 rolls around.

Dana Foti satisfies a young fan's desire for O-Yank souvenirs in 1986.
That was a hot year for a team yo-yo. You just had to have one.
—The Daily Star

16 LAMBROS

One sultry August afternoon in 1966, Joe Buzas sat on Oneonta's Main Street waiting for the stoplight to change. About the time the green signal came on, a young man dashed across the street in front of his car.

Instead of being disturbed by the young man's sprint, the Oneonta Red Sox owner was intrigued.

He turned to his passenger, Neal Bennett general manager of the Sox, and said, "That guy looked like an athlete. Do you know who he is?"

"Everybody knows who he is. That's Nick Lambros. He is one helluva an athlete and he is at the ball park every night doing a lot of cheering for the Yanks and ragging at the other guys."

"Oh, yeah," mused Buzas as they drove away. "I know him."

Buzas remembered Nick Lambros and when he began to put together his plans for the 1967 Oneonta ball club it occurred to him the outspoken Lambros might make a good general manager. He brought that suggestion to Sam Nader and his colleagues and they agreed.

It was an excellent choice.

Lambros proved an adequate replacement for Bennett in the areas of sales and business. But he brought a lot more to the Damaschke Field scene than a native business acumen. He brought a dash and a spirit to the O-Yank team which contributed mightily to the winning record of those early years.

He would work around the park early each day painting, hammering, unloading the bread truck, making calls, selling tickets, greeting visitors, signing players....all the things a minor league general manager has to do during his 14 to 16 hour work day.

But Nick Lambros's day at the ballpark really began when the players showed up. He couldn't wait to get out on the field and compete with the young athletes.

There were people who thought the young son of immigrant Greek parents was too cocky, that there was too much braggadocio in his manner. But, as an old NFL player once said, "It ain't braggin' when you can do it." And Nick Lambros could do it.

Competition and the challenge were a way of life for him. Lambros was a natural and gifted athlete at any sport he tried and he was anxious to take on any and all comers.

He held city tennis championships; city and county golf championships. An all-star basketball and baseball player at Oneonta High and Hartwick College, he led those teams to league and sectional titles.

Deane Winsor, a veteran baseball man who managed the semi-pro Milford Macs through 50 winning seasons, says flat out, "Nick Lambros is the finest all-around athlete I have ever coached."

Many share that opinion.

Lambros impressed baseball people enough so that he had a shot at professional ball with the Dodgers. He went to Vero Beach, Florida and had a great spring training, hitting and fielding with the best.

Benny Borgman and Dale Johnson, major league scouts who worked the Oneonta area for many years, said, "This kid was one of the finest prospects we ever saw. A line drive hitter, an infielder with a great arm and a competitive spirit unequalled in that Dodger camp."

Why the release then?

Nick Lambros was born with one leg shorter than the other and the major league people felt this would hamper him when it came to playing a 154 game big league schedule.

For a few days, the irrepressible little guy was uncharacteristically down. But it didn't last and it wasn't long before he picked up his tennis racket, his golf clubs and his ball glove and returned to competition.

He finished his formal education and it wasn't long before he got his chance to coach basketball at Oneonta High where he had starred as a player.

The winning continued; league and sectional championships came along and huge crowds cheered on the Yellowjackets. As always, Lambros had a flair and his teams were exciting; the games played with considerable elan.

Then Athletic Director Jim Konstanty, an all-star major leaguer himself and a great athlete at Syracuse University, offered Lambros a job coaching basketball at Hartwick College.

Actually, the decision was difficult for Lambros who loved the high school scene and the young athletes. But, after long discussions with wife Sharon, friends and other family members, he took the job he still holds. His winning percentage, by the way, is more than .650. He still loves the job and approaches it with intensity, but regrets the fact it takes time away from his wife and two daughters.

By 1990, the incessant pounding brought on by his intense competitive spirit resulted in serious complaints from his body. Corrective measures had to be taken and so Lambros underwent corrective surgery on the hip opposite his short leg. The years of competition had taken their toll. This operation was no small matter as it involved replacing the hip and yet two weeks after the surgery and still on crutches, Lambros fired a two over par 74 at the difficult Oneonta Country Club course.

Thus, it was quite natural for him, still a young man in the mid 1960's, to want to test himself against the Yankee players.

One day in the early June of 1967, Manager Frank Verdi had his Oneonta Yankee infielders practicing rundowns between third and home. Finally Lambros could no longer control himself and he yelled out, "Hell, I can be the base runner and there is no way you guys are gonna get me out."

"Okay, wise guy, come on out here," yelled Verdi.

Still fast and agile, Lambros went out to third, still wearing street clothes. He got into a rundown and got back to third. The next rundown, he reached home safely—same with the third rundown. Verdi and his players were becoming exasperated.

"All right, that's enough," thundered the O-Yank skipper. "Gimme the goddam ball." And he took his place behind the plate.

This time, they got the hustling Lambros and Verdi applied a vigorous tag which could be heard up in the grandstand.

"That'll hold you," said the dusty, sweating Yankee manager. He held out his hand.

They shook and then Nick said, "I'll be back tomorrow." Then he dusted himself off and headed for the concession stand to get things ready for the night's business.

He threw batting practice for O-Yank clubs all during his tour of duty as general manager which lasted 10 years. He frequently challenged managers like Jerry Walker, who had been a fine major league hurler with Baltimore.

"You can't get me out," he said to Jerry one day. "I'll hit the best you got."

And he did until the frustrated Walker gave him one inside to end the challenge for that day.

Nick Lambros, as O-Yank General Manager, found it easy to relate to young players.

"He was getting angry," Lambros said, "and I wasn't going to take any chances. He could still throw pretty darn good."

Lambros was close to the managers who came through Damaschke Field. An athlete and a coach himself, he under-stood the manager's job and he was able to respond quickly to their requests. Often they became close personal friends. Mike Ferraro was very close to Nick, Verdi stayed at his house before the Verdi clan arrived and the Walkers were frequent companions.

The big pitcher from Ada, Oklahoma loved to make ice cream for his wife and daughters, so one day he asked Lambros if he knew where he could get an ice cream machine.

"No sweat," said Lambros, "let's go." And they drove up over the nearby hills to the little village of Franklin.

At the old-fashioned general store, they found an old style, huge, commercial ice cream machine created for mass production.

"You bonehead," said Walker, "I don't want to go into business, I just wanted to make ice cream for my wife and the kids. Geez, I thought you had some brains."

The genial keeper of the general store listened to the two baseball people for a couple of minutes and then, as they started to leave the store, he said, "You know, I think I can help you."

And he took them into the cluttered back room where, way up on a shelf toward the back was an old-time ice cream maker complete with handle for turning at the critical moment. Walker wasted no time in buying it.

As they left the store, Walker said, "I take back everything I said to you back there. This is terrific." Nick Lambros says Walker's ice cream was the best he ever had.

Looking back over the years at Damaschke and considering the success of the Oneonta Yankees and pondering the question of why Damaschke Field baseball is so special, Nick Lambros suddenly sat upright and said:

"It's the people. It's the owners, the managers, the coaches, the fans, the players - everyone."

After a moment lost in thought, he said, "They're ball park people! Yes, that's it, ball park people. They are special and no matter what their role, they are at home in the ball park."

There is a special bond which makes it possible for people who had been through a season together at Damaschke, to greet each other sincerely and warmly years later at another ball park far removed from Oneonta.

Take, for instance, Lambros meeting Damaso Garcia in Toronto years after Garcia's O-Yank days. Damaso, now an established major league player, ran up to Nick and said, "Look, Nick, I good player now."

When Garcia was in Oneonta, a rookie who spoke little English, Lambros had spent hours hitting ground balls to him and helping him in others ways.

Success is created by guys in the background like Pete Sheehy, clubhouse and equipment man at Yankee Stadium since the days of Babe Ruth, making certain the Oneonta club got the best he could provide.

It is created by community support such as that provided by Hartwick College which makes its academic and physical facilities available to wives of managers, coaches and players to help them through the sometimes long summers. Hartwick and Oneonta State have provided dorm facilities in past years when the room crunch became serious for the young O-Yank players.

But in summing it up..."It is the ball park people."

17 NAMEDROPPING

M any well-known people have turned up at Damaschke Field over the years for a variety of reasons. Some, like television talk show host Sally Jessie Raphael, pop in unannounced just to see a ball game. Others, like Baseball Commissioner Bowie Kuhn, came for the love of the game and an opportunity to see his boyhood hero George Case. Another commissioner, Peter Ueberroth, visited Damaschke Field for a closeup look at minor league baseball.

Pennsylvania Governor Richard Thornburg dropped in one night and Yankee owner George Steinbrenner has been to see a game on several occasions.

Former ballplayers like Ted Williams, Whitey Ford, Yogi Berra, Rocky Colavito and many others have spent days at the old ball yard as coaches. The list is long and includes marquee names like Mickey Mantle and Joe DiMaggio. Jesse Owens was a gracious and charming visitor.

It is the writers who have contributed most toward telling of the Oneonta Yankee story far and wide.

Most of them are from New York, home of the parent Yankees; men and women looking for some relief from the uproar and grind of life in the metropolis and finding it in the trees and greenery of the rural countryside.

They find it in Oneonta which has been featured in the *New York Times*, *The Daily News*, *Sports Illustrated*, *The New Yorker* and many other publications as the seasons roll by and the Oneonta Yankees continue to post winning record after winning record.

Roger Angell, writing for *The New Yorker*, found the bucolic charm he was looking for when, on the advice of friends in New York, he and his wife stopped in Oneonta and visited Damaschke Field in the summer of 1992..

The result of his stay in Oneonta was a long piece in the magazine, an article which people like Sam Nader or Isabel McManus clip, copy, save and/or distribute to friends.

Here's a portion of the way Angell handled the description of an evening at Damaschke:

"I'm sitting in the owner's box, watching the Yankees, and a baby has just crawled under my chair. We're in the second inning, and a delicious coolness has begun to rise out of the grass and spread itself into the deep tree shadows in right field, eating into the warmth of the day."

He goes on to describe activity on the field (getting every player's name correct), then goes on:

"The baby's mother apologetically retrieves her offspring who has been gumming the laces on one of my Keds, and plumps the child down on her lap in an adjoining box.

"I sit back and let my gaze follow the painted foul line out to the foul pole (a white stick above the dark red outfield wall) and beyond, past street lights, to a steeply sloping distant hill, almost a mountain, where I can still make out a horseshoe shaped meadow, just yellow enough to hold its shape against the summer dark.

"This is an ancient diamond, much older than Yankee Stadium - they have been playing baseball here since 1905 - but on this particular evening, just before the Fourth of July weekend, it feels young."

Angell, with his great command of prose, goes on to describe the egg toss, a spectator-oriented event which almost all O-Yank players will remember.

In talking about the players, Angell was perceptive when he said, "They ranged considerably in build and weight, of course, and also in experience (some players from warm weather schools had almost twice as many games under their belts as did Harvard slugger Nick DelVecchio or Jeff Antolick, a pitcher from Lafayette College) but there was something close to a family resemblance among them. I couldn't quite account for that at first, then I got it; they were all young together."

A dozen or so years prior to Roger Angell's visit to Oneonta, a hard-nosed sportswriter named Ken Rappaport visited Damaschke Field when he was doing research for his delightful little book, *Diamonds in the Rough*, which endeavored to tell the story of minor league baseball.

His approach to telling the Oneonta story differed from Roger Angell's in the use and blending of words and phrases.

"The NY-P League players toil in relatively serene conditions in picturesque Oneonta, New York. Damaschke Field, a sturdy, oddly handsome ballpark, is a senior citizen among stadiums. The eye-catching backdrop of the Catskills loom wondrously, the Yankees own 'Green Monster', but unlike the coziness of Fenway Park's legendary relic in left field, there are no easy targets at Damaschke. Only Ruthian clouts go out of the cavernous, tree-lined field.

"Not only is the ball park nestled in a splendid setting, a polished old diamond in Oneonta's charming Neahwa Park, but the tone of play is decidedly low key. In the New York-Penn League they play a schedule less than half of that in the majors.

"It is sort of a halfway house between amateurism and the pros - the first step on a long ladder to the top."

Both writers, and all the others which came before or after them, find themselves charmed by Sam Nader and his family and they wrote volumes about them. All writers explained Oneonta's summer population in not much more than 10,000 and that the O-Yanks draw around 50,000 or more each season.

Phil Pepe, long-time writer for the New York *Daily News*, still visits Damaschke Field. Before him came Gene Ward of the late *Daily Mirror* and a host of others. (Ward, incidentally, was an Oneonta native.)

Writers describe Oneonta's proximity to Cooperstown and the National Baseball Hall of Fame - some 20 miles away - and they write about the Naders' refusal to sell beer in the ball park.

They explain the annual O-Yank budget runs around $250,000 and local business and professional people support the club by buying signs on the ball park fence and advertising in the club's program. And they tell about the fact the slight profit made each year by the Oneonta Yankees goes back into the ball park or the infrastructure supporting it, things like installing whirlpools, painting seats, repairing grandstands and fixing the press box.

It is highly beneficial to the O-Yank operations these travelling writers write positive things about the community and its old ball park and about the people who make up the O-Yank organization. Negatives are few and far between.

That tells you something about Oneonta and its Yankees and helps to explain why winning is part of the tradition of this storied minor league baseball franchise.

The O-Yank "family" poses for a photo with famous Olympian Jesse Owens, in town to speak at the annual "Hot Stove" dinner in 1972. Standing, (from left) are the author, Bob Whittemore, George Pfister, Alice Nader, Sonny House and Bill Hughes. (Middle row): John Nader, Nick Lambros, "Little Alice" Nader, Sam Nader, Front row: Owens, Carole Pfister and Suzanne Nader.

18 'YEROUT!'

George Washington Case's final season as Oneonta Yankee manager will be remembered as long as baseball is played in Oneonta, for a lot of reasons.

The parent Yankees assembled one of the best squads ever for that 1972 season and no less than six members of that roster went on to the major leagues.

Niagara Falls won the pennant after a great race with Oneonta which went down to the final week. And Larry Murray fell just short of winning the stolen base title when he nailed 59. He missed out in the final week for a very good reason: a tired ballplayer by the last week of August, he had trouble getting on base.

Attendance set a season record when 32,429 paid to see the O-Yanks. But that record only lasted until the 1973 season as the period of steady attendance growth was well under way.

But the biggest news of the 1972 season was made by a rival manager Chuck Cottier of the pennant winning Niagara Falls club.

During a clutch game in the heat of August at Damaschke Field, Niagara Falls mounted a strong rally in the ninth inning, a rally which would certainly put the game away.

At a critical stage of that uprising, Base Umpire Steve Palermo called a Niagara runner out for interfering with an Oneonta infielder. Cottier raced onto the field to argue the call and the debate waxed hot and heavy until Cottier, realizing he was close to getting kicked out, finally turned and started toward the third base dugout.

As he crossed the third base line, Cottier turned and yelled something to Palermo. The umpire promptly ejected the Falls pilot who turned, charged out onto the field and tackled Palermo. As the two rolled around in the grass behind the mound, the crowd sat in amazement - not one fan, writer, club official, or player had ever seen that happen before.

"I was dumbfounded," said the veteran Case. "In all my years in the game I had never seen such a thing happen. It is even more surprising to me because Cottier played for me in Hawaii and there was never any indication of a short fuse in his makeup."

Steve Palermo went on to become one of the American League's top umpires. He became a sort of folk hero in 1991 when he was shot and badly hurt in an attempt to rescue a woman from a parking lot mugger.

Palermo, earlier in that campaign, had been teamed with Dave Pallone, making one of the most colorful umpiring teams the NY-P League had ever seen. Before this episode, however, they had been broken up. Pallone, too, made the majors but his career was shortened by controversy which resulted in his leaving the game.

NY-P League president Vincent M. McNamara was surprisingly lenient in taking punitive action against Cottier, suspending him for only three days.

"Niagara Falls was in a pennant race and I have to live there," he was to say when pressed on the matter by O-Yank officials and Jud Magrin, sports editor of the *Oneonta Daily Star.* "I could not drop a manager at that particularly time of the season.

"Most important, however, is the fact that there are mitigating circumstances which I prefer not to reveal. Now let there be an end to it." And he would say no more.

One of the ironies of that situation was Cottier and Palermo were good friends and the Niagara Falls manager had written league officials earlier that season in defense of the umpire who he described in glowing terms as a fine arbiter.

But umpiring in the NY-P League seldom produces praise from anyone and is not one of the easiest jobs in sports.

Pay is low and the travel demanding. Most umpires share the transport costs, one driving on a trip and his mate driving the next. They

Being an umpire is tough anywhere, but calls like these at the plate make any young umpire nervous. Oneonta's Tim Beck applies the tag. —The Daily Star

stay, when possible, in rooming houses and share a motel room when a rooming house is not available. Whereas, in the earlier days, the league umpires were off-duty policemen, school teachers and coaches holding down a summer job, today's umpires are part of a development program which begins in accredited umpiring schools in Florida or in the Southwest.

George Case was among veteran managers who would tell the young umpires, "Make your calls emphatically and don't waver; but don't be hard-nosed and don't try to prove what a big man you think you are. Know the rules and abide by them, just do your job. And remember fans come to the ball park to see players, not umpires. Stay in the game use your head and don't showboat.

The young men are taught to be firm, even aggressive in making and defending their calls, but it is difficult at times when a young arbiter comes up against a veteran manager who played and coached in the big leagues and has years of experience as a minor league manager.

When Eric Gregg, now a veteran National League umpire constantly battling to keep his weight under control, began his career as an umpire, his first assignment was in Oneonta.

Before that night's game, the young Gregg (he was only 19 and couldn't have weighed more than 140 pounds despite a six-foot plus frame) was very nervous. As he talked with a sportswriter, he said no to an offer of lunch.

"I couldn't eat right now," he said, "my stomach is full of butterflies." Then he looked at the writer and said, "Do you realize the Oneonta manager, Mr. Case, has been in baseball almost twice as long as I've been alive?"

The writer assured Gregg he had nothing to fear from Case who realized the importance of umpires and the need to teach them.

The young umpires are fortunate in this respect; they will find managers in the NY-P League who understand their importance to the game's future and are willing to be patient and even help them along the road toward The Show. Older managers like Case are expected to act that way toward the young arbiters, but the umpires are often surprised to find younger managers also can be patient and understanding.

This patience and understanding frequently has to be learned by a young manager, particularly one who has just come in from the big leagues.

In the spring of 1987 at the Yankee minor league complex in Hollywood, Florida, 1985-86 O-Yank pilot Buck Showalter sat rapping with Gary Allenson who was to manage the 1987 Oneonta club. The latter had been in the big leagues with Boston only the year before so it was like starting all over again.

"You may find it difficult at times to accept the umpiring," Showalter said. "Most of the umps are very young and they might try to be very tough if they have come from an umpiring school which teaches that way.

"When you start an argument with one of those kids you must control your temper and exercise extreme patience, even when you know you are right. You have to realize they are young and trying to learn just like your players ." That's not easy in the heat of the game.

"That's easier said than done," replied Allenson. "An umpire is an umpire and they have to be set straight. I can't see it any other way."

But before the 1987 NY-P League campaign was over, it was a fairly common sight after a game to see Gary Allenson lecturing a young umpire on basics.

Despite the difficult life of a minor league umpire, aspiring young men continue to come along. Nearly all are single; the life of a young married man is all but impossible. They cannot have their wife with them so the young couple must live apart.

One young wife showed up before a game at Damaschke Field in the summer of 1992, an infant in her arms. She asked if the umpires had checked in yet and was told they had not.

She returned to her car and waited a few minutes before two young men drove up in a Volkswagen Beetle.

One of them greeted her joyously, gave her a huge hug and picked up the youngster. It was one of the few times the little family would be together all summer. "I drove up from Poughkeepsie to see Dave for a few minutes," the young wife said. "Our little boy doesn't have much chance to see his Dad."

She agreed this was a tough time for them but said her husband had suffered an injury the year before, an injury which ended his playing days at a young age.

"He wants to stay in baseball, he loves the game," she said. "And I'm willing to stick it out for a while to see how it goes.

"I hope he makes it."

There is time for a family later but not during the earlier years of these dedicated young men most of whom, for one reason or another, could not make it as a player and turned to umpiring as a way to stay close to the game. Baseball comes first and a roster of umpires during any NY-P League season, such as l988, will show 12 men - all single.

"It's not an easy life and it's very lonely. You can be certain nobody likes you," said one young umpire during the 1992 season, "But the rewards, if you make it, are great. Like the great Bill Klem said, 'It's not an easy life but you can't beat the hours'."

19 BULLETS

T he guns had already begun to fire heralding the bloodiest war in American history when baseball started in Oneonta. Fort Sumter was only a place "down South somewhere," remote indeed to the young men living in the foothills of the Catskill Mountains. They occupied their time away from chores playing "a game of ball." The games were usually played in the street which, even though unpaved, provided a fairly level ground for their game.

An article in the June 9, 1861 *Oneonta Herald* reveals the game was being played in that village. More than 131 years ago, the editor waxed eloquent about the game.

"The health-giving exercise of such a manly game as ball-playing," he said, "is of itself sufficient reason for its encouragement.

"It establishes a social feeling - a sort of equalization of individual position -that gives us a happier view of life by breaking in the outward crusts of our selfishness and impressing us with the thought that we may be mutually conducive to each other's happiness and pleasure in life if we will but try it.

"The Game of Ball symbolizes, to our minds, a great deal of the game of life and especially in the opportunities it presents for the exercise of social amenities and courtesies."

The verbose editor saw the game as an opportunity to enhance one's social standing. He went on to say the village of Oneonta "is an inviting spot for the clerk, the professional man or the mechanic who may wish to engage in ball-playing and even groups of loungers who enjoy it comfortably."

But this civic minded man had an admonition for those engaged in ball playing. He wanted them to move the site of their games from the streets to "some more appropriate location."

He went on to say that street games were "quite inconvenient to passers-by, particularly the ladies. We know of several instances when ladies passing by have been hit in the face with the ball, causing considerable pain.

"The street is no place to play ball; select some grass plot. We should think it much more preferable and considerably less expensive to some."

It can be assumed that the ballplayers heeded the advice and took to the nearby meadows to indulge in their game. They had an idea of what the field should be like; after all, Gen. Doubleday and his play-mates had drawn up such a field only 22 years before that in a pasture just 20 miles away in Cooperstown.

But the hell and fury of a bloody civil war soon reached into the hilly, backwoods terrain of Otsego County and balls and bats were put away to be replaced by rifles and bayonets. There are no records of or any comment on "the game of ball" until the cannons were silenced in 1865. There are scattered reports of soldiers playing the game during idle days in camp but nothing formal showed up until 1867.

First report of a game in that season 125 years ago was the story of a game between two neighborhood clubs on May 21, 1867. This must have been a nightmare for scorers as Ouleout Baseball Club beat the Unadilla Baseball Club, 89-10. The winners scored 13 runs in the fifth inning, 12 runs in the sixth and again in the seventh and put it away with a 26-run eighth inning. The 16 additional runs in the ninth didn't really matter much.

The account of that game in *The Oneonta Herald* included a box score which listed only outs and runs. It showed, for example, that Edgerton of the Ouleout team was put out twice but scored 13 times.

At the bottom of the box score (we call it "underneath" in today's baseball lingo) the big item was "fly catches made."

Later that year, Oneonta lost to Otego, 30-29.

"A match game of baseball was played on the grounds of the former on Friday last which stood Oneonta 29 Otego 30. Good runs were made by both clubs but at the beginning of the game Oneonta led off very poorly and as they did that Otego thought they must follow their leaders.

"E.B. Jewell and E.G. Bixby were leaders of scores in Oneonta club and Stilson and Bacon in Otego club. Frank Eckert and George Ingalls were the fly-catchers and they did it well."

While the reporter of that long gone era may have been less than lucid in his report of the game, he finished with a knowledgeable flourish by saying, "At the close of the game they adjourned to the Eagle Hotel where an excellent dinner was served."

So that's the way it all began more than a century ago in this old city. Hard working men and "loungers" got involved for the sheer fun of it while eyeing the opportunity to improve their social standing and perhaps catch the eye of a pretty lady.

Nobody then could even dream of what would happen in the next one hundred years.

The 1860's and 1870's came and went. Baseball games were played informally as a recreational and social activity; accounts from that era reveal little about the evolution of the game and the development of the men who played it.

It would appear the first formally organized team showed up in 1876. This baseball team wore sharp uniforms trimmed in black with the club's name, "Atnoeno" (Oneonta spelled backward), written in script on the front of the uniforms. Their success - or lack of it - on the diamond went unrecorded for the most part.

First tremors of what would become major rumblings were felt in the fast-growing community, late in 1878. A brief piece appeared on October 7 that year saying simply, "Oneonta wants a baseball club next year."

Another decade was to pass before the appearance of an organized club in Oneonta, but the groundwork had been done and the scene set.

20 Ugly

Records of the years from the late 1870's until 1888 are non-existent. It is known that baseball, in one form or another, was played in and around Oneonta but because the sport was more of a recreational and social activity, there was precious little publicity.

It seems as if the reasons for the scarcity of baseball news might lie in the fact The *Herald* editor of the day was not in love with the game. In an 1870 editorial he wrote, "We do not discourage any amusement where its tendency is to benefit in a permanent manner, but let Oneonta be rid of baseball playing!" In an 1873 editorial, this worthy was telling of the brutal side of the game and he reported that: "Russell is the first victim of that ugly game, baseball. His thumb will be well in a few days."

But the good old "Atnoeno" nine hung in there and by 1888 things had changed, partly because of the success of the Atnoeno club and partly because city and area fans were already exhibiting their undying love for and interest in "organized" baseball. Those feelings remain to-day and are a major reason this story can be told more than 100 years later.

Also, by 1888, The *Herald* had changed its tune regarding baseball and began to carry game reports, cryptic and brief, to be sure, but there. This story from The *Herald* on August 23, 1888 told the game story this way: "A game of ball between Morris and the Oneonta club was played on Saturday. The Oneonta club, as a matter of course, won. Score 9 to 2."

Umpires in those early days had to have been interesting people. They only used one arbiter and sometimes he was a member of one club or another. At times the umpire was praised for his efforts and at other times he came in for some abuse. Witness this article in The *Herald* of August 30, 1888: "A ball game was played yesterday between two Oneonta clubs, the Blue Labels defeating the Oneontas by a score of 6 to 1. At one time it looked as though the crowd was bent on eating up the umpire."

But, on another occasion in a game against Afton, the writers of the day were most kind. "The game was carried through without a particle of ill will or the least display of temper on either side," wrote one reporter. "The umpire, Mr. Carruth, although himself a member of the

Afton club, rendered his judgment in a spirit of entire fairness. Neither club in a single instance protested against his decisions. It was a delicate position in which to place a man, but Mr. Carruth won honors in it."

Things became a bit more organized as the 1889 season rolled around. Attempts were made to schedule games earlier in the year as part of an effort to be more formal. In April it was announced that "a movement is afoot to organize a baseball nine in Oneonta and to arrange for a series of games with first class clubs. Oneonta has some good material for a nine."

Records of that season are scarce but available clippings reveal consistent winning. And the team kept busy. For example, the week of May 16 and 19 found Oneonta slated for a game against Cooperstown Thursday and against Afton Saturday. The games were normally scheduled for 3:30 pm and the price was right: 25 cents, ladies admitted free. If you wished to sit in the grandstand, there was an extra charge of 10 cents.

The teams for most of the games consisted of Abbott and Tobin, pitchers; Wilson, lf; Giles, 2b; Holmes, c; Bowen, ss; Rogers, cf; Abbott or Tobin, rf and Scully 1b. Reporters of that era seldom used first names nor did they ever reveal the site of the games, other than one vague reference to a field "on the East End", presumably the fairgrounds.

It may be the groundwork for a more active, formal baseball club in 1890 was laid at a meeting on May 20, 1889 after the Afton game when fans (or "cranks" as they were called then) gathered to plan for the future.

The *Herald* on May 16 had suggested a meeting be held on Saturday evening after the game with Afton "and then and there appoint the necessary officers for the government of the team and perfect the final terms with the players."

Status of the players prior to the 1890 season regarding pay for services is uncertain but it is obvious one of the primary purposes of the meeting May 20, 1889 was to plan a pay schedule for what was the first real professional team in Oneonta's baseball history.

Meanwhile, the 1889 season wore along and the Oneonta team won more than its share of games. There were several great performances, but perhaps the most outstanding individual feat was completed by a pitcher named Fournier who struck out 19 in a one hitter against archrival Afton. Each strikeout was credited as an assist in those days and, as Fournier also had a fielding play, he was credited with 20 of Oneonta's 24 assists.

The club finished the season on an October day in New Berlin which was so cold the Oneontans played with their coats on, not warmup jackets but honest-to-goodness overcoats. But with or without coats, the ball club played well. It completed the season with a 20-7 record and Oneonta claimed the mythical Central New York championship.

Despite the team's winning record and spiffy new gray uniforms trimmed in blue, many fans of that era regarded the 1889 team as "an indifferent team, gotten up spasmodically" and called for better things in 1890. The feeling was strong in the city and a serious movement got under way to put together a contending professional club. Money was pledged by interested "cranks" and set aside while the organization movement continued.

In July, 1889 the Oneonta Baseball Association elected David F. Wilber, president; H.E. Bundy, vice-president; William Mills, secretary and W.E. Ford, treasurer. They made up the board of directors together with F.D. Hanford, W.H. Porter and W.G. Stanton.

After two successful meetings in early 1890, The *Herald* was able to report on February 13, "It now seems certain that the town will have a first class club next summer if the citizens will, by the purchase of season tickets, assure a reasonable amount of patronage." Mixing a dash of editorial opinion with a news story, as papers often did in those days, the editor says "the businessmen of the village can well afford to do this in view of the large number of people attracted to town by a fine league game."

In January, area newspapers such as The *Albany Argus* had begun pushing for the formation of a league to include teams from Albany, Troy, Cobleskill, Oneonta, Binghamton and Susquehanna, Pennsylvania. They were successful and in January 30 editions, the *Binghamton Republican* was able to report Albany had brushed off overtures from the International League and would go with the state league concept. The story also said Troy would have a very strong entry, the wealthy backers from the previous year's amateur club showing willingness to jump into the pro ranks.

A meeting in Oneonta on January 27, 1890 firmed up the local entry. It was agreed $2500 would have to be raised if the project was to be launched. Half of that amount was raised at the meeting. Committees were appointed to push other fund-raising endeavors such as stock subscriptions and outright cash donations. By late February, organizers were able to report success all along the line.

So the local club, named The Hustlers, was about to become reality. But, what about the league?

In late February, an organization meeting was held in Albany. Due to train delays along the Albany and Susquehanna Railroad lines, the delegations from Oneonta and Cobleskill were late in arriving and the meeting did not get under way until 10 p.m,. two and a half hours behind schedule.

Albany, Troy, Poughkeepsie, Cobleskill and Oneonta were represented. Although the league setup was still vague, those at the meeting approved a salary limit of $700 per club per month, set a guarantee of $40 per game with the privilege of 50 percent of the gate receipts, and agreed upon a forfeit fee of $250 per club. They also agreed to feel out interests in Utica, Johnstown and Gloversville with regard to joining the circuit. The season was scheduled to begin May 10.

By April 3, Manager Dowling had signed 10 players and Charles F. Shelland of Oneonta had been elected secretary of the new league. Directors agreed upon a home schedule of 42 games for each club, a full schedule of 84 games with the season starting May 10 and closing Sept. 10. Teams from Utica, Schenectady and Johnstown-Gloversville entered the circuit which was to be called The State League. The Oneonta delegation showed it had some clout when it succeeded in preventing the entry of teams from Binghamton and Susquehanna, Pennsylvania.

On April 10, the *Herald* announced, "Manager Dowling has 11 good men engaged, among them three pitchers and two catchers. He is satisfied that he has an excellent club - far better than ever played in Oneonta before - and one which will do valiant battle for the league pennant."

Stories of May 1, 1890 showed these players (again, in the style of newspapers of that era, no first names were listed): "Manager Dowling, 1b, of Syracuse; Conkley, 2b, of Oneida; Burns, ss, of Elmira; Speers, 3b, of Fort Wayne, Ind.; Hassett, lf, of London, Conn.; Gildea, cf, of the New England League; Case, of Oneida and Leary of Concord, N.H. and an unknown, pitchers plus Wente of Utica and Gleason of Canandaigua, catchers."

Friday, May 16 was set for the home opener against Albany and a gala day was planned featuring the Oneonta city band rendering "a choice musical program" and speeches by the appropriate political dignitaries.

The stage was set for the launching of professional baseball in Oneonta.

21 SHAKY

So, the 1890 season got under way. Games were played at the fairgrounds on the east side of the city. That area contained a big track for horse racing, always a highlight of the annual county fair. Now a pleasant residential area known as Belmont Circle, the shape of the track is still there but in the form of paved, well lighted streets.

The Oneonta team got off to a slow start but did show evidence of power in that first week. On one occasion, they walloped favored Albany, 17-6, and the *Albany Journal* writer described it this way: "The 10 earned runs indicate they are the hardest kind of hitters. Alas and alack, the home team fell upon our nine, knocked our twirlers out of their boxes as fast as one relieved the other and so bewildered the others that, before they knew it, they were beaten most ingloriously."

At the end of the first week, Troy, with a 5-1 record, topped the standings. The Cobleskill entry followed with a mark of 3-1. Next came Albany which was playing .500 ball with its 3-3 record. Oneonta checked in with a rather disappointing 2-4 mark and Johnstown-Gloversville was tied with Utica both having won only once while showing three times in the lost column.

As the summer wore on, the Oneonta club stumbled badly and attendance dwindled. Some games were played on "the fine new field in Cooperstown" in an effort to bolster interest but to little avail. On August 11, Manager Dowling was fired and George Geer, who had managed the Mansfield team to the Ohio State League championship, was brought in. With him came several players from the Mansfield club, including Billy Klingman who went on to play 13 years in the big leagues as an infielder. Another was J. Henry Fournier who pitched the one-hitter the previous summer for Oneonta.

In those days there were episodes of all kinds. Much of the travel back then was by horse-drawn vehicles, called buses, and by train. Once when the Oneonta team arrived back in town via horse and carriage after a defeat, some of the local wise guys planned a display of fireworks in mock celebration of the "victory." Unfortunately for the driver (a Mr. Forester), the team was spooked by the fireworks and bolted; the heavy carriage ran over the driver's foot causing a bad break. A purse was collected to help him foot the bill.

Another time, a local reporter saw the umpire's work as the reason for an Oneonta loss to Utica one August day. Unruly Oneonta fans apparently agreed with him. This caused the writer to say, "Umpire Tyler isn't in favor in Oneonta - that's for certain. While he may mean to be fair in his decisions, it is clear to the impartial observer that he 'roasted' the Oneonta boys in the game with the Uticas on Wednesday. Defeat followed and this increased the bitterness against him.

"But because Mr. Tyler is unfitted for the place he holds and renders decisions that are unfair, is no excuse for the disgraceful scenes enacted in this village on Wednesday night.

"Such scenes do Oneonta no credit; they create a prejudice against baseball and they should never be repeated."

Underlying all of these goings on was the fact the Oneonta team was a consistent loser and nobody was very happy about the situation. The new ball team fell into the losing ways of the old club. And so the stage was set for the dismal ending to the 1890 season which had been launched with hopes so high. After a 10-7 loss to Troy on September 2, the team was disbanded. The players were paid off and they went their separate ways, most of them to other league clubs.

One item of considerable general interest transcending baseball was the launching of a new daily newspaper, The *Oneonta Daily Star*. To one of their reporters went the assignment of covering the dismal end of the 1890 season. His story told of low fan interest and the backers' unwillingness to continue shelling out money. But into the story he injected a more insidious note. The last paragraph of his report of September 3, 1890 said, "It was currently reported at Troy last evening that several Oneonta players were not at all sorry because Troy won and that their playing helped very materially in bringing about such a result.

"At any rate, several of the home team were very suspicious as to the honesty of the playing of one or two men."

And that story served as an ignominious end to the first year of real professional baseball in Oneonta.

Oneonta finished fifth in the six-team league with a 36-43 record. The pennant race was a good one elsewhere, with Troy winning the title by 15 percentage points over Cobleskill and Johnstown-Gloversville.

One of the league's best players was Bill Dahlen of Cobleskill, a second baseman who went to the Chicago Cubs the following season. He played 21 years for the Cubs, Giants, Braves and Dodgers, then managed the Dodgers, a club he was piloting when Casey Stengel made his debut in 1912.

And so went Oneonta's first year in professional baseball. It was to be 34 years before the game returned.

22 GAP

If there is one constant thread running through the fabric of Oneonta's baseball history, it is the community's love for the game. No matter how bad things became toward the close of one season, when the following summer rolled around, one could find good baseball being played before sizable crowds. Games were reported with critical enthusiasm by men from the *Oneonta Herald* and, after the turn of the century, by *The Daily Star.*

Despite the rather dubious closing of the 1890 season, the bats and gloves and baseballs and fans were back in 1891.

While there was no attempt to form a professional team in the Gay Nineties, it seemed as if everyone was either playing or going to a game of ball out at the fairgrounds. There were lots of local rivalries to pique the fans' interest. Two teams, The Lewis Hose and Steamer Company and the Wilber Hook and Ladder, represented the fire department. The police department fielded a team as did several fraternal organizations. Company G of the National Guard played a long schedule against teams throughout the area and the Normal School team became a powerhouse and won more than its share of games against varied opposition.

Baseball continued to produce lots of interest and excitement. There were many interesting little episodes. One such episode came in New Berlin in August, 1902 when the Company G team thought it was being misused by the umpire. The Guardsmen demanded a new umpire be brought into the game. When that request was refused, they argued no further, they simply packed up and went home.

In 1905, a most significant event took place when baseball activities were moved to the Elm Park location which was formally dedicated on Memorial Day. (Oneonta lost to Norwich, 11-5 in that day's baseball attraction.) The Elm Park location has been in use ever since. There were some complaints about the "dips in the playing surface, particularly in the outfield" but generally the facility was accepted and enjoyed by the players and the "cranks."

There was one quick advantage to the new location for some folks. By "coincidence", freight cars were parked on the D&H Railroad line just outside the park on game days and these were covered with fans about the time the first pitch was thrown in that day's game.

Oneonta began to move toward developing a stronger team when several players were imported in 1906. These names appeared on the club roster: Gaylord, Hogan, Hennessey, Tiffany, Miller, McMahon, Amsbury, Vortigen, Sandwich, Malarkey, Sullivan and Norton (a local catcher). The players often were given jobs on the railroad as partial "pay." The season was highlighted on August 11 when Oneonta played the Cuban Giants to a 1-1 tie in 16 innings.

The Giant roster consisted primarily of Black players who were not allowed to play in the big leagues, but the team was considered to be the equal of most major league clubs.

By 1908, Oneonta had a strong team in place and a regular schedule was played throughout the summer. Those teams played around 70 games, playing nearly every day and often playing two games in one day—sometimes at different sites. It is incredible to think about the demands upon the players, many of whom had full-time jobs and families to look after. Interest had become so strong in 1908 The *Herald* editorialized on August 20, 1908, saying: "Oneonta is immensely interested in baseball right now, and although there are things more important than baseball, we are inclined to think the interest does the town good.

"Oneonta has a fast team on the diamond and the town feels good over the fact that it is winning more games than it is losing. The games have drawn many people from a wide area and these strangers have been impressed with Oneonta and its progress, its business activity, its thrifty homes and handsome public buildings.

"They are impressed with the fact that Oneonta has a future and that it is alive to the great possibilities that future contains.

"To a great extent, then, baseball advertises a town and helps its growth."

On August 7, 1908, an event of some significance took place when the Cherokee Indians came to town to play a couple of games. In the first game, Maud Nelson pitched for the visitors. Maud, billed as "the best female pitcher in baseball", was treated roughly by the locals who won the game.

But the second game was the key event. The Cherokee club brought its own lights and the first night game in Oneonta's history was played. Some sports enthusiasts believe the larger, softer ball and the shortened base paths used in the game as a concession to the weak lights were the first unknowing steps in the development of the game of softball.

Late in the year another event took place which was to have far-reaching ramifications. Dr. and Mrs. Lewis Rutherford Morris presented 75 acres of land surrounding the Elm Street baseball field to the city for use as a park. They stipulated the park be a multi-purpose facility and suggested that an appropriate Indian name for the park would be satisfactory to them. The park was named "Neahwa", an Iroquois word meaning "gift", in 1911.

Dr. Morris was a direct descendant of Governor Morris, a signer of the Declaration of Independence and of Jacob Morris, an officer in the

American Army during the Revolution who was awarded a large tract of land in Otsego County for his services.

Wooden grandstands were erected in the Neahwa Park baseball field in 1908.

In 1910, 1911 and 1912, most communities were represented on the baseball field by college players, many from the Ivy League. During those years, the Brown University team made Oneonta its summer home; Chic Raymond was the manager.

Ray Chapman played for Richfield Springs during this era, the same Ray Chapman of the Cleveland Indians who was killed a few seasons later when struck by a pitch from Carl Mays of the New York Yankees during an American League game.

During the 1916 season a name still well-known in the annals of Oneonta baseball surfaced for the first time when a story of an Oneonta High game revealed the manager to be one E.C. Damaschke. Physically handicapped, he was small of stature but big in heart. He eventually became known as "Dutch." This man's contribution to Oneonta baseball - indeed to all sports - cannot be overemphasized. He managed or coached scholastic, amateur, collegiate and semi-pro clubs in basketball and baseball for more than 50 years. He was chairman of the Oneonta Recreation Commission for 35 years and devoted his life to the athletes and the children of the city.

Dutch was always one of the first called upon to join an effort to develop or improve sports and was one of the first approached to help with the effort to return organized baseball to Oneonta in the late 1930's and again in the 1960's.

A grateful community and its athletes, men and women. joined in the successful campaign to have the stadium named in "Dutch" Damaschke's honor in 1968.

But the period during which Damaschke first began his career in sports was dominated by another event. World War I came along and the nation turned its eyes toward the winning of the war "to make the world safe for democracy."

In 1919, baseball was back and so was the interest. One of the most interesting aspects of that season was an off-the-field incident in which the so-called "blue laws" were tested when the Oneonta ball club scheduled a Sunday game. Baseball on the Sabbath was prohibited under the local laws of the day but the legal language was vague and there were loopholes, so the Oneonta baseball team decided put the law to the test.

Manager Brown and players Carr and White were arrested and taken away but the game went on. The case of the trio dragged on and on before it finally reached Supreme Court Judge Abraham L. Kellogg of nearby Treadwell. That worthy immediately disqualified himself because of his long and active interest in area sports, particularly baseball. With Lee D. Van Woert attorney for the city and Everett Holmes representing the defendants, the case went before Judge Kiley of Cazenovia. There were more delays but, eventually, the matter was resolved when the men involved were given a reprimand. The basic issue was not cleared up, however, and would turn up again in five years.

An item of interest to area baseball people appeared in the *Utica Daily Press* on October 16, 1919. The story revealed Mike Fogarty and George Oliver of Ilion had joined with one Hardy Richardson (billed as a member of Detroit's Big Four) in writing to suggest a memorial to the game of baseball be erected in Cooperstown. Their memo also suggested a national fund drive be conducted and a game between a team from the National League and a team from the American League be played at a convenient date each summer in Cooperstown. This suggestion came 20 years before the first Hall of Fame ceremonies in Cooperstown in June, 1939.

23 Twenties

In many ways, the 1920's was the most important era in the history of baseball in Oneonta. While it was to be several years before organized baseball returned to the City of the Hills to stay, men and events of those years were important in shaping the events of a later day. Leaders were strong in their love of the game and proved by their actions they were convinced baseball belonged in Oneonta.

There were different motivations. H.P. "Duffer" Weidman couldn't conceal his love for the game any more than he could hide the fact he was a gambler. Gaming was looked at in a different way then and it was commonplace in the stands at ball games. Duffer's idea was to put together a ball club which would win on the field backed by his money. Weidman was well thought of in Oneonta. He had married into the Damaschke family and was widely known - even had a street named for him. He was generous to a fault and usually flush with money. He seldom turned down an acquaintance in need, replying to a plea for money with, "How much do you need?"

He was always around baseball, first surfacing as an umpire during the World War I era. In later years he added a dash of color by having a pet bear who was with Duffer wherever he went. "Why not?" he replied to those who asked why a bear for a pet.

When baseball called, Duffer answered and he was a key player in the development of the game in Oneonta.

In 1920, he decided it was time for the best semi-pro team money could buy. In those days, the term "semi-pro" meant exactly what it said. Many players were hired for the summer and paid. The rest of the team was made up of local players. Weidmann said he didn't mind putting up the money, but added he hoped the fans would come out in support of the winning club he was certain he had assembled.

Two of the imports were Fred Sinstack and Joe Scanlon. Both appeared year after year in the Oneonta lineup, both married local girls and stayed on even after their baseball days were over. Sinstack was 16 years old when he was brought to Oneonta from Naugatuck, Connecticut to play for Weidman. A catcher by trade, he played short or the outfield if needed and first base if necessary. One time he played first base after the regular first sacker was suspended for flattening an umpire during a dispute which led to fisticuffs. Fred's career spanned a quarter century of Oneonta baseball and his lifetime batting average hung at a respectable .267. His family remains in Oneonta today.

Joe Scanlon was a strong, rugged player who could pitch and who could hit as well. He starred for years in an Oneonta uniform and later became fire chief in his adopted city.

Duffer Weidman was certain he had a good team, so certain that he took the train to Binghamton, went to the office of the sporting editor of *The Sun* and said his team would play the E.J. team or the Imperials of Binghamton for a purse of $1,000, whereupon he planked $500 on the desk of the newspaperman, W. Homer Thorne. The sporting editor took up the cudgel for the personable Weidmann and wrote a column which challenged the two Triple Cities clubs to play Oneonta.

He didn't hear immediately from Bill Fischer, manager of the Endicott-Johnson Athletic Association club, but Thorne did get a reply from a Mr. Higgins of the Imperials who said, "I am going to call Mr. Weidman's bluff even if I have to plank down the $500 myself. I am not sure where we will get a diamond but I gave Mr. Weidman my assurance that we would play his team and I offered to bet him another $1,000 that we would beat him."

Betting was commonplace in those days. During games, bettors would wave wads of bills (often a bunch of "singles" rolled into a wad around which was wrapped a more noticeable 10 dollar bill or even a 20) in the stands to attract rival sports.

Weidman's team played well that year, taking on all comers and compiling an outstanding winning record. The victories included wins over the Triple Cities clubs he had called out earlier in the year. It is known Weidman didn't hesitate to bet substantially on his charges and he won much more than he lost.

Miles Dales, who later became a successful real estate broker in Oneonta, was on that 1920 club along with a young dental student from Johnson City named Eddie "Doc" Farrell. He went on to play in The Bigs with the Giants, Braves, Red Sox and Yankees. Farm systems hadn't come about yet in that era and big league scouts found their hopefuls in strong semi-pro clubs like that in Oneonta.

It might be noted, too, the high school team of that year listed names which became familiar to Oneonta fans and to many people in business as well, names such as Farone, Dilello, Delaney, Martin and Brownell.

One of the big events of the 1920 season came in October when Duffer Weidman re-assembled his team to play a special exhibition against a team of touring major leaguers featuring the one and only Babe Ruth.

The *Herald* was so excited about the prospect of seeing the Sultan of Swat that they headlined their story on the game exactly like this in the October 14 edition:

WHEN BABE RUTH BATS
BUSINESS IN ONEONTA WILL SLACKEN
PACE AS EVERYBODY WILL BE GOING

The Babe didn't let them down. The tremendous crowd saw him hit a single, then a double and then a long home run.

Everyone went away happy and excited, most notably Duffer Weidman who made some money on the day and pushed Oneonta baseball up another notch in the process.

Also in 1920, work was completed on field improvements and dugouts were added at Neahwa Park.

A final note on that season: A story in mid-summer about a game included the paragraph which noted: "Burton Hulbert was hit in the face by a foul ball. Further examination revealed his nose was not broken as was originally feared."

24 Spitball

Big Ed Walsh showed up in Oneonta for the 1921 baseball season, the first real major leaguer to manage in the City of the Hills. Walsh would eventually make the National Baseball Hall of Fame in 1946, but that institution didn't even exist when he took over in Oneonta.

Oneonta was fortunate to land Walsh. His was the first big name to be placed on an Oneonta baseball roster and, amazingly enough, he was still strong-armed enough to pitch effectively.

Known as "The Spitball King", Walsh had compiled some impressive numbers for the Chicago White Sox in a career spanning 20 years. For example, he won 40 games for the White Sox in 1908, a year in which he started 56 times! He beat the Cubs twice in the 1906 World Series, striking out 17 batters in one of the games.

He left the Chicago team prior to the infamous Black Sox scandal of the 1919 World Series and was not involved.

Walsh loved Oneonta and the feeling was mutual. As a result, fan support was strong and the team a winner.

It was a strong team; Scanlon and Sinstack were back as was Eddie Farrell and Dorr Hickey. The latter had been with the 1920 Oneonta team, having arrived after working in Newark, New Jersey where he had been a friend of George Weiss, a gentleman generally conceded to have been most responsible for the development of the New York Yankee farm system.

Hickey was from Milford and attended Yale University where his pitching attracted professional attention. But he chose a business career which took him to Newark. He returned to Oneonta in 1920 to join his father in the oil business. He subsequently entered politics, was elected mayor of Oneonta and in the right spot at the right time when Oneonta's chance to enter professional ball came along in 1924 and again in the late 1930's.

Other players on that 1921 club were Ab Hermann who was to become a wealthy trucking executive, secretary to the governor of New Jersey and national chairman of the Republican party. The roster also listed Dewey Steffin, termed "somewhat of a ladies' man" and "Swat" Byrnes, Oneonta's swaggering home run king termed "undoubtedly one of the most popular men ever to play for an Oneonta team."

Mr. Thorne, sporting editor of the *Binghamton Sun*, made frequent trips to see the Oneonta club play and in one of his columns called the team "one of the best semi-pro clubs ever assembled anywhere."

Thurston A. Crounse did the booking for the club and, there being no league for the team, did a remarkable job of scheduling the best teams available - not always an easy task in the days before the interstate highway system.

One game came against the D&H Generals, a game so important that offices in Oneonta and Albany were closed and special trains brought in many of the large crowd which saw Walsh's club win, 3-2.

The joy and enthusiasm of this remarkable season were dimmed in August when word came from Scranton, Pennsylvania that Duffer Weidman had been shot to death early on a Monday morning. Robbery was assumed to be the motive because Weidman had been known to carry large sums of money and reportedly had $5,000 on his person at the time of the murder. Police arrested several men in the case and one man in particular seemed to be the favorite suspect.

But the newspaper stories of the incident and final disposal of the case are difficult to find and researchers believe the case was closed when the suspect was found guilty and jailed.

More than 200 attended Duffer's funeral and an anonymous person penned a touching poem in his memory.

Meanwhile, the 1921 team played on and, when the season ended, club president Dr. F.A. Marx claimed the mythical southern New York championship for the Oneonta club after which Manager Walsh and most of his players went their way.

Another big league man arrived in Oneonta to manage the 1922 club. He was Al Bridwell, best remembered as the man who could have won the National League pennant for the New York Giants in 1908 except for a rookie mistake. With two out in the bottom of the ninth at the Polo Grounds, the Giants and Chicago Cubs were tied. Muddy Reuel was on third for New York and young Fred Merkle on first. Bridwell lined a single to right center and Reuel lumbered home with what appeared to be the winning run. Excited fans poured onto the field and rookie Merkle, fearing the hysterical mob, headed for the clubhouse, never reaching second base.

Alert Cub second baseman Johnny Evers, aware of the mistake, went into the stands after the ball and with a teammate's help wrestled it from a fan. He then raced back onto the field and touched second base. Merkle was called out, the run disallowed and the game ended in a tie. A week later, the season ended with the Cubs and Giants tied. Chicago won the playoff game.

Bridwell's heroic hit was forgotten in the tumult which followed the incident.

Many of the Oneonta regulars from 1921 returned for the next season and the roster was strengthened by the appearance of Owen Carroll, Holy Cross star. He went on to pitch for nine strong seasons in the major leagues after doing well for the Oneonta club in 1922. Actually, he was on the Stamford club's roster but he was "loaned" to Oneonta "for the big games when a lot of money was on the line."

Jim Wiltsie, another pitcher for that club, was to go on to The Bigs, hurling for the Red Sox and the Phillies.

Highlight of the season was an appearance by the St. Louis Cardinals who nipped Oneonta by a 2-1 score. Rogers Hornsby, quite possibly the best hitter the game has known, went three for four that day.

Bridwell was back to manage in 1923 and so was most of his 1922 club. The Cardinals returned for an exhibition in August and prevailed over the Oneonta Giants in another close, well-played game.

A great deal of work was done in and around the ballpark in 1923. The *Herald* reported water mains had been tapped to bring fresh water into the park; a substantial board fence was constructed on land deeded the city by Joseph Molinari; parking space was graded, and a sidewalk was constructed "from the bridge to the grandstand."

The *Herald* article said: "It is hoped the railroad will approve continuing the bridge walk to the D&H tracks. If this is done, the retaining wall will be built up and the watchman's shanty moved down a few feet. Pedestrians will not have to walk in the road." Unfortunately, the 1923 club disbanded before the scheduled closing date simply because good opponents were difficult to come by and fan interest waned. But the club was re-assembled in October for an exhibition against some major league barnstormers and the gate receipts from that well-attended affair helped to alleviate a fiscal crisis.

Oneonta fielded a winner in 1924, called by some writers "the best semi-pro team in New York State." Fred Scinstack (standing, second from left) and Joe Scanlon (kneeling, far right), combined to play 50 years in Oneonta.

25 WILBER

As 1924 arrived, a familiar figure returned to take charge of the flagging Oneonta baseball fortunes. David F. Wilber, who had been president of the Oneonta Community Baseball Association in 1889, attended a meeting in Community Hall on February 20, 1924.

Oneonta was a part-time residence for Wilber by that time as interests in Washington kept him busy. He had not been directly involved with Oneonta baseball since the turn of the century.

But on this cold February night before a jam-packed house, he was at his eloquent best. The meeting had been called to test the community's interest in baseball and its willingness to support it. According to the reports of that meeting, Wilber dealt himself in and "aroused the crowd to a frenzy." He brought the house down when he declared, "I will stick with this to the very end."

Earlier in the year, the Community Athletic Association (as the organization was now known) had announced most of the debt from 1923 had been cleared up and this made it much easier for the group to plan for 1924. As a matter of fact, the fiscal report from the previous year showed a balance of $33.71 so the Association was able to launch 1924 "in the black."

Wilber was elected president that night to succeed Dr. Marx. Some heavy hitters were elected to the board of directors according to the meeting report, like Judge A.L. Kellogg, D.F. Keyes, Harry W. Lee, Chester A. Rote, Frank A. Herrief, George Davis, Harry Butts, Frank B. Sherman and L.H. Townsend.

Under the strong and active leadership of Wilber, things moved along well in 1924. He was determined to field a strong club, saying "Enthusiasm for baseball must be aroused; the stands must be filled at every game and the team given wholehearted support."

By way of proving he meant business, Wilber immediately launched a search for the strongest manager available. He named Dr. Marx and D.F. Keyes to join him as a search committee for the new pilot. Among other things, they wired Branch Rickey of the St. Louis Cardinals and Connie Mack of the Philadelphia Athletics for suggestions. Both responded independently of one another, but with the same name: Roy Thomas, who logged 13 productive years in the major leagues, most of them for Connie Mack.

Acting upon the strong recommendations of two of baseball's most respected men, the Oneonta trio set up an appointment in Philadelphia to interview Thomas. They were impressed and offered him a contract. He wired his acceptance a few days later. He proved to be a popular choice. A huge crowd was on hand to cheer lustily early in March when Wilber introduced the young Thomas to Oneonta and its fans.

One of Wilber's master strokes that season was to bring back the very popular Ed Walsh. The aging pitcher could still get the ball over the plate with some authority and he proved that point by pitching well in the July 25 exhibition game against Mack's Philadelphia Athletics - a game won by Oneonta, 4-3 on a clutch hit by Tommy Wilcox in the tenth inning. Before the Athletics left on the 7:50 D&H train that night, Connie Mack praised the Oneonta community, the ball park and the team.

Thomas's club, which began practice in May, proved a winner from the start. Fans responded to the brand of baseball displayed by the Oneonta team and Thomas became one of the most popular player-managers ever in the city's long baseball history.

On that roster, along with Wilcox, were Sinstack and Scanlon. Wilcox, called one of the best ever to wear an Oneonta uniform, remained in Oneonta, married a local woman and was successful in business, so successful he was asked to run for mayor.

Late in that 1924 season, Oneonta made its first appearance in the NY-P League and its first appearance in a full professional league since 1890. The last-place Utica entry, plagued by a series of losses

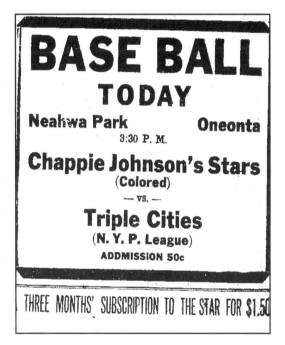

and resulting poor attendance, dropped out of the circuit. The Oneonta team moved in to finish the schedule.

One of the unexpected off-shoots of this action was the revival of the Sunday baseball controversy. The pro leagues played Sunday baseball it was one of the best days for attendance - and to go without that revenue was unthinkable.

But the Oneonta blue laws were still on the books in 1924 and earlier legal activity had failed to settle the problem.

Wilber and Thomas appeared before the Common Council and

pleaded baseball's case. Their eloquence paid off and the Council gave baseball the green light for Sunday action. Although the Council's action brought strong protest from the anti-Sunday folks, the decision held. The Council backed its decision by passing local legislation and Sunday baseball was here to stay.

In the winter of 1924-25, Oneonta indicated an interest in joining the league for the 1925 season, but was passed over by league and club officials who felt the city wasn't large enough to be a real fiscal success.

But Wilber never stopped trying. In December, 1924 he and Charley Bowdish made the trip to Hartford, Connecticut for the National Association meetings to plead for the city's entry into organized baseball. Their mission failed.

Undaunted by all of that, the dedicated Wilber and friends tried to launch a new league in March, 1925, but this project was doomed from the start and, later that month, was dropped altogether.

What might have been a serious gap in Oneonta's baseball history in the ensuing years was filled by Dutch Damaschke who took his Company G team, bolstered by other city and area stalwarts, into a new league called the Schoharie County League.

Red Bursey continued to play as did the indestructible Fred Sinstack and Joe Scanlon. Names like Ritchko, Wilcox, Chase, Delaney and Lee also appeared in the Oneonta lineup.

As so often was the case, efforts of the community's baseball leaders such as D.F. Wilber were not immediately apparent, but the seeds for future growth of the pro game in the City of the Hills had been planted and professional baseball people were to remember Oneonta with favor in future years.

One of the men who spent considerable time and money pursuing the baseball cause for Oneonta was Charley Bowdish. He accompanied Wilber on most of the latter's "missionary" trips trying to convince officials to locate a league operation in Oneonta. He was still around in 1940 when Oneonta's day finally arrived and perhaps more than any other deserves the "unsung hero" award.

26 'DUTCH'

A final effort to assure an Oneonta entry in a state league for the 1925 season having failed when the league officials and executives from the various cities simply could not agree on basic details, baseball appeared headed for limbo in the mid-Twenties.

Enter "Dutch" Damaschke once again, coming in like the Seventh Cavalry to save the day. He moved quickly to organize the Oneonta Red Sox, entered the club in the Schoharie County League along with several area communities, and baseball was assured for 1925 and beyond.

Records for a long period of time are sketchy. It might be noted a box score from a game in 1934 showed Fred Sinstack still catching and Joe Scanlon still pitching.

"Dutch" Damaschke helped assure baseball for Oneonta and the ball park was renamed in his honor.

Night baseball returned for a brief appearance on August 16, 1930 when the travelling California Owls brought in their lighting system and a female first baseman named Mary Nowack. More than 1,500 showed up to see a local team featuring Sinstack, Scanlon, Bursey, Joe Pondolfino, Lefty Blodgett, Stan Kreger and others blitz the Owls, 14-9.

A strong young farm boy named Ken Chase who had been "discovered" by Judge Kellogg became an immediate pitching success, won just about every time out and moved quickly into the big leagues, making his debut with the Washington Senators in 1935. The big left hander had a dynamite fast ball and seemed headed for big things when he was slowed by a chronic sore shoulder. Despite his ability to get batters out, he was forced to retire because of the injury. He returned to Oneonta and ran a dairy farm for years. He often pitched for the Milford Macs, an area amateur team, and his name did much to bring that organization into the limelight.

Other familiar names dotted the roster of Dutch Damaschke's Oneonta Merchants nine, a club considered one of the strongest semi-pro clubs in Central and Southern New York in the middle and late 1930's.

Stan Kreger, Ken Orr, Whitey Anderson, Tom Wilcox, John Azzoli, Paul Ritchko, Jimmy Spencer, Dutch Conte, Les Bursey, "Prof" Perry, Joe Long, Lee Hull, Charley Long, Fran, Art and Kippy Lee, Freddie Sinstack, Lou Pondolfino and Ed Hague were on the roster along with Chase.

Then, things began to happen which would have a direct, positive effect on baseball in Oneonta in 1938.

The Common Council, at its meeting in February, 1938 voted to go ahead with vast renovations at Neahwa Park. The funds would come in part from a bequest in the will of William F. Eggleston which stipulated the money be used for this purpose.

Included in the project proposed by City Engineer Frank M. Gurney were a steel grandstand to seat 500 people, two dressing and shower rooms, public toilets, plus an enlarged and improved playing field. Bids were received, examined and awarded and the WPA brought into the activity.

The work went on over a long period of time while baseball and football competition continued at the ballpark. When the work was completed, Oneonta had a ballpark better than most in the low minors, a ballpark, now known as Damaschke Field, which remains a topic of favorable conversation whenever baseball men gather.

Then, as war broke out in Europe, came the dramatic news for Oneonta. Management of the franchise in Ottawa, Canada was given permission by the Canadian-American League and the National Association of Professional Baseball Leagues (the minors) to move operations to Oneonta for the 1940 campaign. Club officials in Ottawa gave the war as reason for the move, saying Ottawa was, "A great baseball city and we want to remain in the league which is well organized and making money but we must face the reality of all-out war."

On December 20, 1940 Oneonta accepted the responsibility of running a professional baseball club when Mayor Daniel Franklin said, "This city would be glad to take over the franchise of the Senators."

Ottawa made the stipulation that 14 of the 63 home games of the club would be played in Ottawa "conditions permitting."

With the transaction came a working agreement with the Philadelphia Phillies of the National League which included players already under contract; home and road uniforms and two station wagons for transporting the team on road trips. All of the necessary league and Association paperwork was also included.

Cornwall, the other Canadian entry in the league, was making arrangements to take its club to America. That move would seem to take Ogdensburg out of the league because of added transportation costs. In December, 1939 the league consisted of Rome, Amsterdam, Utica, Gloversville and Oswego with Auburn and Schenectady seen as possible successors to Cornwall.

Then, with dramatic suddenness, the picture changed in January, 1940. Demands - financial and otherwise - made by Ottawa General Manager Victor Wagner were ruled unacceptable by the Oneonta interests and the Ottawa to Oneonta transfer collapsed.

But Mayor Franklin and his colleagues Donald H. Grant, Dorr S. Hickey and Charles Bowdish were far from finished. League President Rev. Harold J. Martin had other plans. It seems he recognized a potential in Oneonta despite the city's small size and had quietly suggested to Hickey a deal might be made with the Cornwall people who, he thought, might be interested in a simple sellout with no strings attached.

The good reverend was right and, in relatively short order, the Oneontans came to terms with the Cornwall people and bought that franchise outright. This transaction was sound business from both standpoints: Cornwall was able to turn its attention to an all-out war effort, and Oneonta was assured the franchise would not be moved away suddenly which gave the Oneontans control over their own destiny. The war would catch up soon enough but, in the meantime, organized baseball was back in Oneonta on a solid footing. The Oneonta Sports Association quickly filed papers of incorporation and then sold $10,000 in stock at $5 per share.

Work became more intense at the ballpark as the season opener approached. The huge light poles were brought in and placed, followed by the lights and seating capacity was increased with the addition of new bleachers.

Manager Lee Riley reported in and set up shop ready to tackle a thousand and one details. A new era in Oneonta baseball history was about to be launched.

27 CAN-AM

The Canadian-American League came into being for the 1936 season, the product of the ingenious brain of Joe Carr, promotional assistant to Judge William Bramham, president of the National Association. Carr was no rookie in such matters, having been one of the founders of the National Football League and of the American Basketball League.

Ottawa, Brockville and Perth were the Canadian entries with Oswego, Watertown and Ogdensburg representing the United States. Ottawa newspaperman Walter Gilhooly was elected the loop's first president.

This might be the time to note that Oneonta entered organized baseball in the NY-P League of 1924. That league became the Eastern League in the late 1930's and the NY-P League as Oneonta fans know it today first came along in 1939.

In terms of caliber of play, it has been said many times the Can-Am League was the equivalent of today's class AAA International League because there were a lot of veterans playing their last season or two in organized baseball mixed with the flow of promising young talent which was coming along in 1936.

Over the years, the league makeup changed several times as each year clubs would fold and new ones would replace them. By 1940 the league consisted of Amsterdam, Pittsfield, Gloversville-Johnstown, Quebec City, Rome, Three Rivers, Utica and Oneonta. Kenneth Yager was president of the club in Oneonta with Charley Bowdish, Don Grant, Harold Ford, Ken McEwen, "Dutch" Damaschke, Dorr Hickey, Joe Molinari, Dr. LeRoy S. House, Sid Levine, Tom Wilcox, Frank Gurney and Sam Nader on the board. Fittingly, a lot of those men had been around the Oneonta baseball scene for a long time and had labored mightily to bring about the momentous date of May 10, 1940.

The Can-Am League was on solid footing and attendance increased by leaps and bounds each season. By 1940, it was considered one of the steadiest of all the lower minor leagues. There was a unity, a strength, a fiscal stability which had been lacking in earlier attempts and there was an upsurge of fan interest, brought about by the arrival of night baseball which made the game available to the working man.

Lee Riley, a veteran baseball man considered one of the best hitters in the minors, arrived as manager of the Oneonta club which, by this time, was known as the Indians. Like many of the "old pros" of that day, Riley was a playing manager. He spent much of the season patrolling right field but would play first base occasionally. He was a fine all-around ballplayer, his defensive abilities matching his strength at the plate.

Riley's family joined him in Oneonta and his younger son was born there. An older son, Pat, a tot at the time, had a great time running around Neahwa Park and was a familiar sight to baseball fans. But, as he grew older, he turned to basketball as his first love and is in the process of carving out a memorable career in that sport. As coach of the Los Angeles Lakers, he won a NBA championship and has come close to doing the same thing with the New York Knicks, reaching the final game of the final series in 1994 before bowing out.

His dad was a popular figure around Oneonta. He was highly visible in the community and everyone enjoyed his company when he made his morning swings along Main Street, often with little Pat in tow.

"He was a fine man and a damn good ballplayer," says Sid Levine, a member of the Board of Directors in 1940. "He worked hard and set a great example for his players.

"Remember, he was working with a patchwork club made up of players from all over the place - some going up the ladder and some going down.

"His players loved him and worked hard all season."

There being no major league working agreement available, Riley and the local club officials had to pick up players from wherever they could be found. Competition was heavy because baseball clubs were not in a very good bargaining position. In those days, Class C ball clubs, by the rules of the National Association and the league, were limited to a total monthly payroll of $1,600. Defense contracts were already piling up at various factories around the country and the pay was very good. Baseball clubs without working agreements to guarantee a supply of players had a rough go of it. But, using the contacts developed over years of baseball activity, the Oneonta club people were able to find players. In addition, players were assigned to Oneonta from the Philadelphia Athletics and the Boston Red Sox.

One of the players sent in by Philadelphia was Dick Fowler, a big and strong pitcher who was to make Oneonta his home after marrying a local woman. Fowler won 16 games for Oneonta to lead the staff. He went on to pitch well in the majors, capping his career by throwing a no-hitter against St. Louis on September 9, 1945 just one week after his release from active service with the Canadian Army. After a shoulder injury ended his baseball career, Fowler returned to Oneonta for the rest of his life.

Riley proved he could hit by registering a .340 average in 116 games. He hit 14 home runs and drove 87 runs across. Only Frank Perkowski, with .346, hit better than the skipper. Perkowski led in the RBI department with 104. He was a versatile performer, but his strength was hitting not pitching. His record as a hurler was 1-8 and his ERA was over five.

Chick Genovese was sent to Oneonta by the Red Sox and quickly became a fan favorite. He stood only a little over five feet but he could run like a deer and had a cannon for an arm. Running the bases or chasing fly balls in the outfield, Chick always ran out from under his cap and the fans loved it. He hit .311 in 80 games. Al Tarlecki and Joe Zagami were the only other members of that 1940 club to hit over 300, Tarlecki closing with .316 in 120 games and Zagami with .317 in 80 games. Zagami was a fielding "dandy" and for years was labelled "a real fancy Dan, one of the best first baseman Oneonta ever had."

Oneonta finished fifth in the eight club circuit posting a 62-63 record with two tie games.

Tommy Fine, with his blazing fastball, was the other member of that first Oneonta Can-Am club to make the majors.

The Indians drew 39,851 for the season, not spectacular numbers but good enough for the first time around considering the club was out of the race early that season. The numbers were to get better as Oneonta's rightful place in the world of organized baseball was being firmly established.

28 WINNER!

When 1941 rolled around, things took a dramatic turn for the better around Oneonta's storied old ball park. As a result of an agreement with the Red Sox, Oneonta became a bona fide professional baseball team and, more important, a winner.

Led by Manager Red Barnes, the Sox roared through the regular season to close with a 78-46 record and a pennant by a nine game margin over second place Amsterdam. The Red Sox won the playoff championship as well, topping Rome four games to two and then Pittsfield by a 4-2 margin to win the Shuttleworth trophy.

And the fans came to Neahwa Park in far greater numbers than in the inaugural year as 59,317 paid their way into the stadium. Oneonta, then as now, loved their winners!

One of the big reasons fans flocked to Neahwa Park was a youngster named Austin Knickerbocker, who put together the finest season any player ever had for an Oneonta team. He hung up a .406 batting average in 1941, the only player in Can-Am League history to hit more than four hundred. He was named the league's most valuable player, made the all-star team, drove in 135 runs and set a league record of 202 hits. He had 45 doubles, 10 triples and 12 home runs, hitting three in one game to tie a league record.

Oneonta club owner Sam Nader, who has seen every ballplayer to come through the city since 1940, without hesitation calls Austin Knickerbocker "the best hitter ever to play in Oneonta."

Knickerbocker was never the same after World War II took a heavy physical toll but maintains his interest in baseball. He paid a visit to the Oneonta ball park in 1992 and had a chance to talk with the Damaschke faithful who never forget a player, particularly one of the best ever.

"I signed my first contract with Ottawa," Knickerbocker recalls. "We had our spring training in Ogdensburg and I can recall hitting three doubles off the left field wall. But, I guess, they didn't know where to play me in the field so they sent me to Wausau, Wisconsin in the Northern League."

But the Red Sox found a place for him and he was a success from the first pitch.

The bouncy Genovese was back for the 1941 season and he did

nothing to lose the fan adoration he had developed in 1940. He led the club in homers with 14 and wound up hitting .367 with 97 runs batted in. And he still ran out from under his cap as he toured the bases enough times to lead the Red Sox with 145 runs scored, a league record. He joined Austin Knickerbocker and Ken Chapman on the all-star team. The latter was one of the players who married a local woman and lived out his life in Oneonta. He was a popular and well-known figure around his adopted city for many years.

Zagami was back with his artistry at first base and at the plate where he hit .308 in 125 games. Manager Barnes hit .371 in 106 games; Ed McGah .329; and Tony Sabol .310. No wonder the club was a winner.

Tommy Fine brought his great fastball back to Neahwa Park and proved again he was one of the best Damaschke had ever seen. He won 22 games while losing only nine. And Hal White, on his way to some great major league seasons, was 19 and 6 for the season and Ralph Waite 15-5.

Fine, Emmett O'Neil, Tony Sabol, Earl Rapp, McGah and Knickerbocker also got a shot at the major leagues but, in cases such as that of Austin Knickerbocker, World War II took a great toll from the players of this era and cut short many promising careers. The war cost the lives of a dozen Can-Am players, none from the Oneonta rosters.

World War II had a strong effect on minor league baseball. Travel restrictions made getting to the games on schedule very difficult and players of that time tell of taking a bus to Utica, then a train to a Canadian stop and then back again. Charter buses were heavily restricted by wartime rulings.

Off course, players were scarce because military duty and war plant work diverted many talented athletes into wartime efforts.

Things got so tough that statistics from the 1942 Can-Am season were limited because of an effort to save paper for the war effort.

But those figures which are available show that Ken Chapman, Joe Zagami and Tommy Fine returned to Neahwa Park for another campaign. Zagami continued his solid hitting with a .341 and he led the club with 10 homers. Chapman came up with a .317 batting average, newcomer Vance Dinges hit .338 and rookie Ray Henningsen batted .316. Fine won 13 for the Sox, a number matched by Stan Partenheimer, who was scheduled for a trip to the major leagues. Dinges, too, got a shot at The Bigs.

Emil "Red" Barnes was back as manager and the club finished fourth with a 68-56 record. But the Red Sox won the playoffs for the second year in a row, beating Utica four games to one and Amsterdam, 4-3 for the championship and a second leg on the Shuttleworth trophy.

By the time the playoffs were over it had become obvious that the war had made matters difficult, if not impossible, for the young league.

On February 22, 1943 at a meeting in Albany's Ten Eyck Hotel, the Can-Am voted to suspend operations until the war's end. Most of minor league baseball followed suit as 1943 moved along. The notable exception was the NY-P League which kept going throughout the conflict, buoyed by the high court ruling the game was a sport and by presidential decree was important for home front morale.

The only incident worthy of mention during the down time of 1943, 1944 and 1945 was the election at a meeting in December, 1944 of Al Houghton as president of the league to succeed Rev. Martin who was unceremoniously dumped.

29 62,181

B aseball's return to Oneonta in 1946 was welcomed by a season attendance of 62,181 as the "cranks"—now and forevermore called fans—literally lined up at the gate on game nights.

They were treated to some good baseball as Manager Red Marion's club finished fourth in the Can-Am race, going 68-54 on the year. The Red Sox lost in the playoff semi-finals to Pittsfield, four games to three.

Vern Lehrman was the big winner on the mound for Oneonta with a 15-4 record while Harry Pilarski won 13.

Dick Littlefield, who was to go on to the big leagues where he set some sort of a record by playing for 10 clubs, turned up in Oneonta that season and had a woeful time of it winning only three while losing seven.

Steve Salata, who caught for Oneonta three seasons in that era, was to say of Littlefield, "He was the weirdest runner I ever saw. His feet came up so high behind him he would kick himself in the butt. Honest!"

Marion helped his own cause by hitting .360 and driving in 62 runs. Ted DeGuerero had 73 runs batted in and an average of .310 while John Boryk drove in 68 runs and stole 35 bases. John Hernandez hit .302 for the club but later became best known as the father of Keith, who starred in his own right with the New York Mets. Bill Hornsby was on that club's roster, but failed to show the great hitting ability of his famous dad, Rogers Hornsby.

1947

This team appears to be the one that launched an era in which players increasingly became part of the Oneonta community.

Steve Salata showed up as a regular catcher. A big and burly guy from Bridgeport, Connecticut, he had a gun for an arm and woe betide the pitcher who didn't get out of the way when an opposing runner was on first base in a steal situation.

Salata stayed in Oneonta, went into business with a friend named Joe Rybacki (who was a real sports fan) and still lives in the city's West End. He's still well known around the community and retains his interest in sports, even serving two seasons as a statistician for a friend who was coaching an area high school basketball team.

Another member of that Oneonta team who remained in the community until his death at an early age was Jack Norton. Like Salata, he married a local woman and was active in the community. When the

Oneonta Little League began play in 1955, the four teams were blessed with great coaching. Norton managed one entry; former major leaguers Ken Chase and Dick Fowler each managed a club and the fourth was coached by Eggie Leach who had been an all-star catcher for the strongest semi-pro teams ever fielded in Oneonta.

Dale Long played first base for that 1947 Oneonta team. He was always a friend of Oneonta and, in later years when working for the National Association, he would visit Oneonta each summer to check the ball park lighting and other phases of the Yankee operation.

"Dale was always good to us, always fair," said Sam Nader, Oneonta general manager. "We looked forward to his visits, professionally and socially."

Long set a Can-Am League record in 1947 by hitting safely in 28 consecutive games from August 18 to September 7. During that time he went 40 for 106, including three homers, two triples and five doubles. He had 27 runs batted in and scored 24 times. Later he made his mark in the majors by hitting home runs in eight consecutive games and for playing a few games as a left-handed catcher.

Bob Van Enam hit .327 for that club, Salata .312 and Long .311. Fred Bortolotti led the attack with a RBI total of 76 while Irv Medlinger won 14 games and Norton 10. Medlinger struck out 182 batters in 234 innings.

The league that year was dominated by Schenectady which won 86 games and drew an incredible 175,189 fans. The Blue Jays, managed by the same Lee Riley who had piloted Oneonta in its 1941 Can-Am inaugural, won the regular season race, then captured the playoffs by beating Amsterdam four games to three and Gloversville-Johnstown, 4 to 1. The Glovers had beaten Oneonta, 4-1 in the other semi-final series.

1948

Red Marion returned to manage the Red Sox this campaign and was rewarded with a playoff championship after a third place finish in the regular season.

Pitching did the trick. Bobby Brake won 20 games for the Sox and Charley LeBrun chipped in with 19. LeBrun's ERA of 2.54 led the league. In the playoffs, Brake won four times and LeBrun twice to give Oneonta the league playoff crown and permanent possession of the Shuttleworth trophy as the Sox topped Rome 4 games to 3 and Pittsfield 4-1.

The offense was led by Mike Durock who drove in 74 runs and hit five home runs. Steve Andreski had 68 runs batted in and Cal Burlingame 62. The latter's average of .337 led that department.

1949

This was one of those ball clubs which could very well have won it all. Four of its first line players were headed on a direct route for the big leagues and the club was solid at every position. Little Eddie Popowski, a fiery mite who lived, breathed and ate baseball, was the manager.

The team caught on with Oneonta fans and 63,217 of them turned out for the home dates. The team, however, finished second some 13 and a half games behind one of the best teams ever assembled for Can-Am play, the Quebec club which had no working agreement and assembled its own roster behind the management of Frank McCormick. Quebec won 90 games that year and came back in 1950 with George McQuinn as manager and won 97.

Frank Malzone, the best third baseman ever to grace the aging turf at Damaschke Field, was one of the stars of the 1949 Oneonta team. He remains one of the Boston Red Sox all-time favorites and was fairly recently voted the best third baseman Boston ever had (outdistancing Wade Boggs in that voting).

Malzone hit .329 for Oneonta in 1949 and drove in 92 runs. He played all of Oneonta's 137 games, scoring 107 runs and hitting 26 triples - a Can-Am record. The spacious Neahwa Park field was perfect for a strong line drive hitter like Frank Malzone and he thrilled the hometown fans every night with his smashes up the power alleys. He was second in the MVP voting to Jim Cullinane, playing manager of the Gloversville Glovers. In later years, Cullinane was to say, "I'm proud of that MVP award because the second place man was Frank Malzone."

Frank, quiet to the point of being considered shy, was one of the players who adopted Oneonta as a home town. He married Amy Gennarino and ran a very popular Oneonta restaurant with his brother-in-law, John Gennarino. Malzone did establish a residence in the Boston area and remains one of the most popular sports figures ever in Beantown. He has spent years working for the Jimmy Fund on behalf of children.

Pitcher Ivan "Ike" Delock graced that Oneonta roster as did short-stop Joe DeMaestri and catcher Sammy White. All four of those players reached The Bigs within four seasons after their stay in Oneonta.

RBI leader for the club was Joe Moody with 94 while Steve Salata returned to hit .329 after a 1948 season during which he played in only 23 games.

Tom Herrin won 16 games for Oneonta, Bob Pray 15 and the feisty Delock 12.

Oneonta beat Pittsfield four games to two in the semi-final playoffs that year but was defeated by Quebec, four games to none, in the championship series.

1950

As had become the custom by this time, Oneonta finished this season in the first division, winding up third behind the strong pennant winning Quebec club and second place Schenectady. Oneonta's 86 wins would have been enough to take the flag in any other Can-Am race except for 1949.

Ed Popowski was back as manager for this campaign and enjoyed some strong pitching from John Gilbert, 17 wins; Bob Smith, 13; Jim Sweeney 12 and Bill McMahon 10. Smith went on to pitch in the majors with the Red Sox, Tigers, Pirates and Cardinals.

Quebec defeated Oneonta four games to one in the semi-final play-off action.

Outfielder Arnie Spence hit 14 home runs, scored 116 runs, drove in 80 runs, stole 16 bases and walked 143 times. He also joined the ranks of players who married Oneonta girls and stayed on to live in the City of the Hills. He and wife Mary Lou are parents of son Scott, a successful professional golfer.

Hal Buckwalter was back to lead in batting average with .327 in 126 games. Ed Irons had a gaudy .435 but he put that together in only 14 games. RBI leader was Joe Detoia with 97.

The club, although solid in many ways, didn't have the appeal that some of the teams before it had and attendance dropped off to 45,911 - still respectable for the league's smallest city.

1951

When the first cry of "play ball" sounded the beginning of the 1951 Can-Am League season, few realized it would be the last for this storied circuit.

Fans began to stay home as television had arrived in the "back country" where baseball's farm clubs grew. The league dwindled to six teams, strong franchises like those in Quebec and Schenectady disappeared.

Oneonta was strong. The Red Sox working agreement was still firmly in place and players were arriving. Owen Scheetz reported in as manager, Popowski having moved up the organizational ladder for the parent Boston Red Sox.

For the first and only time, the league was divided into half seasons and Oneonta won both halves, the first by just a half game over Pittsfield and the second by nine over the same club. The club compiled an 83-34 regular season mark for a percentage of .709, a Can-Am League record. The playoffs also went to Oneonta which beat Amsterdam three games to one in the semi-final and Gloversville-Johnstown by the same margin in the final series.

Arnie Spence returned to have another great year, hitting .302, driving in 75 runs and stealing 19 bases. Rich Karl hit .301 and scored 118 runs. RBI leader was John Minarcin who drove in 111. John joined the ranks of players who married an Oneonta woman and stayed. He and his wife enjoyed seeing son John star as an athlete for Oneonta High and later as a professional baseball player.

Pitching was the big reason for this club's brilliant record. Paul

Aylward compiled a 20-4 mark, Joe Ross was 18-6 and George Uhaze 16-3. The staff earned run average for the pitchers of record was under three.

But the ominous portent of what lay ahead could be seen in the Oneonta attendance figures. This club, one of the finest Oneonta had ever seen, drew only 32,503 fans. Overall league attendance dropped from 453,132 in 1950 to 180,382 in 1951. All across the nation, clubs and leagues were folding as the television reached into the grass roots and people stayed home to watch baseball on the tube.

Quebec and Three Rivers went into the rival Provincial League and fiscal problems continued to plague remaining clubs.

Finally, in January, 1952 at a meeting in Schenectady, it was pointed out Oneonta was the only team with a working agreement and that nearly every other club was in fiscal difficulty. At that meeting, the Amsterdam club's secretary, Archie McKee, suggested the league suspend operations until November, 1952 at which time a decision would be made with regard to resuming play in 1953.

That decision was never made and the Can-Am League was dead.

Perhaps the main thrust of this story covering more than 100 years is the Oneonta's consistency in fielding winning ball clubs. The record shows Oneonta to have been the winningest club in Can-Am history and, at this writing, holds the same position in the New York-Pennsylvania League.

But, after the disappointment of 1952, it was to be several years before Oneonta was to get back to proving itself on the baseball field.

30 FIFTIES

Baseball interest didn't die with the Canadian-American League. True, there were no Oneonta Red Sox games at Neahwa Park, no pro baseball at all, but there was baseball and lots of it.

Coach Harold Hunt and his Oneonta High team played home games at the old ballpark. Hunt was the best scholastic coach in the area and proved it week in and week out, year in and year out by winning, many times by simply out-coaching the other guy.

His teams were well drilled in fundamentals; he always told outfielders they were there to do more than catch fly balls and he taught them the importance of fielding ground balls, how to back up one another in the outfield and how to help out by backing up infielders. He taught them how to hit the cutoff man, how to run bases and how to bunt. It was no coincidence that Oneonta High teams were consistent winners.

Hartwick College played home games at Neahwa Park and Oneonta State also played games there. There were American Legion tournament games and high school sectionals plus the Municipal Softball League playoff series.

The high school football team played at Neahwa Park and, when soccer began to grow in fan interest, the colleges played at Neahwa Park.

This activity was made possible by some of the best groundskeeping imaginable. This groundskeeping, by the way, paid off not only for the athletes of that era but for those to come when baseball returned because, when the chance came to show off the facility for pro scouts, the field was ready.

George Rothery was the original groundskeeper and did a most memorable job. When he left Oneonta for other fields, the work was passed to Fran Lee who had, like his brothers, been one of the area's finest athletes.

The soft-spoken Lee soon proved he was an even better groundskeeper than an athlete and his tender loving care of the Neahwa Park field was the source of wonder. His ability to make the change from baseball to football, complete with a re-sodding of the infield "skin," was unmatched. Lee was an employee of the City of Oneonta and his boss was C.M. "Jock" Taylor who headed the Department of Public Works. To say Taylor was a sports fan is the understatement of the decade and his cooperation was in no small degree responsible for the great condition of Neahwa Park's ball diamond.

Launching of the Oneonta Little League also helped keep baseball interest alive. The first year of operation, games were played in Neahwa Park just outside the baseball stadium.

Interest continued to grow in the Little League program as fans were drawn by the games, the kids and by the cast of managers which featured two well-known former major leaguers. In subsequent years, under the leadership of Oren "Doc" Knapp, the league grew in stature and fiscal strength enough to acquire property just a few blocks from the original fields and build its own tidy little stadium.

Things were happening elsewhere to keep baseball alive in the minds of Oneonta fans. Philadelphia pitcher Jim Konstanty had a year in 1950 that rewrote the record book. He was named National League MVP that season, set a record for relief appearances and was one of the keys to the success of the Whiz Kid Phillies. He was picked to start the World Series against the New York Yankees and dueled Yank ace Whitey Ford in losing a 1-0 classic. Konstanty ran a sporting goods store on Elm Street in Oneonta before moving to the Main Street location from where it still operates.

Big Jim was a popular figure in the Oneonta area and officiated college and scholastic basketball for years. After he closed down his active career, he became athletic director at Hartwick College and played a major role in that school's emergence as strong athletic force. He enjoyed watching son Jim, a fine athlete at Oneonta High where he starred in basketball, football and baseball. He played basketball later at Cornell University.

Big Jim died in 1979 and his wife Mary continues in business in Oneonta where she owns an antique store. She and daughter Helen had run the sports store for years. Young Jim became a lawyer and serves as Otsego County attorney.

While the pro baseball scene in Oneonta lay dormant, events which had taken place years before were beginning to get to the point where they were to have a bearing on the City of the Hills.

The New York-Pennsylvania League was churning along full blast, having survived World War II without shutting down. Its president was Vincent M. McNamara, a tough cookie and a baseball man to the core who took over the reins in 1948. He also was involved in many sports activities along the Niagara Frontier, including running the clock in Buffalo's Civic Auditorium.

This man was a wheeler-dealer without peer but he was honest and open, albeit sometimes brutally frank with everyone, and he got the job done. He turned over the league presidency to Leo Pinckney of Auburn in 1984. He in turn was succeeded by Bob Julian of Utica in the early Nineties. Julian is an active administrator and a baseball enthusiast who has already seen the league spread into New Jersey and Vermont in areas where a large urban population promises increased gates.

The first meeting to discuss the possibility of a new league came in November, 1938 when 21 cities sent representatives to Olean, New York. After a series of meetings, the league was officially organized as the

Class D Pennsylvania, Ontario, New York (PONY) League in March, 1939 and Robert C. Stedler was elected president. The league started play that summer and Olean won the pennant with Hamilton, Bradford, Batavia, Niagara Falls and Jamestown finishing in that order.

The league became simply the NY-P League in 1956 as the Ontario clubs left the circuit. They returned in 1986 but the name has not been changed back despite some suggestions it be done.

The loop is considered the strongest short-season Class A circuit in the country and has seen the debut of some of baseball's biggest names.

It also has been the proving ground for some of baseball's most interesting concepts. Bernice Gera, the first female umpire, reached the league and on June 26, 1972 was slated to call a doubleheader between Auburn and Geneva. She worked the first game and then called it quits never to return.

The Designated Hitter and the Wild Card pinch hitter were first tried in the NY-P League during the 1969 season. The designated hitter concept stuck and was formally adopted a few years later, but the wild card idea (which enabled a manager to insert a pinch-hitter once during the game without the original player having to leave the lineup) was a fizzle. The player's name had to be listed on the lineup card before the game, causing minor league managers such as Oneonta's George Case to lament the number of players to be listed on a lineup card not set up even to handle the designated hitter situation. Many managers didn't even bother to use it and the idea was discarded.

More than 20 cities have been represented in the league over the half-century it has operated. Currently, the league functions with a three-division, 14 team format featuring a playoff at season's end.

More than three-quarters of a million fans pay their way into NY-P League parks each season, a fact which does not escape the notice of the major league clubs.

So it was a strong, well organized, healthy league which opened its doors to Oneonta in the mid-1960's.

31 NY-P

B uoyed by the success of the Eastern League game in Oneonta, Mayor Nader lost no time in getting the ball rolling toward the city's re-entry into professional baseball. This time his target was the New York-Pennsylvania League which, having survived World War II and succeeded since then, was doing very well. In the old days it had been known as the PONY League and wore a D classification. Minor league restructuring in the 1950's, brought about by the collapse of several minor leagues (including the Canadian-American League in 1952) resulted in the NY-P League classification as a Class A circuit.

After the Reading-Binghamton exhibition in Neahwa Park, league and club officials took a look at the Oneonta facility in August, 1963 and seemed satisfied with what they saw.

Meanwhile, Nader was cranking up his campaign. First salvo was fired off in wake of that August visit in a letter to Vincent M. McNamara, colorful and feisty president of the NY-P. In that letter, Nader reassured McNamara of Oneonta's "great interest in becoming a member of the NY-P league" and assured the league president he would get "every cooperation of the city administration."

More than two years of meetings, memoranda, telephone calls and frustration followed. The mayor wrote Neil Mahoney, director of the Boston Red Sox minor league system; Phil Piton, president of the National Association; McNamara; major league acquaintances. He went to the winter meetings of the big league people and to the meetings of the NY-P board on invitation from McNamara. The NY-P League president became an ally of the Oneonta cause somewhere along the line and urged major league executives to consider working agreements with NY-P clubs. McNamara insisted his league could expand at brief notice because people in places like Corning, Oswego, Utica, Olean and Erie indicated they were ready.

As 1963 wore away, the major league clubs were showing a cautious side with regard to spending money on their farm systems and were even cutting expenses in some cases. So NY-P League expansion went to the back burner.

But the correspondence and the behind the scenes activity continued. Nader was admitted to most NY-P League board meetings and he continued to go to every meeting anywhere which might lead to Oneonta's return to organized baseball. In that process he was to build a long list of friends who helped him down the line.

By August, 1964 McNamara was able to write Nader with the news

Mr. Piton was going to meet with the NY-P directors to discuss working agreements. "We urge your confidence in this matter," McNamara cautioned Nader. "This is not assurance you will be with us in 1965 as much as we would personally like that. While we are always hopeful of getting back to an eight club league, it would be disastrous for us to stir up too much interest amongst your people only to let them hang."

As 1965 approached, Nader was filling out forms regarding Oneonta's capability to support a professional team and was writing long letters describing his community and the surrounding area for the edification of the major league people. Each letter or memorandum contained the strong assurance city government stood firmly behind this project and cooperation was assured.

Even though Nader received a letter from Mr. Piton in June, 1965 in which the National Association boss bemoaned the fact major league clubs were not expanding farm systems, there was hope in Oneonta that summer. In July, a name surfaced which was to become synonymous with the city's baseball efforts. That name was Joe Buzas, and with the appearance of his name in the records of that day came the news he was considering moving the Wellsville franchise to Oneonta.

Warren LaTarte, area representative of the National Association, had been deeply involved in making arrangements for the switch to Oneonta and he was able to write Nader in August, 1965 offering his congratulations that the deal had been completed and saying that he would spend as much time as necessary in Oneonta to get things under way smoothly.

Nader had also approached his oldest and dearest friend, Sid Levine, on the matter of pro baseball's return to Oneonta.

"Oh heavens, not again," had been Levine's first reaction. He was mindful of the debts left by the collapse of the Can-Am League in 1952.

"You must be nuts, Sam, to want to get involved with all that stuff again. Don't you ever learn?"

"Nope," replied Nader. "Are you in?"

"I've gone this far, I might just as well see it through," said Levine. "Besides, somebody has to keep an eye on you."

Levine is still with the club and remains Nader's key adviser on money matters and many other facets of club operation. Outwardly cynical at times, Levine today is one of Oneonta's most prominent citizens in many areas in addition to his role with the O-Yanks. In 1992, for example, he chaired a successful multi-million dollar drive for an addition to the city's hospital.

Supported by his best friend and other Oneonta stalwarts, Nader was able to turn his attention to negotiations with Buzas regarding the working agreement and a multitude of other matters.

At the insistence of league directors that the pecking order in Oneonta be clearly defined, Buzas was recognized as the franchise holder and Pat McKernan came to Oneonta as business manager, a position he had held with the Buzas club in Pittsfield, Massachusetts in the Eastern League. Buzas also owned a club in Louisville, Kentucky.

Buzas was a colorful character, quick with a quip and equally quick with a reprimand. He was outspoken in many ways and his telephone arguments with NY-P president Vincent McNamara are legendary. He is remembered for wheeling out of Oneonta's Neahwa Park in a cloud of dust, heading for Louisville with a load of uneaten popcorn at the close of an Oneonta home stand.

Because the lengthy agenda made delegates weary and frequent adjournments, the annual meeting of the N Y-P League directors began October 17, 1965 and continued into January, 1966. When it was over, Oneonta was in, the working agreement with the Red Sox in hand and the details of the Buzas arrangement satisfactorily wrapped up. Batavia reached an agreement with the Baltimore Orioles and the league was set. Binghamton, Jamestown, Geneva and Auburn joining Batavia and Oneonta for the 130 game schedule which would get under way April 30 and end September 7.

Oneonta was back at long last.

Binghamton Triplet and Oneonta City officials sign 1964 agreement for an Eastern League game in Oneonta. It was the prelude to Oneonta's return to professional baseball two years later. Signing are Lou Rappaport, Binghamton G.M. and Oneonta Mayor Sam Nader. Standing from left are Dr. John Green, "Dutch" Damaschke, Nelson Ellis and Triplet Business Manager Jerry Toman. Damaschke was Oneonta Recreation Director at the time. Others are Triplet officers.

32 RETURN

O nce the Oneonta group received approval from the NY-P League and from the National Association, once a player development agreement was reached with the Boston Red Sox and once Joe Buzas had been satisfied the move to Oneonta was the right one, plans really began to move ahead in local baseball circles.

It seemed as if every day's mail contained a letter from National Association boss Phil Piton or NY-P League President Vince McNamara or Buzas or Warren LeTarte, Association field man, each containing advice on how to operate and promote or strong suggestions about getting the community involved and, above all, the importance of a working group of citizens.

Buzas was in and out of town and, early in 1966, Neal Bennett arrived to serve as general manager of the new ball club. He had held a similar post in Pittsfield and was experienced in the post, his strength being the ability to sell tickets and advertising in the program and on outfield walls. "Fat Pat" was a wheeler-dealer and just what Oneonta needed at that point.

Acting on the advice of everyone, Nader put together a citizens board consisting of some key community people. Careful even in those days about the allocation of power, his memo to the group at the time of the organization meeting said, "The Red Sox Advisory Board will serve generally in the capacity of Board of Directors. Advice will be given by the board on all matters affecting policy, operations, finances and public relations; but the board will not exercise decision-making or policy creating powers. Final decisions and responsibility must rest with Joseph Buzas, as sole owner."

Nader, in another memo during the same time, wrote: "We expect Joe Buzas to respect and give definite consideration to the Advisory Board's ideas, suggestions and thoughts pertaining to the continuity of baseball in the Oneonta area." The mayor knew something about touching all the bases.

Negotiations with the city for the use of the ball park went well, quite possibly because Mr. Nader was mayor of the community which owned the facility. One of the reasons his career as mayor was so successful became apparent in these negotiations when he was able to hammer out an agreement which was fair to all concerned.

Members of that 1966 Advisory Council in addition to Nader were: Robert Harlem, Sidney Levine, LeRoy S. House, Jr., Larry Gennarino, Henry Bunn, Harold Hollis, Philip Bresee, John Higgins, George Lambros,

Dr. J.O. Whitaker, "Dutch" Damaschke, Ed Somers, Joseph Palko, Edward Super, George Tyler, Alan Gould, Samuel Bertuzzi, Frank A. Lamonica, Robert Leamy and Dr. Samuel Pondolfino.

In naming that group, Nader succeeded in involving every walk of community life.

Work went on getting the park ready although it had been in continuous use since the Can-Am League folded. Oneonta High played baseball and football in the stadium; Hartwick College and State University College played baseball and soccer and, for years, the Municipal Softball League playoffs were held there. In the summers just prior to the return of organized baseball, the local Milford Macs played an amateur schedule in the Neahwa Park facility. American Legion state tournament games were also played there, as was an annual scholastic all-star game put together by Mac Manager Deane Winsor and area high school coaches. All that activity combined to keep baseball alive in the years between leagues.

The New York-Pennsylvania League was still operating under player eligibility rules differing from those which took effect when the league, a year later, wisely decided to play a short-season schedule. There were no limitations in 1966 as to the number of experienced players a roster could contain and, as a result, there were some journeyman players mixed with the rookies on that Red Sox squad.

Among them were colorful athletes like outfielder Harry Greenfield who climbed moving freight trains when necessary in order to reach the ball park in time for a vital workout.

Players were ready for action earlier in the year and, as a result, the Oneonta ball club played a full schedule of games in Florida during the Spring Training period.

So it was a mixture of veterans and rookies which came North with Manager Matt Sczesny for the April 23 opener after compiling a good record in Grapefruit League action.

A series of events for Opening Day were planned by the Red Sox Advisory Board, the Boosters Club, the City of Oneonta and various service organizations. Everybody cooperated except a cantankerous weatherman who saw fit to send cold weather, rain mixed with snow and generally terrible conditions to Oneonta that first week.

One event the weatherman could not stop was a welcome dinner at the Oasis Motor Inn Restaurant which was a heart-warming success. A big crowd turned out to greet the Red Sox and the fans applauded enthusiastically as Manager Sczesny introduced his baseball team to the faithful.

Otherwise, it was tough going as the Sox saw three of their first four games washed out. When they finally got in a game, the temperature sunk to under 40 degrees and, by the seventh inning, snow was falling. The attendance was announced as 811 for the long-awaited return of baseball.

Oneonta lost to Batavia on that chilly day by a 6-2 count. One of Batavia's heroes in that contest was Clarence "Cito" Gaston who went on to manage Toronto to a World Championship in 1992. He was long and lean and the press box denizens of that day said nobody before or since could make the trip around the bases in fewer strides than Gaston.

Billy Hermanson waited three days for his first start and was hit hard in the early going. But he settled down and pitched well the rest of his tour of duty that cold night. Doug Shores was the catcher for the opening day game with John Gecy at first, Ed Mello at second, Lloyd Cobble at short and Amos Otis at third. Joe Silvonic, Jack Mountain and Charlie Bree were in the outfield.

Organizational moves changed the roster soon after that game. Of the infield, only Otis remained and he moved into an outfield position. Katsuhiro Shitanashi took over at third and Greenfield moved into the outfield, joining Mountain, Otis, Silvonic and Fred Wolcott on the picket line. Bob Booth, Wayne Fuzzard and Dave Barbo were in the early season rotation. Later on, Charley Miller arrived and went on to win 11 for the Sox as did Ivy Washington.

The latter, a lean and wiry young athlete, was hailed as a sure thing, his ERA for the season was 1.70. Nobody among the regular starters was even close to that. Along the way, he pitched 138 innings and registered 132 strikeouts to lead the club. John Silva also reported in, appeared in 23 games (11 of which he won) and wrote his name into the Oneonta record book by throwing a seven inning no hitter against Auburn on July 22. It was reported in subsequent seasons Washington threw his arm out and Silva suffered shoulder problems which hurt his career. Many people were to wonder in ensuing years if pitching in the cold weather of that 1966 summer wasn't harmful to the young hurlers.

Jack Mountain, who went on to a long career in AAA baseball but never made it to The Bigs, was a fan favorite as was Washington. Mountain hit .264 and drove in 56 runs second only to his running mate and off-field buddy Silvonic who drove in 58. Mountain led the club in homers with five.

Wolcott hit .275 while Juan Ramos and Dave Casey registered .272 averages. The member of the club who really made it big in the majors was Otis who hit .270 for Oneonta that season. Many fans thought the youngster was inclined to be lazy, but they changed their minds when they found out he had been playing ball every day for more than a year before his arrival in Oneonta helping support his brothers and sisters back in Mobile, Alabama. Even a talented teenager, which Otis was, can get tired after a while.

One summer day, as Bennett, Sczesny and Buzas sat around the tiny Red Sox office in Neahwa Park, a young man poked his head in the door. He walked in, stuck out his hand and said, "Hi, I'm Ken Brett, your new pitcher." The trio greeting him were quick to notice he was not wearing shoes. He had no car, was new in town and was not carrying shoes. They wondered about it but never got around to ask.

He stuck around for the summer, got into 14 games and wound up with a 1-4 record. But he obviously possessed talent and was a fun-loving player who talked a lot about his "little brother Georgie back in California who is a helluva ballplayer - better, even, than me." Baseball fans know he was right on that one as George Brett is a cinch to appear in Cooperstown within a decade.

Ken did okay, however. He remains the youngest player ever to appear in a World Series game. At 19 he played for the Boston club just a year after playing in Oneonta, and became the only pitcher for the Phillies to hit a home run in four consecutive games in 1973.

He returned to Oneonta years later as manager of the Utica Blue Sox in the NY-P League and, true to tradition, gave the press corps a flurry of great quotes, some of which were printable.

The 1966 Oneonta team wound up second in the season's first half with a 32-27 mark but tailed off later in the season and was fourth in the second half. The composite record for the year was 65-59. Attendance was only 24,425 but the weather was responsible for that relatively low figure and things were to improve quickly.

The highlight of that 1966 summer for Oneonta's baseball fans was the appearance of Ted Williams. He came to town in late July as a hitting instructor for the Red Sox. Accompanied by his pal, Bobby Doerr, Williams became a fixture on the Oneonta scene for the week prior to his induction into the Hall of Fame. He and Doerr would stroll along Main Street completely accepted by the locals. He would respond with a "hi ya" to all those who spoke. He was just one of the guys and wasn't hounded by autograph seekers.

Early in the afternoon, he would turn up at the ball park, work out for a while, and then turn his attention to the young Red Sox hitters. After an often long session, he would shower and then move up to the press box where he stayed for the entire game. Asked why he would stick around just to see a minor league game, he replied, "It's a ball game, isn't it?"

Then, almost to himself, he said, "I guess that's why they call me 'Teddy Ball Game'."

A memorable summer for Oneonta baseball fans.

33 Yankees!

During the winter months, the euphoria from the first season of professional baseball in 15 years was to end sharply with a single phone call. It was from Neil Mahoney, the farm director for the Boston Red Sox, who told Sam Nader the Red Sox would not be back for the 1967 season.

He was calling from the winter meeting of the major league clubs with the bad news.

"I was devastated," says Nader. "During the 1966 season, Neil had sat in my box talking about things like upgrading our lights which we said we would do. We had a commitment from the Common Council to help all it could and we had the commitment from the Red Sox.

"To have all this set and ready and then have it taken away without warning was a real blow."

Nader expressed his anger in no uncertain terms to the Red Sox people and to Joe Buzas who was going along with the decision.

"Joe then told me there were other major league clubs interested in getting located in the NY-P and he listed three, one of which was the New York Yankees," Nader said.

"Hell, there was no more point in talking at that time. I had been a Yankee fan all my life and I told Buzas I wanted the Yanks."

Only a few days went by before Nader got a call from Johnny Johnson, farm director for the New York club and one of the best friends Oneonta baseball ever had.

When the conversation was over, the Oneonta-New York agreement had been reached verbally and a historic course had been set. Written agreements were only a formality after that first phone call from Johnson.

Nader and his family had made plans to visit Ocala, Florida during the 1967 spring training period because the Red Sox farm operation was located there. While in Ocala, Nader drove on down to the Yankees' camp in Fort Lauderdale and visited the New York brass.

Johnson was to say later that the New York people were impressed that he would visit them. He said it was the only time he knew of that a mayor had come down to say thanks for locating a club in his city.

From then on, it was smooth sailing. Nader asked Johnson, "What can we do to make things better?" Johnson replied "to just keep on doing what you have been doing. We've heard great things about your community."

So, the Yanks were set for Oneonta and an era of unparalleled baseball success was about to begin.

Sam Nader set about the process of buying the operation from Buzas. He got together with friend and confidant Sid Levine and came up with the idea of forming a corporation to make the purchase and operate the ball club. They sold stock at $1,000 a pop and asked nine men to join them in an effort they deemed beneficial to the Oneonta community. Only one man turned them down. The $10,000 thus raised would enable them to meet Buzas' asking price of $7,500 and leave enough for early operating expenses.

The deal with Buzas was quickly consummated and the Oneonta Athletic Corporation was in business. Nicholas Lambros, Nathan Pendleton, Dr. Alexander Carson, Albert Farone, Henry Bunn, Sterling P. Harrington, Harold deGraw and Steven Low were the original board; Nader's brother-in-law, LeRoy S. House, Jr., came along shortly after the original group was formed.

All were respected business and professional men in Oneonta with strong backgrounds of community service. Most had been involved with baseball since the Can-Am days.

When Nader called Johnny Johnson with the news the local group had bought out Buzas, Johnson's first question was, "What have you bought, Sam?"

He went on to tell the Oneontan that, without the Yankee agreement to come to Oneonta, Buzas really had little to sell.

"What did you get?" Johnson repeated. He wasn't being difficult, he was having fun with the dedicated Oneontan who was trying so hard to do things right.

"Well," reported Sam Nader, "we got 300 chairs, a filing cabinet and a gas stove in the office..." his voice trailed off as he realized his inventory was rather small.

Johnson was through joking. "Don't worry, Sam, we're with you. The Yankees will operate in Oneonta this spring."

Operate they have, bringing Oneonta fans winning baseball for more than a quarter century and developing a host of ball players for the major leagues.

The year 1967 was the first of a new era in minor league baseball, at least at the short-season Class A level. Clubs rated in this category find themselves drastically limited as far as using players with previous minor league experience, although, unlike the rookie leagues, they are allowed three players on their rosters who have had previous experience. These players can remain at the short season Class A level for three years, then it's go up or go out.

The result is that rosters in the NY-P League are made up primarily of first year players, most of them high draft choices because the league is thought of as a good place to launch a professional career.

Most of the players who come into the league now are far different from the players who graced the 1966 Oneonta roster. Nowadays, they are almost all college students, busily building a base for a career away from the ball diamond. They are fully aware of their exceedingly slim chances of making the big leagues and they have a timetable for advancement. There remains a small core of players who will play the game until they are forced out but, by and large, they will drop out if they haven't made appreciable progress within their personal timetables.

The journeyman, the ballplayer who hangs around the minors for years, playing ball and making a modest living, has all but disappeared from all levels below AAA leagues. Therefore, the "color" stories that once abounded in the minor leagues about such players are gone. Now, the serious, dedicated young athlete is all business as he goes about his first year or two as a professional athlete.

A final note on the entire process of change from the Red Sox to the Yankees. Before the 1967 season got under way in Oneonta, Sam Nader got a call from Neil Mahoney asking if the Sox could come back. It seems Mahoney heard about the change in the NY-P League schedule from 130 to 78 games and thought the NY-P League was going to become a rookie league in which he wasn't interested, which is why he called Nader in mid-winter to tell him Boston was out of Oneonta.

As winter began to give way to spring, Mahoney learned the NY-P League was going to be more than a rookie league despite the shorter schedule and his interest returned. So, he called Oneonta back and asked if the Red Sox could return.

"We, of course, turned him down," Nader said. "We had decided to go all out with the Yankees.

"We're glad we did; we've done all right."

Sometimes, Sam Nader is a master of understatement.

34 VERDI

D uring the winter of 1966-67, the New York organization got
busy setting up the new ball club and establishing lines of communication between Oneonta and the Stadium.

The first appointment was a field manager; the Yanks sent in rough
and tumble, outspoken Frank Verdi to be the Oneonta pilot. Verdi was
quick to criticize, quick to praise. His was a loud voice (just ask any of
the umpires of that era or League President McNamara), but he could
be a softy, too. Next to his family, his players came first and he battled
to take care of them even as he chewed them out. It is said of Frank that
his tough attitude toward his superiors cost him a shot at managing in
a higher level and, eventually his job.

But you always knew where you
stood with Verdi and the press corps
covering the Oneonta Yankees loved
him. He would play straight, never duck
a question and was always ready for
the media, even after the most difficult
losses.

Safe to say, then, Frank Verdi is a
baseball man. His son, Mike, followed
in his footsteps having managed at
Elmira in the NY-P League. The elder
Verdi is still at it and in 1993 managed
the Sioux Falls, South Dakota. Canar-
ies in the Northern League, a new circuit designed to give young players who
didn't make a club or who had been
released a chance to play. Mike Verdi
is managing Sioux City, Iowa in the
same league.

Frank Verdi, an outspoken, tough baseball man, was the O-Yanks first pilot in 1967.

Frank Verdi has always been a family man. It isn't too difficult to recall
the early mornings at Damaschke Field when he would be hitting ground
balls to sons Mike at third, Frankie at short, Paul at second and Chris
at first. Doing the catching for those fun sessions was Pauline, lovely
and enduring wife and mom to that busy baseball group.

Verdi turned 67 in June, 1993, an age when most baseball men
think of fly fishing and golf. But son Chris has suffered torn nerve ends
in his lower spine and the Verdis have travelled far and wide in a luck-

less search for successful treatment.

"I'm going back because I'm tired of hanging around and we need the money," Verdi said before heading west.

"It will do him good," said the understanding Pauline.

One believes the young men out in Sioux Falls will be the beneficiaries of Verdi's move because he is a players' manager. He cares about them.

Verdi's concern for his players was apparent the night the O-Yanks arrived in Auburn and were told there was very little room at the inn. The Yank pilot was informed his players would have to sleep two in a bed. The hotel lobby turned blue with the strength of Verdi's reply. After he got his message across to the overpowered desk clerk, Verdi called Sam Nader in Oneonta even though it was late.

After he brought the O-Yank boss up to date on the situation, he added, "There is no way our players are going to sleep two in a bed. Hell, they'd get 30 years for that in the Army!"

Verdi in the firmest possible tones (and he could be firm), told Nader the Oneonta club was either going home or staying in Syracuse where room was available. "I got the damn bus running, so you tell me where to go."

Resisting a momentary urge to do exactly that, Nader calmed down and said, "Go on to Syracuse."

That 1967 ball club was the first to play the short-season schedule of 80 games. The players didn't arrive in Oneonta until 10 days or so before the campaign got under way in mid-June. The roster was a mix of some veteran ballplayers like Ingram "Arch" Haley and Ron Cook, both of whom had played in Binghamton the year before, and rookies like the apple-cheek teenager Terry Echan who was so thrilled at being named to the starting lineup for opening day he raced to Western Union to get a wire off to his folks in Santa Ana, California.

This was a special youngster, one many thought was short-changed as a prospect because scouts labelled him too small. But it's easy to recall the game he won by hitting a double, stealing third during the intentional pass to the next hitter and scoring on a sacrifice fly. He also can be remembered for being called in from the outfield to play second base after a sixth inning injury to regular keystoner Walter Peto and turning a key double play on the very next pitch. Echanhit .311 for the season and scored 38 runs while driving in another 21.

Peto ranks as one of the best second baseman ever to play for the Oneonta Yankees and was an offensive force as well. His 46 runs led the team in that category and his 16 stolen bases were second only to Echan's 21. Walter was back strong for the 1968 season and had a good year but said an emotional farewell early in the 1969 campaign because he felt his young wife and two small children came first and, despite his obvious talent, his career wasn't going fast enough.

That club had power. Gary Washington, a big and strong athlete from Paragould, Arkansas, smashed a grand slam over the centerfield fence some 410 feet from the plate in the bottom of the ninth to win an early season game. Chuck Lelas hit 12 home runs to set a club record which stood until 1984; Washington added six and Bobby Carson four to the club total of 31. Carson's batting average of .358 topped the club and kept him in the league race until the final days of the campaign. Lelas's 59 was tops in the RBI figures for the club.

Catcher Steve Mezich from Seattle, Washington was a fan favorite from day one and his battle cry of "c'mon now, everbuddy hep out" still is recalled by the Oneonta Faithful. Steve and his wife Nancy were popular folks around the ball park and around town.

Outfielder Cesar Geronimo played in four games that year and then moved rapidly up the ladder on his way to becoming an all-star outfielder in the major leagues. Pitchers Gary Timberlake, who was the starter for opening day, and Larry Gowell also made it to The Bigs as did Rusty Torres who played in only eight games for the O-Yanks.

Gowell came from Auburn, Maine and at one time dazzled all connected with the Oneonta club when he disappeared one Friday night. He was quickly located at home in Auburn where he had gone unannounced for the weekend. He was a member of a religious sect which did not permit him to play on Sunday so he simply decided to go home in time to attend church.

A highlight for O-Yank players that season, and for those covering the O-Yanks, was the appearance in Oneonta of Hall of Fame pitcher Ed "Whitey" Ford.

Shortly after abruptly leaving the mound during a game in Detroit to close out a brilliant major league career, Ford turned up unannounced in Damaschke Field to coach the young O-Yank pitchers.

At first he was evasive when writers turned up, tired of talking about his sudden departure from the big club. But he warmed up after former New York Yankee teammate Jim Konstanty, a resident of Oneonta, introduced Ford to a writer and told him the writer could be trusted to be fair and accurate.

Before he left Oneonta, Ford sat with that writer in an Oneonta restaurant and talked about his decision to retire. "I walked away because I realized I could no longer do the things what I wanted to do with the baseball. The curve wasn't biting anymore, the fast ball had no pop," Ford said.

"Nobody had to tell me it was time to leave. It wasn't easy but it was the right thing to do."

That 1967 Oneonta team finished third in the six-team NY-P League race behind Auburn and Batavia. There were no playoffs, a fact which disappointed Oneonta fans who thought the team was playing its best ball at the close of the campaign. But that season left behind great memories of exciting players, a salty manager and a great pitcher who arrived to help launch the winning Oneonta Yankee tradition.

35 PENNANT

F rank Verdi and his family packed their bags at the close of the 1967 campaign, the first at Damaschke Field under agreement with the New York Yankees, and headed home. They left an atmosphere never quite equalled in the annals of Oneonta baseball.

In their place came the Jerry Walker family when June 1968 rolled around. Walker was ready to try his hand at managing a baseball team, even though he was still young and strong enough to be throwing in the big leagues; however, a bad shoulder ruled that out.

So Jerry set to work. He was confident his baseball knowledge and experience would offset his inexperience as a manager. He was right.

The Yankees sent help in the form of Cloyd Boyer, assigned as pitching coach. Boyer learned quickly about life in the minors: his first Oneonta assignment was to help General Manager Nick Lambros clean up the concession stand. Coming from a large family (brothers Clete and Ken made the majors), Cloyd knew how to handle a broom and cleaning cloth. He received high marks from the fussy general manager.

Walker and Boyer set to work on their diverse pitching staff which consisted of Larry Gowell, back from the 1967 club; "Bullet Bob" Elliott, a bonus baby who had problems controlling his live fastball on the field and himself off the field; Wayne "Boom-Boom" Crowder, who finished the season with an ERA of 27.00, and Dante Schirrippa, who sometimes concentrated so hard while running in the outfield during practice he would crash into the fence, also returned. Doug Hansen won eight games and pitched to an ERA of 1.67 despite a poor strikeouts to walks ratio.

The work of Walker and Boyer paid off and the staff was the key to a club which brought the first NY-P League playoff title. Steady Ken Lange won seven games and crafty Ray DeRiggi, like Elliott, won six.

Steve Mezich returned from the 1967 club but was forced to share the catching chores with a big redhead from Denver named Jim Diedel who went on to the major leagues. Diedel hit .322 in 38 games after joining the club in mid-season.

Walt Peto turned in another solid season at second, playing alongside steel-eyed Jeff Mason at short and Dan Bohannon at third base. Bob Hefflinger logged 57 games at first base and, while not a strong hitter, proved invaluable in the field. Outfielder Dave Kent led the offense by driving in 31 runs and hitting .282 and Bob McDaniel contributed a solid year at the plate despite battling a chronic sore arm.

Mason, with that hard stare of his, loved to tell gullible Easterners about the "jackelopes" which ran wild in his native Iowa. The animal, he explained without the trace of a smile, was a cross between a jackass and an antelope. "You ought to see those suckers jump," he would say.

Andy Bottin arrived from Edmonds, Washington and played in 43 games, joining McDaniel and Kent in the outfield. Andy's baseball career was short-circuited shortly after the season as he was caught up in the Viet Nam war. While on active duty there, he tangled with a land mine and suffered terrible leg wounds. But the spirit was strong and the desire to get back to baseball obsessive and he recovered to return to Oneonta in 1971.

Kent returned to Oneonta as a coach in 1990.

Elliott, after receiving a substantial bonus from the Yankees, arrived in Oneonta in a cloud of dust stirred up by his high-powered sports car. He did everything with a noticeable flourish and, asked one day why he acted like a hot dog, he replied, "I don't know. I'm a bonus guy and I guess that's the way I am supposed to act."

There was an umpire in the league at that time named Ross Cruscilla. He was small of stature and always wore a glove similar to a batting glove while working. Nobody ever knew why. One night in Geneva he was working behind the plate and Elliott was pitching. On a close play at first base with Elliott covering, the base ump called the Geneva runner "safe" thus incurring the wrath of the big O-Yank pitcher. As the argument heated up, Cruscilla rushed to the scene from his position behind the plate but, before he could say a word, Elliott shouted at him, "Keep out of this, muskrat" (using a nickname all players had for the feisty little ump). The little umpire reacted by bumping up against the much taller Elliott and throwing him out of the game using his strongest voice and his most dramatic flourish.

"I was out of the game," said Elliott afterward, "but I brought out the best that little umpire had."

All agreed Elliott's fast ball was one of the best ever seen at Damaschke Field and, as Walker said, "When this kid concentrates, when he is really on, nobody is going to beat him."

Crowder would complain to the official scorer, "Geez, nobody, not even me, has an ERA of 27.00." But it was true and "Boom-Boom" really wasn't the best pitcher on the O-Yank roster that year.

Curious about the Canadian native and how he came to be signed, an O-Yank beat writer asked him one day as the players sat around the pool at a motel in Batavia.

"Well," drawled Boom-Boom, "I was on a trip through the boondocks one time selling shoes - that was my job, selling shoes -and I was hanging around the ball park in this little town one Sunday watching a pickup game. Somebody there remembered I told him I played ball so they asked me to play. When they asked me what position, I said I guessed I could pitch even though I hadn't pitched very much.

"The game was going on when, all of a sudden, this guy comes off the sidelines, says he's from the New York Yankees and tells me I'm a pitcher and wants to pay me. Who was I to argue with him? I signed on the spot, got some expense money and headed for Oneonta."

He arrived in town with a car full of unsold shoes, some of which he was able to unload on his teammates.

In fairness to ol' Boom-Boom, it might be pointed out he was back in Oneonta the following season, got his ERA down to 4.35 and won six games while losing only three.

One of the highlights of that 1968 season came in August when the Neahwa Park facility was named Damaschke Field in honor of the little man who had been so big for so long in the annals of Oneonta sport, E.C. "Dutch" Damaschke.

The Yanks lost the opener, came back to beat Newark the second night and then sat out a week of bad weather. When they got going, Walker's ball club made a race of it, at one time knocking off a five game win streak.

Williamsport clung to the lead in the first third of the season with Oneonta right behind. But the leaders faltered and sunk from contention and, by the second week of August, the O-Yanks had also slipped. They went into a real tailspin going 2-10 over one stretch so that they were in fourth place by August 15. Typically, they picked themselves up, got it together and by the regular season's end were the best club in the NY-P League. They finished second to Auburn and ahead of Williamsport and Newark and were ready for the playoffs.

"I didn't have to psyche these guys up," said Walker. "They did it for themselves. They wanted to win, believed they could, and then went out and proved it."

Oneonta blasted Newark, 12-4, in the one-game semi-final and then turned to arch rival Auburn.

Jeff Mason, with three hits and two runs batted in, and Jim Deidel, who had the game-winning hit in the eighth, were the offensive stars in support of Doug Hansen who pitched the game of his life as Oneonta won, 3-2.

The game was a classic and well remembered by Oneonta Yankee fans. Many more NY-P League titles followed, but this was the first and the memory of that campaign will linger as long as baseball is played at old Damaschke Field.

36 BREEZIN'

For one short season, kids on the 1969 Oneonta Yankee club were willing to give what it took to win. Under wily manager George Case who, despite the age gap, communicated well with his young charges, the O-Yanks breezed in to the pennant by an eight game margin over Batavia. Newark finished third, a half game out of second place. Williamsport, Jamestown, Auburn, Geneva and Corning finished in that order.

Billy Olsen returned to the mound for Oneonta and had an outstanding season, going 8-0 with an ERA of just 1.23. "Boom-Boom" Crowder came back to Oneonta looking like a real pitcher and throwing like one as he won six games, dropping his ERA to a decent 4.35. Dante Schirrippa, too, returned and also hung up six wins. (And he never once ran into the wall while doing the running required of all pitchers.)

Chuck Lelas came back to Damaschke but the pop was gone from his bat. He hit only .237 and nailed only four home runs and a promising career was gone.

Catcher Jim Diedel also came back but was heading in the other direction. The big guy led in runs batted in with 45 and hit for a solid .320 average. Jeff Mason had another solid year but it was a newcomer named Paul Baretta who captured the Damaschke fans.

A little guy out of Western Connecticut College, he had more range at shortstop than any O-Yank before or since. And fans were amazed at his ability to get off the long throw from behind third base despite his small stature. Case welcomed the little guy with open arms because he saw a bunter in this hustling athlete. Baretta played in 72 games and scored a club-leading 53 runs. He also stroked 16 doubles and had 15 stolen bases.

A local pitcher, Steve McMullen from Sidney, was signed by the Yanks and won three games for Oneonta despite giving up a grand slam to the first batter he faced as a pro.

Another fan favorite was Nephtale Mora, signed out of Brooklyn as a catcher and nicknamed "Papo" Mora. He once precipitated a bench clearing brawl at Damaschke Field by sliding into home plate and spiking a Batavia catcher in the shoulder.

The shoulder?

"Yeah, I guess you could say I came in a little high that night," said

Papo during a conversation at the Yankee minor league facility one day in 1992. "I didn't know much then and I was trying so hard to make the team I played out of control. I had been a big star in high school sports and it was tough going to Oneonta and being a third string catcher."

Mora, now several pounds over his playing weight, is a popular figure around the Yankees' Tampa complex with his wide, bright smile and willingness to help where needed.

The NY-P League had done away with playoffs in 1969 and so the O-Yank season really ended before most were ready to see it close. The club was winning, everyone was happy and George Case was proving to be a manager of whom almost everyone approved.

He was named Manager of the Year and the choice was a popular one.

"Seldom has the selection of the year's best manager been easier than it was this year," said President Vince McNamara. "It was a pleasure to see that team develop into a winner under the direction of such a fine baseball man.

"George Case is a special man and the game could use more like him."

37 Grits

To the delight of everyone connected with Oneonta Yankee baseball, George Case returned as manager of the O-Yanks for the 1970 season.

In early June the veteran manager greeted a fine collection of young ballplayers, one of the best to represent Oneonta. (Meanwhile, a cagey baseball man named Boyd Coffie arrived to manage over at Auburn and he, too, greeted a good collection of baseball aspirants including people like pitcher Mark Wiley and catcher Rick Dempsey. In August, these luminaries spoiled a great O-Yank season and touched off a wild Auburn celebration.)

Watching early drills on a fine June morning in Oneonta became a pleasure for fans as they could see pitcher George "Doc" Medich throwing strikes, Dave Pagan tossing up his tantalizing curve, lumbering Chris "Baby Huey" Barker trying his best to do any thing he could and a variety of strong young players working out all over the field.

Medich, who had played football at the University of Pittsburgh as well as baseball, moved rapidly up the baseball ladder into Yankee Stadium as did Pagan. Medich, who played 11 years in the big leagues and closed his career with a career ERA of 3.78, will probably always be remembered best for responding to the call for a doctor by leaving the field during a major league game and saving a stricken man in the stands.

Big George studied medicine at Pitt and went on to continue his studies and receive his shingle as an M.D. He and his wife Nancy, who was about half his size, are well remembered by the Damaschke Field faithful. Medich loved to fish and a friendly sportswriter arranged a couple of productive angling trips along the Ouleout for the grateful pitcher.

Pagan, a tall and slender Canadian, was 21 when he arrived in Oneonta for the 1970 season. By 1973 he was at Yankee Stadium to begin a five-year major league career. Pagan was easy to take, mindful of his career yet always pleasant company. After his big league career, he retired to his native Saskatchewan where he and his family still live.

Pagan won four in 1970 as did Clark Babbitt, Tom Couples, Dan Dalonzo and Robin "Ty" Hippi. Dave Hazelip led the pack with five victories while Medich, Tom Hannibal and Al Tetrault each won three.

Couples is the older brother of golfer Fred Couples who was named by PGA players as Player of the Year in 1992 and has established himself as one of this era's finest golfers.

Infielder John Shaw, a pink-cheeked blond youngster from Oxford, Mississippi reported in with his new bride Libby. His first question to the Damaschke Field folks hanging around was, "Do you know where we can get some grits? We haven't been able to find any."

Grits aren't a common table food in the North like they are in Dixie, but after his plea was reported in *The Daily Star* the following day, a couple of pounds showed up at Damaschke Field later in the afternoon.

Papo Mora was back and he improved to .290 at the plate. He shared catching duties with Irv Homs, an athlete who truly danced to a different drummer. Homs, after two years as a backstop in Oneonta, turned up for this third NY-P League season as a relief pitcher for Jamestown. The first warmup pitch he threw when he returned to Damaschke with Jamestown sailed high up into the press box, a notice to "the guys upstairs" that Irv Homs was back. A few pitches later, a ball was hit sharply back to the box and Homs, ever true to form, turned his back to the ball and hid his head in his hands. The ball struck him squarely in the fanny and was duly recorded as a base hit.

"A fluke hit," said Homs after the game. "He was lucky to get a piece of that pitch."

Tom O'Connor led the 1970 Oneonta club in runs batted in with 50, in home runs with seven and runs scored with 56. He also was a class act around first base and appeared a potential sure thing to make The Bigs. He never did.

Angel Muniz hit .389 in 42 games and proved a strong outfielder. He also proved hard-headed (in the literal sense). He was running bases and stood at third one night when the opposing catcher fired a pickoff attempt to third. The ball hit Muniz squarely in the head with a loud pop. Observers in the press box, watching as Muniz lay unconscious on the ground, said,"It's a good thing he had a helmet on." A more observant member of the press box crew said, "He wasn't wearing his helmet." There was a moment of near silence as concern rippled through the stands.

Oneonta firemen got him into the ambulance and to Fox Hospital quickly and efficiently. Play resumed but the fate of the little ballplayer was in everyone's mind as the game wore on.

But, by the seventh inning, a ripple of applause went through the crowd as Angel returned to the ball park and took a seat with the pitchers who were charting the game in the box seats. There were no ill effects and he played out the season with his customary dash and fire. Many players from that team said in later years Muniz was the best player on the club.

Ed Waters played his second year for the O-Yanks and saw his batting average slip a few points even as his defensive outfield play improved. He was a fan favorite and returns frequently to Damaschke when he can get away from his coaching chores at a Florida high school.

And there was infielder John Bakis, affectionately called "Iron Glove" by teammates.

Of him, the Skip was to say, "John will bobble the ball frequently but, when the chips are really down, I'll go with him any time."

Offensively, he was strong. He scored 38 runs and drove in a like number. He hit four homers, four triples and 13 doubles and his 12 stolen bases placed him second only to Waters in that department. "Iron Glove" always came to play.

The pennant race was a dandy as the Yanks battled the Auburn Twins down to the final four days of the campaign. In the final week, Coffie brought his Auburn club to Damaschke for the make or break series. The Twins came in with a two game lead and two games to play so the O-Yanks had to win both games to tie. A win that first night was a must or the 1970 race was history.

Case decided to start a young left-handed rookie named Terry Vargason against the Twins in that game Vargason, a 17-year-old from Boise, Idaho, had shown a strong strikeout pitch in the brief time he was with the O-Yanks. The more experienced Jerry Johnson wasn't available because he pitched a couple of nights before. Case liked the idea of going with an unknown in a situation like this.

Hours before game time, a call from Yankee Stadium changed Case's mind. The caller asked the Oneonta skipper to start Steve Snyder, a left hander whose ERA of 6.60 led the club, but who also led the club in wild pitches. The Player Development people, prevailed upon by the field scouts involved with his signing, felt he had shown promise and wanted to see him in a pressure situation.

In the top of the first inning a base on balls, a single and another walk loaded the bases for Auburn outfielder Jack Smith. He promptly cranked one over the left field fence for a grand slam, an Auburn lead and eventually, the 1970 NY-P League pennant. Oneonta battled back to come within a run but lost 5-4.

The Auburn club had a victory party that night at the Oasis Motor Inn which lasted into the wee hours.

There was a game to be played the next night and Coffie saw a woeful sight when he looked into the dugout trying to find nine guys who could play. He found a few live bodies for the field positions then searched the forlorn dugout for a pitcher. Finally, as game time drew near, Catcher Rick Dempsey looked at Coffie and said, "Gimme the goddam ball." Coffie complied and Dempsey wobbled out to the mound. The umpire told him to put his hat on straight before he tossed the first pitch. Oneonta won that game, called by the writer who covered it "quite possibly the worst game ever played at Damsachke Field", by a big score and the season was over.

Young Vargason, who pitched well in relief during the game, might just epitomize the problem of that era when the Class A manager had no help. He was to lament that at 17, he was pretty young and inexperienced to be used in relief exclusively. "I never pitched a pro game that I wasn't in trouble to start with," he said.

Case, again using the youngster as an example, said, "It always bothered me that, being alone and having so many things to look after, I never had a chance to really study kids like Terry Vargason and make a proper evaluation."

So, the season ended and Yankee fans had a long winter ahead, broken only by the annual February Hot Stove dinner. It was well attended by Yankee brass, Yankee major league players and distinguished baseball guests such as Umpire Ron Luciano and thoroughly enjoyed by area fans for several years before the cost made the event fiscally impossible.

38 ANDY

Winter finally released its grip and spring made its welcome return to Damaschke Field. High school and college athletes played out their baseball seasons and gave way to the Oneonta Yankee hopefuls as the 1971 NY-P League campaign approached.

One of the early arrivals in the O-Yank camp that June was Andy Bottin. The big kid had fought his way back from the terrible wounds suffered in Vietnam and was ready to give pro baseball another shot.

His wife, Jenny, came along. She was a help and an inspiration to Andy. During the days when they were alone at the field, she would stand out behind second base with a stop watch sometimes for an entire morning timing her husband as he ran across the spacious Damaschke outfield from one foul line to another, battling to get his legs back in shape. Nights, when they were alone in their tiny apartment, she would offer words of encouragement when her husband wondered if he should keep going or pack it in and head for home.

"Baseball means so much to Andy," Jenny would say. "We just have to get it out of our systems one way or another. I'm with him and we'll hang in there together until the good Lord points our direction."

Manager George Case checked in an set up shop in his little office which once was described a being as big as the back seat of a Toyota. He had been named NY-P League Manager of the Year in 1969, gave way to arch-rival Boyd Coffie of Auburn for that honor after the dramatic 1970 season and was destined to win the award again for 1971. The stretch drive this time was not as dramatic as the previous year's, but Auburn did keep it interesting right down to the final week before Oneonta put it away by a four game margin.

As the season got under way, word came to Damaschke Field that the double play combination from Tulsa University had been signed by the Yankees and that second baseman Roger Adams and shortstop Phil Honeycutt would report as soon as the College World Series was over.

That word proved true and those two brought defensive strength up the middle. Tom O'Connor at first base and Phil Still at third gave the O-Yanks a very strong infield. Billy Stearns, a hard worker behind the plate, caught 46 games but struggled as a hitter. Powerful Rich Bianchi shared catching duties for the Yanks.

Pitching was the strength of this club. Like all of Case's teams, the wins were fairly evenly distributed among several pitchers: stylish Dave Lawson won seven, Bert Raschke and Clark Babbitt six each. One of Raschke's victories was a seven inning no-hit, no-run victory over Newark on August 11. Rob Arnold and Joe Blake each won four. Blake, whose son played in the NY-P League during the 1992 season, returned for a visit during that summer and remarked about the special atmosphere of Damaschke Field. "It hasn't changed," he said, "and there's no place like it in baseball."

Babbitt was one of those players who remains a happy memory in the minds of Damaschke fans. Called "Dracula" by his team mates and by some of the insiders, Babbitt appeared to be in his own world some of the time. But, when the chips were down, he could be tough.

The final week of the season found the O-Yanks at Williamsport with a chance to put the pennant away. They were scheduled for a doubleheader, it was Kid's Night at the park and the weatherman tossed in a little rain for good measure. Although a few days remained in the schedule, several of the Oneonta players were scheduled to leave after that night's action because of commitments such as college. So Case and Company were determined to wrap it up that night.

The Yanks won the first game and got into a tight match in the second. Finally, it came down to the bottom of the seventh. The clock showed it to be almost one in the morning and the scoreboard showed Oneonta ahead by a single run.

The Williamsport club loaded the bases with one out and the tying run, in the person of Jim Rice who went on to star for the Boston Red Sox during a long career, at third.

Roy Jefferson, who was having a good night, came to the plate. Catcher Rich Bianchi went to the mound to talk to Babbitt who had come on in relief. "Don't throw this guy a slider," said Bianchi to Babbitt, "he kills a slider."

"Not my slider," said Babbitt to Bianchi.

"You haven't got a real slider," said Bianchi to Babbitt.

"Tonight I have," said Babbitt to Bianchi.

"Dracula" knew of what he spoke. He struck out Jefferson on three pitches, all sliders, got the next hitter on a pop to second and it was all over.

Innkeepers at a watering spot on the top of the Route 15 hill south of Williamsport endeared themselves to the Yankee contingent that night by staying open late to accommodate the modest O-Yank celebration which included the Nader family who had driven down in two cars for what they hoped would be the pennant winner.

One of the players who enjoyed the pennant celebration with mixed emotions was Andy Bottin. He played in 49 games that season but was finally halted by the injured legs. On an August night in Damaschke Field, he smashed a long drive to right center field and started around the bases, feeling he had an inside the park home run. But, as he roared down the third base line toward what would have been a close play at the plate, his legs suddenly gave out and he collapsed before reaching the plate. Andy was tagged out and his professional baseball career was over.

Billy Sheets, a promising youngster who went 3-1 during the campaign while pitching to an 1.96 ERA, was killed later that year in a logging accident in his native Oregon.

Adams at .302 was the only regular to hit better than .300 and he added 26 RBIs. O'Connor led the club in that department with 39, Honeycutt added 30 and Bottin 23.

The party at the end of the season back in Oneonta wrapped up the season in an aura of sincere emotion; the camaraderie which had existed all year long was evident. It was as if each person there realized he had been part of something very special, something which might not come his way again.

One of the great moments came when the players honored batboy Randy Georgia. Randy, now a married man with a family, stood outside the locker room at Damaschke Field and cried his eyes out when the team left for the final road trip, sobbing, "I can't believe it is all over. I don't want them to go." The players remembered that just as they remembered all that Randy had done during the season.

Sam Nader capped the evening by giving out championship rings, something that very few minor league clubs do and a gesture which deepens the feelings players have for the Oneonta Yankees long after they have departed Damaschke.

Andy Bottin, the shattering Vietnam War behind him, slides in to score for the O-Yanks. His season and career ended soon after.

—The Daily Star

39 SPEED

Talent abounded on the Oneonta Yankee team of 1972 and speed was the keynote. It was the kind of club that Manager Case, who worshipped the stolen base, could really relate.

Jamestown manager Walt Hriniak, in a bit of overstatement after he had suffered a one-run loss to the O-Yanks in the bottom of the ninth, described that O-Yank club best when he said, "It's the bottom of the ninth and we're ahead by three. I go to get a drink of water and look up to see the game is over and we've lost. How did it happen?"

It would happen with a couple of bunts, a double steal, a squeeze, a hit and run—whatever it took involving speed on the bases. All Case's clubs were like that but this one, led by Larry Murray's 59 steals, was particularly adept and could snatch a victory away while the victim wasn't looking. They were the most exciting O-Yank club ever in that respect.

Roger Adams and Phil Honeycutt were back at second and short respectively and Honeycutt got his average up to a solid .317. Daryl Jones had a strong year, closing with a .300 average and leading the RBI list with 55 while Murray was driving 42 across.

One of the brightest lights, and certainly the brightest smile, came from 19-year-old Terry Whitfield, a lithe speedster from Blythe, California and one of the nicest kids ever to wear an Oneonta uniform. He had ten solid years in the majors after starring in Oneonta and Syracuse on the way up. He finished by playing a couple of seasons in Japan and now coaches high school sports in California.

It was a searing hot day in California desert country when Whitfield was spotted by a Yankee bird dog in 1971. He was competing in a track meet that day and playing in a baseball game. After winning (with one leap) the long jump and earlier, two sprints, Terry raced over to the ball diamond, put on a uniform and, in the words of the scout who signed him, "proceeded to hit hell out of the ball."

One year later, he arrived in Oneonta to the delight of George Case who saw him lead the club in home runs and wind up second in stolen bases.

When he made the opening day lineup, the first thing Terry Whitfield wanted to do was call his beloved "gramma" in Blythe, California to give her the good news.

One of the things that made Terry Whitfield special was he never forgot friends from the early days. The year he played in Oneonta, he joined Dick Cavanagh and Dick's son Pat for the annual Hall of Fame game in Cooperstown. The Dodgers were playing that day and Terry wanted to get the autograph of his idol, Tommy Davis. As the bus pulled up to where Terry and Pat stood they moved toward the bus door. When the door opened, the first Dodger off the bus rudely shoved everyone aside and there were no autographs that day. Terry turned to young Pat and said, "One thing I promise: if I ever make it, I'll never do something like that."

Years later, when Terry was with the San Francisco Giants, they were playing the Mets at Shea Stadium. When the Giants got off the bus, there was Pat Cavanagh looking for Terry Whitfield. The Giant players were being hustled through the crowd toward the clubhouse past autograph seekers. But, when Pat hollered to Terry Whitfield "remember Oneonta and Cooperstown," the player stopped, looked, and then came over to the youngster. Not only did Terry recall the early days but he stayed around to chat and sign autographs until the Giant clubhouse man came to fetch him.

The 1972 season Hard Luck Award would have gone to pitcher Billy Kostrba. Late in the season he went into the top of the ninth against league-leading Niagara Falls with a no-hitter and the Yanks holding a 1-0 lead. After getting the leadoff hitter, he walked a runner. This set the stage for Tom Nieman who responded by hitting a towering fly ball to left center field some 400 feet from home plate at spacious Damaschke Field. The speedy Murray, playing center field, got under the ball but couldn't reach it as it hit the top of the fence and bounced out into the street for a home run. It cost Kostrba his no-hitter and Oneonta the game by a 2-1 score.

Scott Larsen won nine games for Oneonta in that 1972 campaign

Larry Murray racks up another stolen base for the O-Yanks in 1972. He holds the club's all-time base stealing record with 59.

and didn't lose a game. Colorful Caleb Glover, who from time to time would slip up to the press box and work with the radio man, won eight for Oneonta and Bob Artemenko seven.

Tippy Martinez, on his way to the big leagues, stopped for a brief time with Oneonta and appeared in only two games, but quickly became a fan favorite.

The day Martinez reported to Oneonta, he came in via commuter aircraft to Oneonta's modest airport. General Manager Sam Nader was to meet him there and, as he got into his car for the drive up to the airport, he asked Manager Case if he wanted to ride along.

The Skip responded immediately and off they went. They met Martinez at the airport and drove him to "Myrtle Manor," where he would be staying during his time with the O-Yanks. Myrtle Manor was a private home but it was like a dorm for the Yankee players and as many as eight stayed there at one time. It was called Myrtle Manor simply because it was on Myrtle Avenue in the heart of Oneonta's residential section.

As they approached the house, Case carried one of Tippy's bags and Nader another.

On the porch, Case dropped a bag and looked at Martinez as Nader struggled up the stairs with the other piece of luggage.

"Mark this moment well, Tippy," said Case to his young pitcher. "This is the only time in your baseball career that the manager and the club owner will carry your bags."

"You know," Martinez was to say years later as he recalled his Oneonta days, "the Skipper was right."

Whitfield, Murray, Jones and Kammeyer joined Tippy as members of that squad who made it to the big leagues.

At the close of the campaign, George Case repeated as winner of the President's Award for being named the NY-P League manager of the year, the third time he won the award in his four years at Oneonta.

He died in December, 1989 but will never be forgotten. George Washington Case, "The Skip," will always be Manager of the Year in Oneonta.

Oneonta first baseman Ron Spann goes high to haul in errant throw and save an extra base in a 1972 game.

40 Guess?

C lub officials, manager, coaches, sportscasters and writers, along with fans, annually play a game at Damaschke Field, the game in which they try to figure who among the young players will make it to the big leagues.

Some players, such as Roger Adams, Chuck Lelas or Tom O'Connor, show great talent while in the NY-P League, put up great numbers, sometimes play a year or two at the next level and then just disappear from the baseball world.

Others, like Amos Otis, Willie McGee or Willie Upshaw, fail to impress at the short-season Class A level and fans don't have much regard for their chances yet, they go on to excellent major league careers.

And then comes the player who leaves little doubt in anyone's mind he is headed for the majors.

Such a player, in the form of a teenage shortstop, came to Damaschke Field with the Newark Co-Pilots in the 1973 season and everyone knew immediately this was a special player.

His name was Robin Yount and he was in the major leagues the next season at 18 years of age. He recently retired with more than 3,000 hits and a gang of MVP awards, and is set for immortality at Cooperstown.

Oneonta, under new manager Hank Majeski, had a player in its own right as Kerry Dineen won the league batting championship with a .352 average and the NY-P League's Kinsella Award as rookie of the year. Yount captured the Stedler award, indicative of scorers' and managers' opinions he was the player they thought had the best future in baseball. Dineen went on to the major leagues, as did teammate Del Alston who had a .321 batting average for Oneonta.

Mickey Klutts, a shortstop with a golden glove, a sharp bat and a cannon for an arm, played well enough to make the big club for the 1976 season but a broken thumb suffered in the last exhibition game that spring cost Mickey his spot in the starting lineup and hurt his overall major league career.

O-Yank pitcher Bob Polinsky who attracted interest with an 8-3 record and an ERA of 2.55 paled in comparison to Neal Mersch who went 11-0 and pitched to an ERA of 1.18. His 11-0 mark is an O-Yank club record, his 114 innings pitched are second only to Bob Majczan's 115 as a club record. Majczan's 12 complete games also stand as a club mark.

But Mersch and Majzcan didn't make it, nor did Steve Coulson, fondly remembered by Oneonta fans for setting a club record of 95 hits that season and driving in 41 runs.

Caleb Glover returned and won five games for Oneonta, also managing to slip up to the press box from time to time to continue his "broadcasting career." He was a fun guy.

Majeski, best known for his years holding down third base for the Chicago Cubs, brought a relaxed party atmosphere to the clubhouse and Damaschke Field. He was quiet but he had a flock of old friends from his major league days with the Cubs and enjoyed having them around.

Sometimes, during the pre-season workouts at Damaschke, his friends would lounge in camp chairs around the outfield until chased beyond the foul lines by a field attendant. On one occasion he planned to take a half dozen pals with him for a road trip, but O-Yank officials didn't think that was too great an idea and informed Hank accordingly.

But this had nothing to do with his baseball ability and he managed the O-Yanks to a 44-26 record and a second place finish 2 1/2 games behind Auburn. He was liked by the players and the media folk who followed the club and, although he was a generally "laid back" personality, he was pleasant to be around.

41 RUNAWAY

T he designated hitter rule arrived for keeps in 1974 along with new manager Mike Ferraro and, quite possibly, the most talented ballclub the Oneonta Yankees ever put on the field. Combined, the ingredients meshed to form a record-breaking ball club, one which played to a .768 percentage which has never been bettered. The team set a record by winning 53 games, a mark which stood until Buck Showalter's 1986 Oneonta team won 59.

The 1974 O-Yanks captured the league pennant by 17 1/2 games over Auburn. The race was over early as Ferraro's club got off to a strong start and never looked back.

Dave Bergman won the league batting crown with a .348; Fred Anyzeski the pitching crown with a 10-1 record and an ERA of 1.61 and Ferraro was a shoo-in as manager of the year.

This club had everything. Greg Diehl pitched a perfect game against Newark July 7, the second such game in the league's long history. (The other was by John Herbert of Erie on July 23, 1956 over Hornell.) Diehl closed the season with an 8-2 mark, Scott Delgatti was 9-1 and Rick Fleshman 9-5.

Bergman went on to a long and successful major league career which lasted 17 years, finally ending in the spring of 1993. Most of the years were spent with the Detroit Tigers and his business career in the Motor City has been as successful as his baseball career.

With Oneonta, he hit 10 homers and drove in 48 runs, third behind Dennis Werth's 61 and Pat Petersen's 53. The latter sported a .330 batting average for the year.

Mike Heath, who became a strong major league player for more than a decade, was another reason for that club's success while Werth, who many fans thought was the best player on the club, came in with a .336. Heath's major league career spanned 15 seasons and included post-season playoff and World Series action while Werth's career in The Bigs lasted four seasons.

Detroit Manager Sparky Anderson said of Heath, "I like that guy. He's like having a manager on the field. And he'll give you 100 percent every time."

But Marv Thompson, who also posted some good numbers, and Peterson never made the majors.

People covering the club were quick to point out this was a happy clubhouse. That isn't always the case in baseball which demands so much mentally and physically from players and managers.

But Ferraro found the key and instinctively knew when to sternly reprimand a young athlete and when to offer some quiet advice or listen to a youngster's lament.

It's a difficult line managers must walk at this level and many of those who try it find they are not up to what the job demands.

42 QUIET

Returning as a manager after a banner season is not the easiest thing for any baseball man. Mike Ferraro's 1974 Oneonta Yankee club was a record-shattering pennant winner, a tough act to follow in any event.

But it was obvious early in the 1975 season Mike did not have to worry about topping 1974.

The team got off to a slow start and was never in contention. But the O-Yanks played well in the second half, turning a losing record into a winner and finishing third behind Newark and Elmira, 13 games off the pace.

Language was a problem. There were several youngsters on the team who could not speak English; some had never been to the United States before. Communication at critical times in a game was difficult to say the least. But the kids hustled every day.

Instead of chattering to support the pitcher, the Latin Americans chirped. This caused one veteran Damaschke Field fan to remark, "What the hell's going on? This place sounds like a swamp on a hot summer night."

Team batting was off, the team averaging only .233 and the average of .268 by Damaso Garcia was highest on the club.

The O-Yanks hit only 14 home runs all year. Jim McDonald, who did not make it to the big leagues, led the club with a .284, led with 37 runs batted in, and was the only O-Yank to play in all 69 games. Willie Upshaw, who went on to a solid major league career, hit only .088.

Upshaw, Garcia, Terry Bevington, Mike Fischlin, Domingo Ramos all reached the big leagues, as did pitchers Gil Patterson, Jim Beattie and Randy Nieman.

Years later Upshaw, who played in more than 1300 major league games and had a lifetime batting average of more than .260, came back to Cooperstown with the Cleveland Indians for the annual Hall of Fame game. Before the game, he was talking to the locals about his batting average in Oneonta.

"I was really struggling," he said. "But, you know, nobody ever got on my butt, nobody ever gave me a really hard time. I heard some yells about bonus baby a couple of times but mostly it seems as if everyone was pulling for me. I'll always remember Oneonta."

Domingo Ramos, who was with Upshaw in Oneonta, was a member of that 1988 Cleveland team as was Mark Wiley, pitching coach. It was the same Mark Wiley who stopped Oneonta for Auburn in the climactic final days of the 1970 NY-P League pennant race.

And the same Chuck Cottier who charged the umpire in the zany 1972 episode was a coach for the Chicago Cubs who played Cleveland in Cooperstown in Doubleday Field on August 1, 1988.

During a pre-game chat, some of the former Oneonta players fell to talking about Oneonta fans.

Upshaw said the Damaschke Field crowds were the quietest he ever played before, a recurring theme among O-Yank "graduates."

"Sometimes, if you didn't look right at the stands, you would wonder if there was anybody there. It was just plain quiet, almost to the point of being weird.

"But there was never any question that they were with the O-Yanks all the way."

In later years, Willie was told, some of the young Yankees thought the fans weren't with them and really didn't care much about the outcome.

But by the time September rolls around, Oneonta fans have always been able to convince O-Yank players they have been with them all season, cheering them in Damaschke and following them on the road.

The 1975 season wound down to its conclusion and the Yanks left town, not really satisfied with their 35-34 record and third place finish, but happy with the thought they were a better team in September than they were in July.

Mike Ferraro went on to coach in Yankee Stadium and then manage Cleveland in the American League.

Like all of the Oneonta Yankee teams over a quarter century, the 1975 edition left its owncollection of memories. That's one of the nice things about organized baseball in a small town.

43 CELLAR

N apoleon came to town in 1976 but he didn't conquer. He wasn't banished into exile, either. Ed Napoleon, a career baseball man, came to Damaschke Field as manager and left as the only manager other than Bill Livesey to finish last in the long history of the Oneonta Yankees. Oneonta owner Sam Nader and most of the Damaschke Field faithful say, "1976 wasn't Eddie's fault. He was and is a damn good baseball man who has lived his life for the game. He gave it every effort but things just didn't click."

Again, the age-old and yet unsolved mystery of what happens to players after they compile great records in a short-season Class A baseball league surfaced in the wake of the 1976 season.

Garry Smith hit .391 to capture the NY-P League batting championship and was presented the Stedler award as the player league managers and official scorers deem likely to go farthest in baseball. His .391 average is the highest ever recorded by an O-Yank over a long haul. He appeared in 44 games, more than half the team's total, led the team in RBIs with 34 and had 169 times at bat which should have been enough to give him recognition in the O-Yank record book.

Kerry Dineen, who is listed as the best O-Yank hitter in terms of averages, hit .362 in 1973, going to bat 250 official times.

Benny Perez hit .325, Darnell Waters .320 and Don Hogestyn .305 for the 1976 club. Hogestyn turned away from baseball shortly after his time in Oneonta and became an actor. He still appears regularly in the daytime television series "The Young and the Restless" and has a long career in daytime soaps behind him. He is the second former Oneonta player to make a career in television. John Dockery, who was with the Oneonta Red Sox when baseball returned to Oneonta in 1966, appears regularly as a sports commentator for network events.

The team finished the campaign with a 26-46 record, a percentage of .343, by far the worst in Oneonta history.

Fischlin and Bevington returned from the 1975 team but Bevington appeared in only two games and Fischlin but 14 before they moved onward and upward. Pat Tabler played in 65 games for the O-Yanks as a youngster just out of high school. He fought a violent case of homesickness and there were times when he really wanted to pack it in and go back to home in Cincinnati. But he played in 65 games and, although he hit only .231, Tabler showed enough to convince major league people he had the tools. He did, because his career is still very much alive after 12 years during which he has hit a career .287.

Ted Wilborn, also on his way to The Show, stopped off in Oneonta for 28 games but he hit only .188 and was unable to show any indication he was headed for the top rung.

Pitching was the basic problem with this ball club. The staff ERA of 4.43 was the second highest in O-Yank history (topped only by the 4.72 of the 1983 team).

Calvin Rigger, with a 5-4 record, was the only winning pitcher unless you count Rafael Carmarena who was 1-0 in 10 starts.

One of the most telling statistics of this pitching staff is it had more bases on balls than any other team in Oneonta Yankee history. No other staff is even close to the 382 walks the 1976 pitchers gave up.

The effects of this slippage in the team's record were felt at the gate when attendance slipped to 21,082 after nine years of steady increases.

The bright side of the Napoleon story came as the 1992 major league season got under way. During his long minor league career, he managed a young and promising athlete named Buck Showalter who came to believe Napoleon had a most positive effect on his career. When Showalter was named New York Yankee manager, Napoleon was appointed first base coach and, as the 1993 campaign got under way at Yankee Stadium, Ed Napoleon sat beside Buck Showalter as bench coach.

44 TURNAROUND

O neonta had finished 1976 dead last in the NY-P League race, something that has happened only twice in franchise history. Art Mazmanian showed up in June, 1977 and things began to turn around almost immediately.

In short-season, Class A baseball the turnover among players each season is close to 100 percent. As a result, only five from the 1976 team were among the players at Damaschke when drills got under way June 10.

One was an athlete who had toiled in Oneonta as a pitcher for two seasons and was now back as an infielder. Rafael Santana proved the decision makers correct when he forgot pitching and embarked as an infielder on a path which was to take him all he way to the big leagues. He became a solid starting shortstop for the New York Mets and produced four good seasons for them, including the championship year of 1986 when the kid from the Dominican Republic earned a World Series ring.

The term "kid" is not loosely applied, as Raf was only 16 when he first reported to Oneonta. He won a car on Jalopy Night at Damaschke Field that year but couldn't drive it away because he was too young to have a license.

Others back from the 1976 failure were pitcher Leonce Laurent and position players Rodrigo Bellony, Benny Lloyd and Mark Plantery.

So, Mazmanian started from scratch. The start was not awesome and the O-Yanks struggled through the early going. But then came one of the hot streaks which became the hallmark of Maz's clubs. Utica put up a good struggle but Oneonta won the key games down the stretch and took the Eastern Division flag by four and a half games over the Blue Sox. The Yanks won the playoff series by taking two straight over Western Division champion Batavia.

The total turnaround showed the 1977 O-Yank record to be 47-23 as opposed to the 24-46 record of 1976. And the fans showed they were paying attention because attendance for 1977 was almost double what it was the previous year.

One of the players on that club was a slender speedster from San Francisco who was to go on to great things in the majors, topped by his 1985 season when he was named the National League's most valuable player. His name is Willie McGee and he was 18 years old when he launched his career in Oneonta. He played in 65 of 70 games that year but hit only .236, had only nine extra base hits and stole only 13 bases.

"He was just a kid," Mazmanian said about Willie in later years. "He had the basics, including speed, but he really didn't know the game at that point in his career. But he was willing, he worked awfully hard and took instruction really well.

"And, obviously, he learned about how to use the carpet,"(a reference was to the artificial surface in St. Louis where Willie McGee had his greatest years).

Jeff Tillman's 43 runs batted in led the club in that department while Dwayne Gray hit a solid .324 and Ken Baker stole 17.

Mike McLeod won nine, Paul Semall and Chris Welsh eight each for the Yanks. Welsh and Jamie Werly, who each won seven, were destined to reach the majors.

In 1978, the Yankees sent Oneonta another group of talented players and Mazmanian knew how to use them. His charges zipped through the NY-P League schedule, winning 51 games and taking the Yawkey Division flag by 14 and a half games over Utica. But the playoff championship eluded Mazmanian's club for the only time during his reign in Oneonta when an equally good Geneva team won the playoffs two games to none.

No fewer than nine members of that Oneonta team went on to the major leagues. Pitchers Don Cooper, Tom Filer and Andy McGaffigan went on to the top rung, although it was John Franks (8-1), Dan Ledduke (6-0), Rich Carluccis (6-1), Karl Steffen (6-2) and Jeff Taylor (6-2) who did the winning for Oneonta. Cooper, Filer and McGaffigan stopped only briefly at Damaschke. Taylor returned to Oneonta in 1988 as pitching coach after arm problems ended is playing career.

Rex Hudler, a 17-year-old shortstop from California, was one of the popular players that season with the fans and with the New York organization which paid him a substantial bonus to sign. For the O-Yanks he hit .281 in 58 games and sparkled in the field, flashing what scouts liked to call "a major league arm."

Speaking about the reported $100,000 bonus which snatched him away from a football career at Notre Dame, Hudler said, "I know I am young and have a lot of learning to do. But the players on the big club all went through this at one time or another and I figure, God willing, in a few years I'll be there."

He made it and he's still there.

Hudler would usually have a wad of tobacco to chew on, emulating, like so many youngsters of that era, their big league heroes of an earlier era. Now, of course, we are in the bubble gum age.

Baseball people love to say "pitchers dance to a different beat, they aren't the same as other ballplayers." Coaches and managers realize one of the most difficult things for a young pitcher to do is to prepare himself mentally for a start.

On that 1978 O-Yank squad was Brian Ryder who, at 18, was starting his baseball career. He was from Shrewsbury, Massachusetts but signed with the Yanks rather than his native Red Sox.

Each pitcher has his own way of getting ready for a starting slot;

some are superstitious.

"It can be difficult to get yourself up for a game, especially when you are on the road and you might have to hang around the hotel all day like we're doing right now," Ryder told a sportswriter one afternoon on the road. "This is a big part of what you are here to learn."

Young Ryder, who had an exceptionally adult outlook for someone so young and inexperienced, said part of the learning process was defeating the homesickness which usually hits young players their first week. This has to be accomplished before the player can settle down to concentrate on his work.

"Everyone told me that by the time I was 22, I should be in the big leagues. But I knew all I had was a fastball and I knew I had to learn another pitch, hopefully more than that," Ryder said one night, showing a wisdom beyond his years.

He went on to have a decent season in Oneonta with a 5-3 record and an ERA of 3.55, but the big leagues were not in his future.

Ted Wilborn was in his third year of pro ball and, by 1978, was beginning to have doubts about his future.

"It seems like I'll never get to the majors," he said on an introspective night in the Damaschke Field dugout. "All those great players on the Yankees plus my age (he was 20 then) it seems like such a long way off. But I'll stick with it for maybe two more seasons."

O-Yank super salesman LeRoy "Sonny" House takes a breather before the game begins.

He did stick with it and didn't have to wait long; he was in the majors the very next year with Toronto.

Part of what made them go after Wilborn was his stolen base record. He stole 57 that season in Oneonta, second on the all-time O-Yank list behind Larry Murray. And Ted hit .309 here while scoring 63 runs.

Big man at the plate for the O-Yanks in 1978 was Brian Dayett who stands among the Oneonta leaders in seasonal offensive categories like runs batted in (tops with 63), home runs (third with 11), doubles (third with 20), total bases (best with 140). He also went on to a big league career.

Others from that 1978 team, including Victor Mata, Rafael Villaman and Matt Winters, made The Bigs, although Winters returned for another season at Damaschke.

Mazmanian was high on Villaman, seeing a lot of himself in the scrappy little teenage speedster. Villaman had surprising strength and once in a while would get the ball out of the park.

"One night we're losing 2-1 in the seventh inning and Villaman comes to the plate. He has that crouching stance like Pete Rose and they're laughing in the dugout. Then he hits the ball over the center field fence and nobody is laughing, they're cheering," Mazmanian recalls.

That 1978 O-Yank club also sported an international flavor with a couple of Japanese names appearing on the roster. Fugio Tamura and Haruhkiko Nakano were products of an informal agreement reached when Gabe Paul was a Yankee official.

"Gabe made an agreement with Japanese baseball people to try a few players and give them a chance to learn. We are not committed to play these kids but get them in when we can," said Sam Nader.

They played 20 games for the O-Yanks that year.

The Japanese players were joined by a half dozen players from Latin American countries, giving an added dimension to the challenge tossed at Manager Mazmanian.

"I sometimes found myself talking Spanish to Japanese players," Maz was to say one night in recalling that season. "But we got it straightened out."

The record of 1978 shows that he did, indeed, get things straightened out.

45 Artful

O ver his years as manager of the Oneonta Yankees, Art Mazmanian showed remarkable talent in many directions. His ability to judge players for their spiritual drive, as well as their physical capabilities, helped him become the winningest manager in Oneonta history.

There are many cases in which the importance of the little manager's tactics manifested themselves but none more dramatic and effective than what passed between he and Don Mattingly in 1979.

Mattingly had been living through a period of adjustment in the early days of the 1979 campaign. He wasn't playing first base because bonus baby Todd Demeter was holding down that position. Mattingly was being used as a designated hitter and an outfielder and was platooned, sitting down against left-handed pitching.

He never complained, accepting each day's assignment without a whimper. But Mazmanian, an artful manager, had kept an eye on this eager rookie

Manager Art Mazmanian's "artful" handling of rookie Don Mattingly gave a boost to the future superstar's confidence.   —The Daily Star

and, when Mattingly suggested he could hit lefties, the Oneonta pilot responded and Mattingly played regularly the rest of the season. He had a key role in the winning charge.

Nine members of that team reached the major leagues (Demeter was not one of them), so Mattingly was among some good players and not as easily recognized as some of his teammates. Matt Winters, for example, was much better known than Mattingly.

Although jeered at times by the fans who thought he was goofing off, the highly visible Winters became a Damaschke Field favorite before the season was over. He left town a hero after capping the season by hitting two home runs in the finale at Geneva to lead Oneonta to the championship.

Oneonta had lost the playoff opener in Damaschke Field and the Yanks headed for Geneva one game down to the Cubs.

Stefan Weaver stepped front and center on that late summer Saturday night in Geneva. Boosted by Mattingly's timely hitting, he stopped the Cubs cold, shutting them out, 3-0, on five singles and setting the stage for Sunday's title game.

The championship game was exciting, typical of so many during Mazmanian's years in Oneonta. Home runs by Winters and Demeter gave Oneonta an early lead but starter Pete Filson - a late arrival in the O-Yank camp - gave up four runs on a combination of walks and timely hits in the bottom of the second and the Yankees trailed, 4-2. Mazmanian turned to relief pitcher Curt Kaufman who responded with a beautiful effort, shutting down the Cubs the rest of the way.

Dave Buffamoyer homered in the fourth and Winters came through in the ninth with a two-run shot which gave Oneonta a 5-4 victory and the championship.

Winters hit 12 home runs for the Oneonta ball club that year while hitting .282. Third baseman Glen Swires hit .283 and led the club in total bases (114) and runs batted in with 41.

Freddie Tolliver led a strong pitching staff by going 10-2 with an ERA of 2.10. He went on to the big leagues as did Filson, Kaufman and Weaver. Victor Mata, Ed Rodriguez, Keith Smith and Winters also went on to the major leagues although Smith returned for another season in Oneonta.

In early June of 1980, Art and Shirley Mazmanian made the long journey across the country from California to Oneonta where another crop of eager young Yankee hopefuls greeted him.

One of the most engaging things about Mazmanian's approach to managing was his enthusiasm which never waned.

"I consider myself a coach and a teacher as much as a manager," he said. "And the mission is important. These young men have much to learn about life as well as baseball and I hope to be able to provide some valuable lessons."

Those nearest the ballclub in those years believe he succeeded brilliantly in teaching as well as winning.

"We all believe you don't have to lose to learn," is the way John Nader puts it. "There's nothing wrong with winning and the lessons derived from winning are invaluable.

"In baseball, you lose from time to time and you learn from that experience as well. But here at Damaschke Field we believe we can win without sacrificing one measure of our belief in good sportsmanship."

As in every year of Maz's incredible reign in Oneonta, the Yankees won another pennant and another playoff championship. They finished the regular season 49-25, beating out second place Little Falls by 8½ games and captured the playoff series two games to one over Geneva.

This just might have been the little Californian's best year as a manager. The team's composite batting average was the lowest of all his teams and no less than 36 players passed through the Damaschke Field clubhouse that summer. Doug Latrenta's .294 was the top batting average. Jeff Reynolds led the team in runs batted in with 56 and in homers with seven.

Mark Mendez led the pitching department with a 9-3 record but didn't make The Bigs; Clay Christiansen (4-3 with the O-Yanks) and Ed Olwine (2-1 with an 1.00 ERA) did.

Mazmanian said later he got as much satisfaction winning with this 1980 club as with any he managed during at Oneonta.

46 Farewell

A nd then came 1981. When the season started, Art Mazmanian didn't realize this was to be the last of his years in Oneonta. As a matter of fact, when the season ended, he thought he would be returning to the city he and his wife had come to consider a second home.

Whereas, 1980 had come and gone quietly and produced another championship, 1981 was a season of greater excitement and colorful individuals.

It has been said by players like Russ Davis, currently moving up through the Yankee organization with his eyes on third base at The Stadium, "If you can play third base at Damaschke Field in Oneonta, you can play third base just about anywhere."

There is a lip just in front of the bag at the hot corner and the ball hit just right will shoot off that lip and right at the third sacker. If he's not careful, he'll be taking meals through a straw for a long time.

One of the most colorful, and most popular, players ever to hold down third at Damaschke came along in 1981. That was Mike Pagliarulo ("Pags" to just about everyone) whose uniform would be dirtier after pre-game warmups than most players' uniforms would be after an entire game.

"He was dedicated to the belief there was not a ground ball hit toward third that would get by him and, you know what, he was right," says Nick Lambros, a ball park regular, former O-Yank general manager and a fine third baseman himself in his younger days.

"Mike was a tough, chin out player and he was 100 percent every day. Not much got by him."

To this day, he has a running (and friendly) argument with General Manager Sam Nader about the money he owes the ballclub for broken bats. Nader says he broke 34 that summer.

Pags will look at you and say, "How the hell could I have broken 34 bats? I only hit .216 that year. Besides, they were lousy bats.

"And tell Sam Nader he still owes me bonus money for my home runs and doubles hit during the year."

For the record, Nader says, Pagliarulo only had two home runs and nine doubles for the season. One gets the feeling the argument will never be settled as the combatants are enjoying it too much.

The Yankees' number one draft choice reported to camp in June and left in September leaving nobody in doubt as to why he was drafted so high. Catcher Scott Bradley turned in a fine season behind the plate, showing a rifle arm and an ability to handle pitchers which belied his tender years. He was strong at the plate, too, hitting .308 in 71 games and leading the club in runs batted in with 54.

Bradley was a pleasant kid - he reminded one of Mattingly with his work ethic and desire to succeed - but he had a fun side, too, and helped make a lot of long bus rides easier to take.

Bradley moved on to a strong major league career which is still humming along. He caught most of the games he played in the earlier big league years but now is doing a lot of games as a designated hitter and has played third base, first base and the outfield. His lifetime batting average has stayed around .270.

Roberto Dennis at .322, John Hughes at .309 and Ed Rodriguez at .308 were other regulars hitting over the three century mark as the team batting average moved up to .265 for the season.

Keith Smith returned for a third consecutive year at Oneonta, a rarity for a short-season Class A player, but his perseverance paid off as he reached the major leagues in 1984.

As always, pitching played a big part in the club's success. Pitching coach Q.V. Lowe had a large role in the steadying of the staff.

One pitcher that didn't need much steadying was Bob Tewksbury, a big right hander from Concord, New Hampshire who has become one of the game's millionaires. He won seven for that team, second only to Kevin Quirk who appeared in 27 games for that club, picking up seven wins while losing only twice.

Tewksbury won 16 games in the majors in 1992 and was awarded a major arbitration verdict for the 1993 season, indicating he is established as a major league pitcher.

But in 1981, he was a young ballplayer who always seemed to be around the ball park, early to arrive and among the last to leave.

One Sunday, after the O-Yanks had played an early game, he got involved as a "plumber." It seems that Pat Cavanagh, son of public address announcer Dick, had played in a Babe Ruth game at Damaschke earlier in the day and became angry at himself for being picked off first base.

As he approached the first base dugout, he tossed his helmet toward the dugout. It bounced into the dugout and hit the aging water fountain, breaking it and causing it to leak.

Groundskeeper John Falk was summoned and got the water turned off before the O-Yank dugout was thoroughly flooded and, when the O-Yanks arrived for their game, the drinking fountain was out of order but the dugout was dry.

Dick Cavanagh being the kind of man he is wouldn't let it go at that. He was determined to fix the water fountain himself. He gathered buddies Dave Rivino, Bernie White and Grover Baker, collected some plumbing tools and waited for the game to end. After players and fans left, they moved into the target area. Pitching coach Lowe came along and he immediately got involved. "They needed advice, lots of it," he said next day with a chuckle.

Then along came Tewksbury who had heard earlier in the day about Cavanagh's project and was so intrigued he decided to get in on the action.

So this diverse crew went to work in the darkened, shadowy dugout, "looking like a band of commandos from World War II," Lowe said.

Their plan was to solder the broken pipe. They wrapped towels around it and started to work. But the heat from the soldering iron kept causing the water to surge through the broken pipe, dampening the gallant workers.

Finally, Baker suggested that bread could be the answer.

"Bread?" asked Cavanagh, leader of the crew.

"Yup," said Baker. "You put that in the pipe and it will soak up the water. After a while the bread will dissipate and disappear once the pipe is fixed and the water is running again."

Bread was not handy but Lowe had the answer. He went to the concession stand and returned with a half dozen hot dog rolls for immediate use.

Tewksbury and Lowe stuffed the rolls down the three-eighth inch pipe and Baker completed the soldering work. When they were done, the crew stood around chatting and admiring their handiwork.

Suddenly the pipe began to shudder and shake and make strange noises.

"All of a sudden," said Tewksbury in recounting the episode the next day, "these hot dog rolls came squirting out of the pipe like a snake. The next thing I knew, I was covered with wet dough while the old guys just stood around and laughed.

"Q.V. said something like 'welcome to pro baseball Bob' and I couldn't help laughing."

Cavanagh said the water fountain never was used again, the club was going to remove it eventually anyway.

"But," he added, "the sight of this fine young pitcher standing there with all that dough dripping off is one that I will never forget. He is a great guy and I wish him continued success."

And so the season rolled along. There was fun, excitement, color and, again, winning. The O-Yanks took the regular season division flag by seven and a half over Utica and beat Western Division winner Jamestown two games to one for the championship.

Art Mazmanian left for California the last time as Oneonta Yankee manager. He would return to Damaschke Field before leaving the NY-P League scene forever but in a different role.

His legacy to the winning Oneonta baseball tradition? Five pennants, four playoff championships and a 237-118 record which figures out to a winning percentage of .668. Small wonder the bouncy little guy with the white hair and the sunburned face will be remembered as long as there is baseball in Oneonta.

47 Hustle

K en Berry was to find his managerial skills tried to the limit during an exciting and unusual Oneonta Yankee campaign in 1982. Following the most successful skipper in Oneonta baseball history, working for a young female general manager and handling an athletic superstar as part of his squad were all challenges for the new manager.

He met all challenges head on and won. He captured the regular season pennant, worked beautifully with the young lady who ran the club and managed to mesh football star John Elway with the rest of his players in smooth and easy style.

Elway drew a crowd wherever he went; TV, radio and print media types were all over the place during his stay at Damaschke Field and it's a wonder the distraction didn't throw the O-Yanks completely off track. In August, Elway made his decision, opting for football over baseball and he left Oneonta accompanied by a horde of media people.

After the excitement and emotions subsided in the wake of Elway's departure, Berry and his players turned back to the pennant race. They were trailing a pesky Utica club in the division scramble and needed to put together a win streak. That's exactly what they did.

One of the athletes who finally got a chance to play after Elway's departure was Dan O'Regan. He patiently "rode the pine" while Elway got his trial and then finally got a chance. Before his first week of action was out he had done something few O-Yanks have ever done: hit a home run to straightaway center field more than 410 feet from home plate.

Another player who turned up in those climactic closing days was Dan Pasqua who swung into Oneonta from Paintsville, Ky. on his way to The Bigs. He hit a couple of dingers during his quick stop, appearing in only four games.

Mike Brown, who covered the 1982 club for his newspaper, *The Sporting Eye*, said, in a roundup at the end of the season, "The three big names to remember from this club are pitchers Jim DeShaies and Paul Doty and first baseman Orestes Destrade. DeShaies and Doty, along with Chuck Tomaselli, had 100 or more strikeouts and were practically unbeatable during the month of August."

Mike was on the money with DeShaies and Destrade but arm trouble forced a premature end to Doty's career.

Jim Riggs was a fan favorite and a player Berry thought could make it big.

"Jimmy has the best bat on the club. He hits righties and lefties equally well and if he improves his quickness and works out to build his upper body, he could move up fast."

The pennant race was a dandy. Utica walloped Oneonta five straight times early on before the Yanks got it together. At one point Berry's club won 10 straight and another time won 17 of 20 games in the late going. They faltered a bit in the final few days but hung on to win clutch games at the end and take the division flag by a game and a half.

Fall fever caught the club as the playoffs with Niagara Falls got under way. A letdown from the pressure-packed pennant race was inevitable and the players were homesick.

"It's been very tough for us the past couple of weeks," said Manager Berry at season's end. He looked as tired as his players as they packed to head home.

"Come the last week of August, people start thinking of getting home, football, girl friends, wives and families. It's been tough to stay sharp."

Errors ruined a three-hit pitching job by Doty in the series opener but Oneonta came back to win the second game 5-4 with a stirring rally in the bottom of the ninth inning. A good crowd roared its approval throughout one of the most exciting nights Damaschke Field has ever seen.

But Sunday night was as forgettable as Saturday night was memorable and Niagara Falls left town playoff champions after six Oneonta errors gave the Rapids a 6-2 victory.

It had been a memorable season, to say the least.

Berry, whose long major league career gave him plenty of experience with the vagaries of baseball, was philosophical when the O-Yank season was over.

"The secret is to look back over a fine regular season and a championship rather than dwell on one loss, no matter how costly.

"I see it as a fine season for a good bunch of young athletes who never stopped hustling."

Everybody was hustling, including author Bob Whittemore shown heading back to the Press Box after picking up his quotes.

48 Chemistry

Six regular season championships in a row. The euphoria floating around aging Damaschke Field in the wake of the Art Mazmanian run and the surprise pennant won by Ken Berry's charges soon evaporated as the 1983 O-Yank season rolled along.

It was obvious the chemistry which had so excited Damaschke Field faithful was missing.

Bill Livesey, a career baseball man who now holds the top player development job with the parent New York club, took on the job as manager in 1983. He had some tough acts to follow.

One of the biggest problems that year was the constant movement of players in and out of Oneonta. It was difficult to get a set lineup each day.

Before the year was out, 23 pitchers had passed through the Damaschke field gates and 28 position players appeared on Yankee lineup cards.

The team batting average of .234 came within a point of being the lowest in the club's history and the composite fielding average remains the lowest ever by an O-Yank club. The .271 average compiled by Richard Lewallen in 69 games was the season's highest and his 37 runs batted in led that department.

The hitters' strikeouts to walk ratio showed just about twice as many "Ks" on the scorecard as "BB."

There's more statistical data to show this wasn't the best O-Yank club by any means. And the fact he had to handle more than 50 players as the season wore on made it even more difficult for Livesey and his staff.

One of the bright spots was Rich Mattocks who played in 75 games, hit .271 and drove in 26 runs. But his best statistic was 34 stolen bases.

Livesey has always been a scout. He's been with the Yankee organization for more than a quarter century and is credited in many quarters as being one of the primary reasons the Yankee farm system is considered one of the best in baseball. Early in 1993, he was promoted to vice president, Player Development and Scouting with headquarters in the Yankee Stadium complex.

He can be philosophical about his two seasons in Oneonta during which his teams finished next to last the first year and dead last the following season.

"Scouting and appraising talent is one thing," he said during a spring training gabfest in 1993. "Managing is something else. I guess I was just not cut out to be a manager, but it's one of those things you have to find out for yourself."

He does say he looked upon his job during his tour here the same as he always looks at it: the primary concern is player development.

"So you experiment and switch and shuffle in an effort to find out what kids can do in given situations. As a result, a game can be sacrificed quickly in the name of development," he says.

Livesey is a stocky, red-faced man who bears a resemblance to Stump Merrill (until you see them together). He literally has given his life to baseball and is considered one of the best judges of talent in the game.

"I know my managerial record comes up for critical comment from time to time," he says with a chuckle. "And that's no problem.

"Let those who have so much to say give it a try sometime; it would be an awakening."

Now Livesey is an executive. But it is a fair bet that he will spend as much time on a baseball field somewhere and away from the desk as he possibly can.

Highlight of that year came in an incredible game in Geneva when Oneonta pitcher Bill Fulton entered the ninth with a no-hitter going. What made the game unusual was the Geneva pitcher was also working on a no-hitter as the ninth inning came along.

Oneonta broke the no hitter in the top of the inning and scratched out a run. Fulton held off Geneva in the bottom of the ninth, the O-Yanks had a 1-0 victory and Fulton a place in the NY-P League record book.

Pitchers Jim Corsi and Steve Frey off that roster made it to The Bigs for a brief stop.

Another player who reached The Bigs was Roberto Kelly who hit only .216 but showed obvious all-around talents. He went on to become a solid outfielder and a decent hitter for New York before his trade to Cincinnati in 1992.

Kelly was among players on that 1983 roster who spoke almost no English and communication was sometimes very difficult.

49 MONK

H e has a pigeon-toed walk, a brusque manner and frequently uses language which would blister paint. But he was a fine athlete, has a warm heart as big as a house and generally gets his point across to other managers, umpires and particularly players.

His name is Russell Charles "Monk" Meyer and he is one of the most beloved men ever to hit Damaschke Field. Many pitchers who have gone through the New York Yankee system are quick to say that Monk Meyer did more for them than any other coach.

Meyer always said his strength was in his teaching ability and he enjoyed working in the minor leagues with the young pitchers. But, as the years slipped by and he grew older, Monk would say, almost wistfully, "I would like to get back to the Bigs, even if only for a year."

He made it, spending the 1992 season at Yankee Stadium as bench coach on the big club for Buck Showalter with whom he had shared great minor league success.

After a boisterous major league career spanning 13 seasons and three World Series, Meyer retired in 1959 and, to all intents and purposes, disappeared from the baseball scene. He ran a bowling alley in his home town of Peru, Illinois for many years, always secretly longing to get back into professional baseball one fine day.

Russell "Monk" Meyer, an Oneonta Yankee legend, has been a longtime mentor and friend of NY Yankee Manager Buck Showalter.
—The Daily Star

Monk kept in touch with baseball by coaching at Illinois Valley Community College during the 1980 and 1981 seasons. The long-awaited call from professional baseball came late in 1981 when the New York Yankees offered him the opportunity to become pitching evaluator in their minor league system. "To say I leaped at the chance would be an understatement," he said.

"Let me say this right now," he said, taking a deep pull on his cigarette, "people can say what they want about George Steinbrenner. But he gave me the chance to get back into baseball and, if he asked, I would run through a wall for him."

Meyer moved on to Bradenton as pitching coach for the 1982 season and reported to Oneonta for the 1983 campaign.

Meyer's major league career had been interesting to say the least. His nickname of "Monk" was a shorter version of "The Mad Monk" which is the way he is listed in the *Encyclopedia of Baseball*. Other nicknames such as "Russell the Red-Nose Reindeer" or "R.A." (used by Dick Young of the *Daily News*) attested to his performance and to incidents such as the time that, in anger at being yanked, he tossed the resin bag so far in the air he forgot it and it came down and hit him on the head.

Monk didn't mind chewing out his infielders after a costly error and had no trouble doing the same with managers and club officials if he deemed it appropriate. His teammates and most officials lived with it because they understood the man's burning desire to play well and to win and much of his anger was actually pointed at himself. Win he did, the record book showing 74 major league victories.

Echoing the words of George Case several years before, Meyer said of his young Class A charges in Oneonta: "They are already fine players; they are here to learn how to be professionals and how to cope with baseball life - the terrible hours, the long bus rides - all of it.

"And," harking back to his own career, "they must learn to accept the bad breaks and not get the red neck every time something goes wrong."

He pointed to a young pitcher who had given up a two-run homer the night before.   "He benefitted from that gaffe," Meyer said. "A year ago he would have folded up after a mistake like that. Last night he pitched better and came out with a win."

His philosophy as a coach? "Some kids you have to kick butt to get them going; others you have to sit and reason with. Once you've figured out which kid is which way, you've taken a big step." Buck Showalter, who had two great years in Oneonta with Monk Meyer, said it best when talking about the feisty pitching coach.

"The thing about Monk is that he has nothing more to prove. He has made it big. But he is here because he cares about these young athletes, I mean he really cares.

"All of us, players, coaches, managers and fans are winners as a result."

Bill Livesey returned in 1984 looking for better things in terms of winning but it was not to be. The club finished last with a 29-45 record, some 14½ games off the pace set by the winning Little Falls Mets.

Meyer was back as pitching coach. The coaching staff was rounded out by Joe Hughes whose promising playing career had been cut short by illness. He can still hit the long ball which he has done consistently in recent years with the nationally known Macs, a strong amateur club headquartered in a village 12 miles from Oneonta. Joe is now head baseball coach at Oneonta High and sells tickets at Damaschke Field.

Meyer's coaching talent became apparent that season. A young pitcher named Dody Rather was on the roster of that 1984 O-Yank club and his pitching was in tune with the team's losing record. He went 0-4 and his ERA of 5.92 brought few cheers.

But Monk saw something in the kid and worked with him that season and in camp the following spring.

Dody Rather came back to Damaschke in 1985, went 8-0 with ERA of 0.31, lowest in the long history of the NY-P League. He walked only 15 hitters while striking out 88.

Livesey struggled hard in that 1984 campaign. He battled himself through the short-season schedule which seemed to those involved as if it were the longest season in baseball history.

Meyer stewed and kicked butt and pleaded and cajoled but nothing seemed to work. Young Hughes just suffered. But he said, in a retrospective moment, he learned a lot from the experience and, though he disliked losing, the season was time well spent.

Jeff Pries, a first round draft choice from UCLA, showed a good arm, pitched to a very good ERA but wound up 3-4 as poor hitting continued to plague Oneonta.

Al Leiter, a promising young pitcher, was only 17 when he reported to Oneonta but he had "good stuff" in baseball parlance. An arm problem soon surfaced, something that didn't seem like much then but never did go away. He was one of only three winning pitchers on the staff (Pat Dougherty and Tony Sarno were the others). Though battling a chronic arm problem throughout his career, he reached The Bigs and was still seeing active duty with Toronto during the 1994 campaign.

There were some strong players on that 1984 O-Yank club. Darren Mandel started like gang busters, hitting four homers in the first four games. But he tailed off later in the season and hit only nine the rest of the way. His 13 dingers left him in a tie with Ruben Rivera for the best season total in O-Yank history.

When he was struggling later in the season, Mandel sat in the dugout one night rubbing his bat with a ham bone. When asked, he replied that the process was supposed to put more pop in his bat.

A passing player heard the comment and said "you ought to put the damn thing in a pot with some peas and make soup. It'll do more good that way."

Mandel drove in 40 runs, only three behind team leader and University of Miami team mate Phil Lane. Gary Cathcart also had a decent year on a team which again failed to produce a three hundred hitter. Lane's .291 was tops.

There were light moments like the night when a skunk showed up in right field and Lane didn't see it. Gary Cathcart in center did see it, however, and yelled to Lane "I'm shading over toward left, you've got right center." This puzzled Lane because the hitter moving up to the plate was a left-handed pull hitter and everyone knew it.

Suddenly, he saw the striped intruder and, being a man of action, headed for the dugout on the double. As he did, he saw Cathcart standing way over in left field with Randy Foyt watching Lane's hasty departure.

Jose Canseco's brother Osvaldo was with that 1984 O-Yank club. A nice kid who didn't possess his brother's talent, he left Oneonta a winner after marrying a pretty woman from a nearby village.

And so the 1984 season faded into the memory book. From the standpoint of winning, it was zilch but it produced its share of memories and served to make the next two years a couple of the best ever in Damaschke Field.

And it was one of those seasons which helped make Russell "Monk" Meyer the living legend he is among the Damaschke Field faithful.

50 Rain

L ean years followed the six straight championship years manufac-
tured by Art Mazmanian and Ken Berry and the Oneonta fans
were looking for the Oneonta Yankees to return to the winner's
circle in 1985.

A young unknown named William Nathaniel "Buck" Showalter was
given the job of putting the pennant flag back on the centerfield flagpole
at Damaschke Field.

Asked about the pressure of managing the New York Yankees com-
pared to pressure as a minor leaguer, Buck answered, "I was more
nervous when we lined up along the first base line for the NY-P opener
at Little Falls in 1985 than when I started at Yankee Stadium."

His club certainly didn't feel any pressure. The O-Yanks got out of
the gate with a rush and never looked back. They stormed through the
campaign winning night after night as the team pitching showed an
incredible 1.87 and team batting was a respectable .268.

Dody Rather won eight and didn't lose a game. His ERA of 0.31 is an
NY-P League record which will probably never be broken. He walked
only 16 batters while striking out 88. His no-hitter was thrown on July
24 against Watertown over the nine inning route.

"The way that kid was pitching that season, it's a wonder he didn't
have a no-hitter every time out," said coach Monk Meyer. "I think it's
the best season pitching performance I have ever seen at any level."

When asked about his repertoire of pitchers, Dody would smile that
sheepish little grin and say "my slurve is my best pitch and Monk has
helped me develop it."

Slurve?

Yep. Rather said it's a combination of slider and curve ball and he
said it with a straight face. Meyer says the pitch does exist and "when
it's biting, it cannot be hit." You can't argue with 88 strikeouts and an
ERA of 0.31.

Unfortunately, Dody Rather blew his arm out in the next year and
was through as a pitcher. He never made The Bigs although he appeared destined to make The Show when he played for Oneonta.

Troy Evers made not have thrown a biting slurve but he was a strong
and durable pitcher who hung up 10 victories against one loss for
Oneonta.

He was a power pitcher who fanned 85 during the year and closed
the season with an ERA of 1.18. He was at his best when the chips were
down and proved it by pitching a no-hitter against Geneva in the nine-

inning playoff semi-final while his proud Dad, in from Appleton, Wisconsin for the occasion, looked on.

Mike Christopher was 8-1 on the season and fanned 84 as the Oneonta staff simply overpowered the league.

Scott Shaw and Shane Turner, both of whom made The Bigs, anchored a strong infield and hit well, Shaw going 5 for 5 in a game at Niagara Falls on July 12. First baseman Rob Sepanek out of Michigan had a strong season as did just about everyone.

Tragedy almost marred this great season when Buck Showalter was injured over the Fourth of July weekend. Todd Ezold, a catcher, had shown a strong arm and somebody suggested they take a look at him as a pitching prospect. Naturally, it was Showalter who stood in as a hitter while Todd tossed some pitches.

One fast ball got away from the young athlete and struck Buck Showalter squarely on the right temple. He wasn't wearing a batting helmet and he went down as if clubbed. He was rushed to the hospital where he remained for three days with Angela at his bedside and Alice Nader looking after Allie. Strong spiritually and physically, Buck was out of the hospital on the fourth day but it was months before he finally shook off the effects of the blow. It was a frightening time for everyone in the Yankee camp.

Buck recovered and returned to action and the campaign wore on to its inevitable end: an Oneonta division title.

In the last week of the season, with the O-Yank roster diminished by injury and early departures, Ted Higgins reported in from Florida. He had only one time at bat as an O-Yank but it was memorable. He smashed a home run which many Damaschke Field fans believe was the longest ever hit there. It not only cleared the right field wall but the trees which stand outside the fence in right and club officials theorize the blast carried somewhere around 500 feet.

Higgins was declared ineligible for the playoffs and left town shortly after his only appearance.

Oneonta beat Geneva in the semi-final, 2-0, behind Evers' no-hitter and the O-Yanks headed for Auburn and the Wednesday night opener of the best two out of three title series.

A potential controversy loomed over that final series. The annual Mayor's Cup college soccer tournament involving Oneonta State and Hartwick College was scheduled in Damaschke Field the coming weekend. If the O-Yanks and Auburn split their first two playoff games, they would playing the final on Friday night at the same time the Mayor's Cup action would get under way.

Some frenzied negotiations produced suggestions such as the Yanks should play their entire final series at Auburn or at a neutral site such as Utica or even Doubleday Field in Cooperstown.

On a Wednesday night in Auburn as the Yanks were warming up for the first game of the final series, Showalter approached a sportswriter and asked about the status of the soccer vs. baseball negotiations.

Told that things were still up in the air, the O-Yank manager said,

"Well, I just got a call from Woody Woodward in the New York office to tell me 'The Boss' just told him 'the Oneonta Yankees will play their game where it is supposed to be played, when it is supposed to be played or else, period!'"

Locals immediately felt the "or else" carried a thinly veiled threat as to the future of the New York-Oneonta relationship. Woodward, a New York vice president at the time, told Buck, "Mr. Steinbrenner meant exactly what he said."

The O-Yanks took the issue off the negotiating table and onto the baseball field with a display of spirit and competitive desire which had been the hallmark of this club all season. In that series opener at Auburn, the O-Yanks were trailing by a 6-2 count at the start of the seventh inning.

Auburn appeared in control, the Yanks weren't hitting and Auburn was. In the dugout, Auburn players were already exchanging high fives and shouting at the Oneonta club. The fans were jeering the Yanks and things looked tough.

Suddenly, the Yanks came alive. A couple of walks, a couple of hits and two runs were across and the bases were loaded for little Johnny Pliecones. The fans really got on him. One fan was heard to say, "Things are so tough the Yanks are using Little League players." (This was in reference to the small stature of Pliecones who had hit only .222 during the year.)

O-Yank Manager Buck Showalter pauses during a practice session to take a call from Yankee Stadium.

But the little guy with the big heart, who afterwards said he heard the taunts, lined a double to right center clearing the bases and giving Oneonta the lead which they held until the end for the opening night win.

The next night, Thursday, the teams moved into Oneonta. In late afternoon, it began to rain and things looked tough. A postponement would mean playing Friday and this would certainly rekindle the dormant flame of the soccer vs baseball controversy.

Determined to get the game in, the Yankee people went to work. They brought in all the Kwik Dri they could get. Sam Nader and his son John were wielding shovels, groundskeeper John Falk was raking along with manager Showalter and some of the players and Alice Nader was bringing in wheelbarrow after wheelbarrow full of sand and dry dirt to the infield.

The umpires were consulted as was NY-P League President Vincent McNamara. All realized the serious nature of the problem and decided to go ahead with the game. There was steady rain and frequent stoppages of play to work over the diamond but, thanks to the unique drainage system at Damaschke and some willing people, the full nine innings were played. Oneonta clubbed Auburn into submission 14-0 and it was over.

The next night, thanks to an all night effort by a skilled and hard working city public works crew, the soccer games went on as scheduled.

Roy White, the ex-Yankee great who at that time was working in the player development program, watched in wonder from the comfort of the crowded press box. As the game went on White said, "I've never seen anything like this. I just can't believe there are people like this or an operation like this ball club from top to bottom. I love it."

Roy's remark summed up that fabulous season which saw, as Sam Nader had predicted nine months earlier, Oneonta's return to winning ways.

Buck Showalter's 1986 O-Yank NY-P champions set a league record for victories (59) while losing only 18.

51 Encore

W hen it came time in early 1986 to announce the Oneonta Yankee manager for the coming NY-P League season, Sam Nader didn't have to spend much time getting out a long release. Everyone knew who Buck Showalter was and the announcement he had been named to a second year at Damaschke Field brought cheers all around.

Back came Buck, Angela, Allie and Russell Charles "Monk" Meyer to help re-open the "Buck and Monk Show."

"What do we do for an encore?" said Showalter, repeating a reporter's question. "We do better than last year, that's what we do."

There was no braggadocio in the little guy; he meant what he said.

The New York organization's "casting office" sent him a cast to do it with and, when September rolled around, the Buck and Monk Show encore was a beauty, a league record of 59 wins and a

Popular O-Yank Andy Stankiewicz poses for a quick picture with O-Yank batboy "Tank" Cavanagh.

winning percentage of .766, second only to the NY-P League record of .768 set by the 1974 O-Yanks. They won the pennant by 22 1/2 games over Little Falls.

The O-Yanks were particularly fond of Damaschke Field where they won 33 games while losing only six and where almost 50,000 fans paid to watch the happy events.

Oneonta set a fielding record of .971 as a team while the club walked away with the two primary individual awards: first baseman Hal Morris earning the Kinsella award and pitcher Ken Patterson the Stedler award.

Morris, like Robin Yount of Newark a few years earlier, was one of those athletes who left no doubt he would make it all the way. He was that good. He fielded first base like a veteran, hit .378 and drove in 30 runs in only 36 games. He moved up to Class AA Albany halfway through the season and went on to the majors just two seasons later. Traded to Cincinnati in 1990, he has become an established star with a salary in the millions.

The supply line of talent continued for Oneonta as Kevin Maas was sent in to fill the first base spot. Kevin didn't do too badly, hitting .356 in 28 games.

Patterson, a Monk Meyer project from the previous year, came on like gang busters. He had a 9-3 record and an ERA of 1.35 with 102 strikeouts. He set or equalled club records in five pitching categories and went on to a successful career in the majors, mostly in Chicago where he pitched for the White Sox and the Cubs.

Patterson was a colorful character and frequented the press box on nights when he wasn't working. He loved to argue scorer's calls (although not seriously) and loved to talk about things back in McGregor, Texas, his home town. He always joined the press box pool on attendance figures and left in September mumbling about how "those press box guys still owe me eight bucks."

One night, he appeared to be pondering a serious matter. Pushed by the curious press box crew, he admitted his Daddy had called and said he wanted to buy a steer he'd seen, but wasn't sure if he should go ahead as the cost was around $3,000. He was seeking his son's advice "and perhaps a couple of bucks," said Patterson.

The conversation went on for an inning or two and finally the scorer said, "Ken, do you think he should buy the steer?"

The big left hander fidgeted with his ever-present painter's cap for a minute and then said, "Yup, I think it's a good deal."

"Well then, dammit, get on the phone and call your Dad and tell him!"

Patterson pondered for a minute and then said, "You know that McGregor is a long way from here? It's near Waco."

"Call him," shouted the scorer.

He did. The deal was done and, when the scorer talked with Patterson the next spring in training camp at Hollywood, Florida, the pitcher thanked him and explained that things had worked out real fine.

Dean Wilkins pushed his slender frame to the limit and finished 9-0 after a stylish performance all season long. Rick Scheid won nine, Steve Adkins eight and young Rick Balabon showed great promise. Oscar Azocar won two games and subsequently made the big leagues, but as an outfielder, not a pitcher. Outstanding relief pitcher Dana Ridenour saved eight games and appeared headed for the show. He didn't make it but Steve Rosenberg, who stopped in Oneonta for a cup of coffee, did.

Fred Carter, kid brother of Toronto World Series star Joe, was hitting .385 before injury ended his season and Yanko Haraudo hit .340

before moving on to Fort Lauderdale.

Darling of the Damaschke Field faithful that season was a little second baseman with a funny, arm-flopping trot and a great attitude. It was Andy Stankiewicz and he captured the fans by running to the plate for his time at bat, running hard to first base after a base on balls and playing the game he loves right to the hilt every day.

His idol was Phil Rizzuto and from the beginning had modelled his baseball efforts after the Yankee all-star.

"There's no other way for a little guy to make it," he said. "I know I'm small and I know that baseball people don't get too excited about little guys."

He was great to be around. He would talk and spend extra time working with kids like John Rivino who says the things he learned from Andy Stankiewicz helped him play well in college baseball and entertain a glimmer of hope for a career in professional baseball.

Andy hit .296 in 59 games for that 1986 club and led a strong defense which featured the likes of Morris and Maas and Casey Close at first, Tim Becker at short and Luc Berube at third. Some people believe Becker is the best shortstop the O-Yanks ever had and he contributed mightily to the fact this was the best NY-P League fielding team ever.

Oneonta Public Address Announcer Dick Cavanagh greets former O-Yank and NY Yankee Pitcher Ken Patterson before a game in the Bronx.

The fans, and most club officials, think the 1986 team was the best ever to represent Oneonta in the NY-P League.

But when the final curtain came down in September, there was no encore for the Buck and Monk Show.

Villian of the final act was a man who had been a hero just a few years earlier for the Oneonta fans. Art Mazmanian was managing the Newark entry that year and got his team into the playoffs as a wild card entry in the three-division, 12 team league setup.

Mazmanian forecast the Oneonta downfall. His team came into Oneonta for a two game set late in the regular season. Newark appeared set for post-season play and apparently would be meeting Oneonta in a one game semi-final.

"If that does happen, and we do play Oneonta in a one game set, we'll beat them," Maz told a sportswriter.

"Unlikely," thought the sportswriter as he completed his conversation with old friend Mazmanian and set off to begin the night's work.

That opinion was shared by just about everyone around the ball club. There was no way Newark, a team that had finished the season just a bit over .500, could play with the Yankees, far and away the league's best.

Perhaps over-confidence was the problem. In any case, Maz and his Newark kids made his prediction stick by knocking the Yankees out of the playoffs with a 2-1 victory in the one game series. It was a tight, tense ball game, one in which Oneonta just could not get the clutch hits. Mazmanian had his team sky high and they were making plays that ordinarily might not have been made.

When it was over, shock set in with the realization the greatest season in Oneonta Yankee history was over; the final prize had eluded the O-Yanks. After the game, the clubhouse was as somber as a funeral parlor; the champagne was quietly carted away unopened; most players dressed quickly and left to pack for the trip home.

Hours after the incredible events, the sportswriter, his work done for the night, returned to Damaschke Field out of curiosity. To his surprise, several players were still sitting around in a state of shock. They didn't talk much, just kept saying, "I cannot believe it" over and over again. Some of the players stayed there all night, not even leaving to grab something to eat.

One player said, "What bothers me most is that we let Buck Showalter down."

Showalter, a little more experienced with the vagaries of the game of baseball, shrugged that thought off and managed to be philosophical about the turn of events.

"These things often happen," he said, "it's the nature of the game. But it's never easy."

He looked up at his writer friend, his stare intense in the Showalter manner. "I didn't have our guys prepared. We were all guilty of overconfidence, we did nothing to combat it and they took advantage of it.

"This is the reason I dislike these one game playoffs. Ordinarily, with two more games to go, we could tighten our belts, take stock, review our mistakes and come back to play another game. We were good enough to win if we had that opportunity.

"But I hope we've all learned something from this experience."

With that typical Buck Showalter thought, they parted company and the young manager moved on to the next step.

Ahead was more success on a road which was to lead him to the top job: manager at Yankee Stadium and American League Manager of the Year in 1994.

Behind was the memory of the greatest regular season Oneonta ever had in the New York-Pennsylvania League.

52 Cloninger

The "Buck and Monk Show" moved on, The 1986 summer was history, a mix of brilliant regular season victory and bitter play-off defeat. Oneonta Yankee fans were wondering who would pilot the 1987 edition.

The answer was Gary Allenson, still a major league catcher in 1986 who had decided to hang up the tools and try his hand at managing.

The Boston Red Sox had no spots open but the Yankees did. So the young man, deep down very uncertain about the abrupt switch from player to manager, came to Oneonta. He also harbored some doubts about working for an organization which had been a bitter rival of the Red Sox for so long.

The panacea for such doubts is often to bear down and get to work and that's what young Mr. Allenson decided to do.

The work began in early June. Allenson got a real lift right off the bat with the assignment of strong coaches in the bull pen and along the coaching lines.

Tony Cloninger, returning to baseball after a long time away from the game, came to Oneonta as pitching coach. Brian Butterfield, who had been a popular O-Yank player in 1979, returned as infield coach and Jack Gillis came back to spend his sixth season as an Oneonta coach.

Cloninger had a solid major league record, spending 12 seasons in The Bigs, winning 113 games, all in the national League. He probably is best remembered for hitting two grand slams in one game and for winning 24 games in 1965. Tony caught the eye of Whit Wyatt in 1962 when he was a pitching coach for the Braves. Dan Parker, well-known and well-remembered columnist for the *New York Daily Mirror*, had this to say in a column on March 26, 1962: "Whit Wyatt, former Ebbetts Field favorite now coaching the Braves pitching staff, is paying special attention to Tony Cloninger, 21-year-old right hander now starting his fifth season in pro baseball."

Tony Cloninger has nothing but good feelings for George Steinbrenner, the often controversial head man of the New York Yankees.

"Let me tell you something about Mr. Steinbrenner," he said one day at Damaschke Field while the raindrops slanted across the old ballpark. "He's the man who gave me my chance to get back into baseball after a long time away from the game. I will always be grateful and some day I hope I will be able to show my gratitude in a solid way."

Cloninger got his chance; the big guy from Lincoln, North Carolina started the 1993 New York Yankee campaign as pitching coach with the major league club. He was there because Manager Buck Showalter and the 1992 mound staff realized how much he contributed during his season as bull pen coach. And his cause was enhanced by testimonials from the young Yank pitchers who did not hesitate to say how much they learned from the soft spoken, warm-hearted man.

He is also respected throughout baseball as a fine player. During the Hall of Fame weekend in Cooperstown that 1987 summer, Cloninger agreed to do color commentary for the radio broadcast of the annual Hall of Fame game by Oneonta station WDOS.

Tony and his broadcast colleague decided to walk to the Otesaga Hotel to partake of the noontime buffet, one of the weekend's highlights each year.

As they walked down the street, Cloninger and his colleague were approached by a running man who came up dragging his wife behind. He shook hands with Cloninger, turned to his wife and said: "Honey, this is the guy who almost drove me out of baseball. He was just about the toughest pitcher I ever faced."

The two former major leaguers chatted for a few moments before Tony Cloninger turned to his Oneonta radio colleague and said, "Bob, I would like you to meet Willie Mays."

Although the personalities were different, the Allenson-Cloninger team developed a working process much like that of Buck Showalter and Monk Meyer the previous two seasons at Oneonta. Each respected the other as a pro and each trusted the other to make the right baseball decisions.

The result was a 41-34 record and a second place finish in 1987 and a championship in 1988.

Allenson still places the burden for the second place finish in 1987 on his own shoulders.

"It was a learning experience in so many ways," he was to say years later. "The fall, winter and spring of 1987-1988 were reflective months for me and I was able to digest what I had learned; able to reflect on my own mistakes.

"As I look back now, I think the club we had in 1987 was good enough to win it all and we might have done it had I been the same manager I was in 1988 and the seasons since then."

There was a heavier than usual turnover in the pitching staff that season and, frequently, a pitcher under the tutelage of Cloninger and the watchful eye of Allenson developed quickly to the point he was ready for the next level. Other moves, too, were critical to the team's pennant aspirations.

"While you always strive to win the pennant at any level," Allenson said one day, "your primary job at the class A level is to help young players develop and we were pleased so many of our guys got the chance."

Gary Allenson returned to the Red Sox organization in 1989 and, after successfully managing in Lynchburg, Virginia and New Britain,

Connecticut, went up to the big club as bull pen coach. After the 1992 disaster at Fenway Park, the Red Sox had a poor spring training in 1993 and the fate of Butch Hobson as Red Sox manager hung in the balance. People around the Red Sox organization said Allenson had a shot at the top job but Gary would not even discuss that. Hobson is a close friend and Allenson said he only wanted to work hard for Butch and the Red Sox no matter what his assignment. In 1994, he was third base coach in Boston.

On the field, that 1987 Oneonta club contended all the way and proved one of the most entertaining teams the O-Yanks ever had. Speed was a keynote. Little Lew Hill played only a few games before injury cut him down. But his defensive speed was a delight to watch.

Speed was also the key for a couple of other outfielders who passed through town. Bernie and Gerry Williams played here that year, Bernie hitting .344 in 25 games and Gerry .365 in 29 games. Most O-Yank followers believe their presence all season in Oneonta would have meant another NY-P League pennant. It was said of Bernie, one of the big stars of the 1994 New York Yankee season, with him in center field, you could dispense with the left fielder and use him someplace else because Bernie could cover the whole area.

Dave Turgeon, who hit .281 in 48 games also showed some speed by leading the club with 23 stolen bases.

Luc Berube proved a durable infielder, appearing in 72 games and hitting .302 while whacking seven homers. Mark Mitchell also drew notice with his .344 average in 45 games. Tom Weeks, who led the club with 57 RBIs, was the other regular to finish over .300.

Cloninger worked with some interesting people in the pitching department. Billy Voeltz and Randy Foster each won six games for the O-Yanks. Foster was a commuter that season, as he came from nearby Norwich.

Anthony "Red" Morrison led the staff with 79 strikeouts but, his team mates kiddingly said, that was because he really didn't know where the ball was going when he let it go in the general direction of the plate and few hitters dug in.

"The ball sometimes has a mind of its own," he chuckled one day, "but, I tell you, once I get command of that little rascal, I'll be one tough pitcher."

At last report, the baseball still had a mind of its own but Red was hangin' in there.

If the loss of the Williams boys was felt during that season, the early departure of Rodney Imes and Dave Eiland also made a big difference in the pennant hopes of that 1987 club. Both went 4-0, both pitched to a great ERA. (Imes 0.33 and Eiland 1.84) and both had great strikeouts to walks ratio. Eiland later made an appearance with the big club but Imes never did make it big.

Tom Popplewell, Jay Makemson and Doug Gogolewski carried on. Makemson, a fun-loving Californian, was a fan favorite and a press box visitor when not on pitching duty. He was to return in 1988 and be part of the most colorful, well-loved championship team ever to perform in Damaschke Field.

Gogolewski, "Gogo" to everybody close to the club, was second only to Red Morrison in the base-on-balls department. He was a gregarious, happy youngster and another frequent press box visitor.

One night he came up to the press box beaming all over. He happily announced he just purchased an expensive brand new car. He named the make of car and then asked public address announcer Dick Cavanagh (who was in the automobile business) what he thought.

"It's a piece of junk," said the frank Mr. Cavanagh. "You got taken, my friend."

Taken back by that reply, the gregarious Gogo was shocked into uncharacteristic silence.

But Cavanagh has a warm heart and, after seeing the youngster ponder that news for a couple of minutes and seeing him wonder about his money, he told Gogo he made a good choice and bought himself an excellent vehicle.

Gogo's ready smile quickly returned and he shook hands all around before heading downstairs to tell his teammates about his new car.

The season wore down and Oneonta couldn't stop Watertown's march to the division title. The Pirates, who had finished eleventh the year before in the overall 12-team standings, played well all season and won the flag by beating the O-Yanks in Oneonta to touch off a wild celebration among a large contingent of fans who had journeyed down from the North Country hoping for just that opportunity.

They lost the playoff to Geneva in two games and the 1987 season was history.

Back in Oneonta, there was no doubt in anyone's mind that, had the O-Yanks been able to hang on to Bernie and Gerald Williams, Eiland, Imes and a couple of other players who left early, the pennant would have been celebrated by Oneonta fans that night in late August, 1987.

53 Stretch

Events of the previous season may have bothered some minor league managers as they entered their second year as a pilot, but not Gary "Mugsy" Allenson.

In 1987, his rookie year as manager of the Oneonta Yankees, Allenson saw the workings of a minor league organization at first hand. He stood by as promising players were moved up after brilliant performances for the O-Yanks, quickly realizing player development was more important than winning at the Class A level. But it was difficult nonetheless to accept the fact that, except for the promotions, he had a flag winner.

But as 1988 got under way, he felt good about the talent coming in and he felt good about himself. He was ready for the coming challenge.

Once again he was blessed with strong coaching. Jeff Taylor, who pitched for the O-Yanks in 1987 and whose promising career was cut short by injury, became an effective pitching coach ("improving with age," he said) and big Jim Saul, a long coaching record behind him at all levels of the game, contributed as a most versatile aide, a "cheerleader", a quiet counselor and a supplement to Mugsy in the clubhouse.

The statistics would bear out those who talked about this club not being blessed with outstanding talent. Only two players hit more than .300. One was the acrobatic second baseman Pat Kelly, who hit .329 in 71 games and the other was first baseman John Seeberger who was at .333 when promoted to Fort Lauderdale after 22 games.

Long-time O-Yank fan Isabelle McManus has rarely missed a game since the 1967 season. Here she "babysits" Kevin Allenson (the manager's young son) in the stands.

Shortstop Bobby DeJardin put up some good numbers while playing in 69 games as did Rey Fernandez and Skip Nelloms. Promising outfielder Bobby Zeihen moved up after 27 games and Jay Knoblauh suffered a broken hand just about the time he was ready to break loose.

The lineup for this club most days saw Jason Bridges at first, Kelly at second, DeJardin at short and Herbie Erhardt or Hector Vargas at third. Erhardt also spent some time at first and Rey Fernandez played third occasionally.

Rod Ehrhard did most of the catching with Jeff Livesey alternating.

Brad Ausmus, a red hot prospect who made it to The Show in 1994, got into a few games behind the plate.

Nelloms was in center most of the time with Knoblauh, Fernandez and Miguel Torres also on the picket line.

Short of talent as far as numbers were concerned but long on heart was this O-Yank team. Few of these kids worked harder or made more use of their talent than Ehrhard whose clutch hitting and gritty defensive play despite nagging injuries keyed the late Oneonta drive. He and DeJardin exemplified the grit and determination of this team more than any other.

In St. Catharines, Ontario one incredibly hot and muggy Saturday, DeJardin was huddled in the corner of the dugout looking quite ill. He assured everyone he was OK, just tired and bothered a bit by the heat but, he said, "I'm ready to play." He looked more ready for the hospital emergency room.

He went 3 for 4 at the plate that day and joined Kelly in three double plays as the O-Yanks won a key game from the Blue Jays. Typical.

Bobby roomed with the irrepressible Herbie Erhard, with his happy-go-lucky ways and easy grin.

One day when the O-Yanks were checking out of their Jamestown motel, Erhard could be seen in a heated exchange with the desk clerk. It seems he had a phone bill of $488 which, he said, was quite impossible.

Herbie did say he had called his girl friend in Florida that night but, "we only talked for a little while."

"Call my roommate, Mr. DeJardin, he'll verify that," pleaded Erhard The rather slow-witted clerk did, had a short conversation, and hung up.

"Well?" asked Herbie, desperate to get the matter squared away.

"Mr. DeJardin said he never heard of you," said the clerk.

Startled, Herbie wasn't really sure what to do next. He had some uncomfortable moments until a sportswriter who was travelling with the club interceded. Negotiations improved and by the time DeJardin, who had enjoyed his little bit of fun at Herbie's expense showed up, the clerk was beginning to see the light.

This sort of thing was another reason for the strong camaraderie of the 1988 O-Yanks. They had a happy-go-lucky style which kept them loose and they had a manager and coaches smart enough to realize this was a plus.

And yet, when they took the field that night, the word which best seemed to apply to them was "competent." They knew their job and they did it, reacting the same way whether up or down 10 runs.

As Ken Greer said one night when the team was boarding the bus in Erie for the short run to the park, "Well, here goes another day at the office."

Greer, who in spring training at the start of the 1993 season appeared to have a shot at The Bigs, had to work hard to get there. His "day at the office" remark may have been misleading for he was a fierce competitor. During the September 1988 title game in Damaschke Field, he pitched brilliantly for eight innings, but severely damaged his shoulder when he threw out a runner at second base on a bunt play which might have been easily made at first. It was Kenny's competitive drive which made him want to cut down that lead runner.

There was time for fun among the pitching staff, too. There's no place in sports quite like a baseball bullpen and that's a fact.

For instance, the bullpen crew of that 1988 club adopted two skunks who had been hanging around the park for years. They fed them and took care of them and the animals were too smart to louse up a good thing by spraying the players. The skunks became so much a part of the scene that, when they entered the box seat area one evening, they were introduced by public address man Cavanagh as "Pepi LePew and his wife."

When ardent bow hunter Herbie Erhardt wanted to bump them off with his bow and arrow, he was shouted down.

When the season had about a week to go, college students returned to Oneonta and rooms became scarce so Greer, Jay Makemson, Ehrhard and Erhardt rounded up some mattresses and spent the last few days of the season living in the clubhouse. They fed the skunks well during those final days.

Top prospects Andy Cook (8-4), Jeff Johnson (6-1) and Jerry Nielsen (6-2) produced as expected while Makemson surprised even himself with a 4-1 mark. Johnson and Nielsen made the major leagues while Cook was just a breath away as 1993 spring training ended. The staff ERA

Just another quiet night in the O-Yankee bullpen. Not a skunk in sight.

was a brilliant 2.86. When last heard from, Jay Makemson was selling jewelry in California.

One of the pitchers who won his way to the big leagues after starting with the 1988 Oneonta Yankees was Frank Seminara. He was a walk-on who played his collegiate baseball at Columbia University and who stood up well under the constant taunts of those who chided him on Columbia's terrible record on the football field. He also withstood the taunts and criticisms of those who told him he didn't have a prayer of going anywhere.

Cavanagh along with Sam Nader constantly encouraged Frankie, telling him to keep working, keep developing his three basic pitches, keep believing in himself and he would make it.

He did.

The 1988 O-Yanks got out of the gate well, lost some players to transfer and injury, stumbled with fatigue in late mid-season and then came on to win 14 of their last 17 in the most stirring stretch charge in O-Yank annals. Night after night they rallied to pull out a victory and night after night, they produced heroes like Rod Ehrhard, Pat Kelly, Bob DeJardin, Skip Nelloms, Jason Bridges and Rey Fernandez.

An unlikely hero in that stretch run was little Johnny Broxton whose heart was as big as his body. He arrived late but just in time to pick up a victory and four saves in about 10 days of action. Only Bruce Prybylinski's eight saves topped the little guy's record.

Broxton's effort remains one of the most outstanding feats for the Oneonta Yankees, a baseball club which each year seems to bring out a special effort from its players.

And he helped Gary Allenson leave Oneonta wearing a grin instead of his game face. Mugsy drove away a happy man. He left a legacy of winning attitude, happy players and love for the game of baseball.

A very special man.

54 BUTTER

F or Brian Butterfield, the 1989 Oneonta Yankee season was a case of being in the right place at the wrong time. "Butter" came to town familiar with the old ballpark, the Nader family, the Oneonta fans - that group which sits in Damaschke night after night pulling for the O-Yanks and enjoying baseball but in such a quiet way you hardly know they're around. He played in 58 games for the O-Yanks just 10 years earlier.

Butterfield is the only man to have played (1979), coached (1987) and managed (1989) for the Oneonta Yankees.

His 1989 Oneonta club won 48 games, enough to have meant the pennant in 14 previous NY-P League seasons but not enough to win this race. Pittsfield turned up with a solid ball club, featuring great pitching, and turned aside every Oneonta challenge to capture the regular season division championship by four and a half games over the Yanks.

"We had a strong club," Butterfield said in later years. "We might very well have won it all but Pittsfield had one of the best short-season, Class A clubs we had ever seen. The Watertown club that season was also very tough.

"But we're proud of the fact that so many of the players from that club were in the majors or close when the 1993 season got under way."

A quick check as the major league season began showed Frank Seminara a full time pitcher with San Diego at a salary of $150,000; Sherman Obando with Baltimore at $109,000 and J.T. Snow with California at $110,000.

Brad Ausmus, Russ Davis, Mark Hutton and Mike Gardella were very close to The Bigs.

Upward movement was also in the works for the young manager, Butterfield progressing through the New York organization to reach the Stadium first base coaching box for the 1994 campaign. He fit there very nicely.

Former O-Yank players Dave Kent and Jeff Taylor returned as coaches for the 1989 club and were joined by newcomer Rich Arena. Taylor continued his effective work as pitching coach while Kent, who played in Oneonta for the 1968 champions, coached first base and Arena third.

Gardella set the club record for 19 saves, won two games and had an ERA of 1.67. And he was consistent.

Seminara, back after a shaky first year in Oneonta, proved that he belonged in the starting rotation. The Columbia graduate, who had been a "walk-on" for the Yankees in 1988, never faltered in his belief he could make it and he pitched with confidence. His dedication and hard work have paid off and he has proven himself a solid professional.

Seminara won seven games for the 1989 O-Yanks while Artie Canestro, with his broad "Noo Yawk" accent and a charmer of the opposite sex, also won seven while losing only two. A firm believer of the "it ain't braggin' if you can do it" school, Artie held his ERA at an outstanding 1.05. Quiet Ken Juarbe won seven and registered 73 strikeouts along the way, second only to Jim Moody's 81.

Snow at first base, Davis at third and Ausmus behind the plate showed early they had major league potential. Snow, playing in more games than any other Yankee (73), led in runs batted in with 51 and homers with eight while averaging .292. His fielding was every bit as good as his hitting and he is generally regarded as one of the best first sackers ever to play in Damaschke.

His dad, Jack Snow, once an all-star end for the Los Angeles Rams in the NFL, was a frequent visitor in Oneonta during that 1989 season.

"Baseball was strictly J.T.'s choice," he said one day of his son. "He might have gone on in football but he had a solid opportunity in baseball and made his decision."

Snow was back in California as the 1993 season began, having been traded to the Angels in the deal which brought Jim Abbott to New York. He had a home run in his first game as a major leaguer.

"It was difficult to let a player like J.T. go," said New York Manager Buck Showalter, "but, as the world knew, we had to have pitching and to get quality you have to give up quality."

Obando had a productive year for Butterfield's club, too. He was second in RBIs with 45, hit .312 and had six home runs. Davis had seven homers, drove in 42 runs and averaged a solid .288 in 65 games. His fielding in the tough third base spot at Damaschke was superb and he had a gun for an arm. Rich Barnwell stole 39 bases, third on the all-time O-Yanks list behind Larry Murray and Ted Wilborn. Ricky Strickland batted .353 for the O-Yanks but appeared in only 18 games.

The race was a good one from wire to wire and the Yanks were in it to the final week. In the end, the strong Met pitching tipped the scales in Pittsfield's favor.

As a developer of baseball talent, his primary job with the New York Yankees, Butterfield left Oneonta pleased with having helped some promising players along the way to The Show, title or no title.

55 TREY

Pitching and speed, elements just right for Manager Trey Hillman's approach to baseball, were the strengths of the 1990 Oneonta Yankee champions.

Sam Militello, in the starting rotation at Yankee Stadium as the 1993 American League season got underway, was the mainstay of the 1990 O-Yank staff. He won eight games while losing only two and struck out 119. He was one of three pitchers on that staff to register an ERA under 2.00; Kirt Ojala and Darren Hodges were the other two.

Militello's story has taken a strange turn and 1994 found him locked in a struggle to regain his control which he suddenly and inexplicably lost.

Many are pulling for the young man because Militello is a polite, quiet and reserved person, pleasant to talk with and dedicated to the game.

"I just go out and try hard every tine," he said back in 1990. "I know I've got good guys behind me and I just try to keep the ball in the strike zone."

That he did with regularity as he marched through the Yankee organization all the way to the top.

Mark Shiflett, who pitched for Oneonta in 1981, returned as pitching coach of this 1990 club and enjoyed the summer with the great talent he had available. Mark is generally credited with aiding in the development of that young but talented staff.

One young pitcher who made Mark's life interesting was unpredictable Greg "Bo" Siberz who, in one game, walked five consecutive batters to tie the score and then struck out the side.

"He was a guy who could change the boos to cheers and cheers to boos quicker than any player I every coached," said Shiflett one night.

Ojala won six as did Ron Frazier, Darren Hodges, Steve Perry and Raf Quirico and the staff ERA wound up at a very respectable 2.60.

Ricky Strickland led off most of the time with Kevin Jordan hitting second., Strickland and Jalal Leach were exciting players with their great speed and combine to steal 52 bases and score 78 runs.

"They were important," said Hillman, "because this club didn't hit the long ball that much and it was important to have them in position to score on a single."

Brian Turner went most of the way at first base with Jordan at second, Robert Eenhorn and Rich Lantrip at third. Jordan was an exciting player in the filed who showed great range and he led the club at the plate with a .333 average in 73 games. He also led with 54 RBIs and 47 runs scored; his all around play brought him a place on the league all-star team.

Eenhorn is the talented kid from Holland who went down late in the season with a stomach ailment. But he impressed a lot of people with his bat and his defensive play and has moved up steadily through the Yankee organization.

Mike Hankins was popular around Damaschke Field and proved to be one of the best utility players every in Oneonta, even pitching - and winning - a couple of games.

In the semi-final against Geneva, Oneonta trailed going in to into the bottom of the sixth by a 2-0 count. But a costly Geneva error and RBI hits by Leach, Jordan and Luis Gallardo gave Oneonta two runs in the sixth and two more in the seventh for a 4-2 victory. Ron Frazier got the win and the irrepressible Siberz a save when he retired the side in order in the ninth, two on strikeouts.

Troublesome Erie faced Oneonta in the championship series. They had won the Stedler division and then topped Jamestown in the one game semi-final.

Oneonta had to journey to Erie for the opener of the best of three title series, but came back with a win.

Erie came into Damaschke Field and got a great game from Jack Mikkelson who shut down the Yanks on three hits for a 2-0 Erie victory which evened the series.

Militello got the call once again and he responded as the Yankee beat Erie, 11-2 to win the championship. He was a tired pitcher and not at this best. But he was tough in the clutch and left nine Erie runners stranded. He struck out seven. Brian Faw and Siberz finished up, ol' Bo retiring the side in order in the ninth.

The Yanks put it away with five run bursts in the fifth and in the seventh as Ricky Strickland had a triple and three singles, driving in three runs. Scott Romano had two RBIs and also hit a triple as the Oneonta club breezed.

And then it was over. There came that inevitable September day when Oneonta says goodbye to its Boys of Summer and accepts the fact another season of Oneonta Yankee baseball is over.

The pennant hasn't flown over Damaschke Field since that year, all the more reason to remember Trey Hillman and his troupe with affection.

56 Courage

Most men would have folded up under the events of early 1991, but not Albert S. "Sam" Nader. His beloved wife Alice died in an auto accident early in the year in Atlanta, Georgia and Sam was badly injured.

But, calling on the courage which had been his strength for so many years, rallied by son John and daughters Alice and Suzanne, supported by his loyal brother-in-law Leroy "Sonny" House and by his longtime friend Sid Levine, Sam Nader came back to lead the 1991 Oneonta Yankees in defense of their NY-P League pennant.

The ball club has been uppermost in his life for a quarter century, second only to his family, and from his hospital bed in the Spring of 1991, he directed operations in preparing for the O-Yank season.

"His love of this baseball club was a key to his recovering from the tragedy of Alice's loss and his critical injuries," said House whose own courage in the loss of his sister set a solid example for all around the ball club.

Cards and letters and calls from baseball people at all levels also helped buoy Sam Nader through the difficult period. People as highly placed as George Steinbrenner remembered the Oneonta owner as did some of the many people he helped along the way.

His association with baseball people at the highest levels remain one of the joys of Sam's life and the winter meetings are an annual highlight for him.

The 1991 season was dedicated to Alice's memory and the program for the season read, in part:

"Alice performed many, many tasks and services around the ball park on behalf of the club and those people who made it up.

"She preferred to do these things quietly and without notice and words of praise or thanks would usually be greeted by a humorous retort or a quick shrug, actions designed to hide her embarrassment."

She had duties as an officer of the corporation that ran the Yankees and she did a lot of work at home, handling phone calls and many duties regarding ball club business. But she is best remembered for her humanitarian work on behalf of players, coaches and managers.

She earned the title "den mother" because she cared for the players and their wives and girl friends without patronizing them. People were comfortable with her and she always seemed to do the right thing at the right time, whether it was the early morning coffee and Danish to greet early arrivals to Oneonta or a change of diapers in the ball park business office while she was looking after a young manager's child.

At times, she would care for a young athlete in her home if he was too ill to be left alone.

Ballplayers' parents, when they visited Oneonta, would often receive the warm, gracious hospitality of Alice Nader and many baseball dignitaries received the same congenial treatment. Small wonder that activity in the comfortable home at 95 River Street ran almost 24 hours a day.

She would find apartments, help clean up living quarters, cook, do laundry, transport players and, perhaps most important, give the young athletes a feel of home whether through great home cooking or a bit of counselling to a youngster too proud to admit he's homesick.

The dedicatory program, sold nightly at Damaschke Field during the season, went on to describe the positive effect her efforts had upon the young players passing through Oneonta. To this day, big league players who launched their careers in Oneonta recall their days fondly and will ask, "How's Sam?" and say, "Gosh, that was sad about Mrs. Nader. She was a great lady."

Alice Nader was missed in 1991 and in 1992 and will be missed as long as baseball is played in Damaschke Field. But, the ball club, the players, coaches, managers and fans of those years and the years to come will always be aware of this fine lady and what she has meant to the Oneonta Yankees.

Sam Nader, though hampered by his injuries, managed to sit down at the typewriter and bat our a press release announcing the appointment of Jack Gillis as manager of the 1991 Oneonta Yankees. The release also said Mark Rose, who pitched for the 1986 team, would be pitching coach and that Gillis' buddy, Bill Schmidt, would be a coach.

It was a tough year for Gillis as injuries constantly hampered the team.

"I have never seen the like of it," said experienced trainer Mark Littlefield. "It seems my training room is an emergency ward because so many guys are coming in with this injury or that. And, I spend a lot of time making out reports."

Oneonta did manage a 42-35 record, good for second place in the McNamara East division, winding up nine games behind a strong, veteran Pittsfield club which won 51 games.

One of the problems with an injury situation was that Gillis had difficulty trying to put together a regular starting lineup, particularly in the infield.

"These guys need time working together, getting used to one another, particularly around second base," he said one night. "I can't put together a starting lineup until Mark Littlefield has had sick call."

But Mark Hubbard and Tate Seefried each got in 73 games, Jorge Posada 71 and Lyle Mouton 70. Tim Flannelly survived 65 games at third base, hitting .272 and driving in 46 runs.

Mouton, a big, strong kid from Louisiana, hit the long ball and wound up with seven home runs. He was a scholar and spent most of the time on long bus rides reading books. His mother was a member of the Louisiana State Legislature. He closed the season hitting a respectable .309, the only regular to hit more than .300. Steve Anderson registered a .351 average but was used sparingly and got into only 47 games.

Seefried's batting average was only .246 but he led the club in runs batted in with 51.

Steve Phillips, a lean youngster with great speed, was hobbled by knees which had been banged up when he was a running back for the University of Kentucky football team. But he still hit .260 and drove in 43 runs.

Pitching, which had been so strong in the recent years, tailed off during the 1991 campaign. The staff ERA was 4.35 and Grant Sullivan, with six wins, led in that department. But he also lost six games and had an ERA of 4.29. Andy Croghan, Bert Inman and Frank Laviano each won five.

Gillis and Schmidt returned for the 1992 season at Damaschke, joined by pitching coach Fernando Arango and coach Joel Grampietro.

The club finished under .500 for the year and was never really in the pennant race.

The player with the best name, "Poom-Poom" Cumberbatch, left early in the season just as the fans were anticipating the call of his name by public address announcer Dick Cavanagh in his own special style.

Nick Delvecchio supplied some power to the club by hitting 12 home runs and finishing at .274 with 35 RBIs.

One should remember when the home run figures are listed for Oneonta players they perform half their season in one of the minor leagues' largest ball parks and many long shots which are caught at Damaschke Field would be out of nearly every other NY-P park.

Second baseman Robert Hinds proved to be one of the best keystoners ever to perform at Damaschke. His range was unequalled, particularly to his right, and he had a great sense for the game.

"The kid knows how to play baseball," said Gillis. "He has a tremendous feel for it and he instinctively seems to get to the right place at the right time."

Blaze Kozeniewski at third also showed plenty of promise with a strong arm and a lot of courage in charging the ball in Damaschke's dangerous third base territory. His arm was too strong at times and his errors, when they came, were nearly always on the throw.

Ray Suplee had a great arm and his throws to home plate from the deep, dark right field corner surprised a lot of opposing runners and delighted the Yankee fans. Unfortunately for Ray, his bat never came around and he finished with a .224 average for 63 games.

Kent Wallace led the pitching staff with a good 8-4 record and a respectable 2.55 ERA. Bert Inman returned to win six games and Ryan Karp also rung up six victories.

There was a lot of movement among pitchers during the 1992 season and 16 athletes wore the O-Yank uniform as the campaign wore on.

The Yankees finished with a 37-38 record for third place in the

McNamara Division behind Utica and Pittsfield.

As the 1993 season approached, Oneonta Yankee fans were watching the big club in Yankee Stadium and its struggle to reach contention under Buck Showalter, among the most popular of all O-Yank managers.

They were looking back over the glory days in Damaschke Field as a lot of fine athletes had teamed with a dedicated front office staff to produce the best won-lost record in all of organized baseball.

And they were looking ahead to the coming season hoping to see the NY-P League pennant hanging once again in its rightful center field location at the old ball park.

O-Yank Nick Delvecchio shows off a big league swing during a 1992 game.
—The Daily Star

57 Dry

K en Dominguez left Oneonta after the 1994 season with the bitter pill of disappointment lodged firmly in his throat. Since his appearance as a coach with the 1990 NY-P League champion O-Yank club he had dreamed of returning to Oneonta as a manager; and he had worked very hard to live that dream.

In 1993, his dream came true and in June he came north as manager of the Oneonta Yankees, one of organized baseball's most successful operations in terms of wins and losses.

But dreams and reality are two different things and the dedicated, hard working pilot soon came face to face with the reality of baseball. His 1993 team raced to a solid winning record early and were 31-16 as the final third of the season began. Fans were looking ahead to the playoffs once again.

But Ruben Rivera, one of the brightest young stars in the Yankee firmament who had equalled the O-Yank home run record of 13 before mid-season, went down with a broken wrist, "Poom-Poom" Cumberbatch was among several players transferred and the Yanks fell apart. They finished with 36-40 record, going 5-24 the final third of the season.

Dominguez's 1994 club started poorly, never did get under way and struggled to a 30-45 record.

This was a difficult thing for Dominguez whose life is baseball and who had seen the Oneonta job as a stepping stone to better things. Also he felt he had let the fans down.

"These are the best fans I know," he said after the 1994 season. "They deserved better from me than they got."

Although they grew impatient, the fans are certain Ken Dominguez will see things during his fall and winter of introspection he might have overlooked because of his disappointment.

He will see, for example, club officials were quick to point out they felt one of the reasons for the poor record was the constant turnover of personnel. This is a way of life in the lower minors and managers everywhere with all clubs have endured constant through constant roster changes.

As Bill Livesey had said after a similar experience in Oneonta 10 years earlier, Dominguez similarly commented, "Such movement makes it tough to develop any continuity or consistency between the lines. I understand the movement, and I'm pleased for the young players who are promoted. That's what it is all about.

"It's frustrating from the team standpoint and from the position of looking at the lineup card every night."

But the young manager is quick to add, "It's great for the organization that we're moving guys up the ladder."

It is not too difficult to see the ripple effect of the major league activity upon organizations like Oneonta. It appears as if, having failed in an effort to buy a winning team through the free agent market, the New York Yankees, like other more affluent baseball organizations, are pushing their farm systems to produce talented players in greater numbers and more quickly.

The result is a lot of player movement from Tampa to Oneonta, to Greensboro, to Albany, to Columbus and, hopefully, to The Stadium or to the attractive trade market.

The 1994 club was one of the youngest to wear the pinstripes in Oneonta. The oldest players on the squad were 23 and there was only a handful of them. Average age of the team was 19. Looking at the player movement, the tender age of the players and the late signings among the newly drafted players, it's easy to understand what happened to Ken Dominguez and many other managers caught in this whirlwind of change in the baseball world.

Everyone involved with Class A baseball now realizes player development is the key reason for a club's existence. And the news from that side of the organization's activity was good. Rivera went on to put up great numbers in Greensboro in the 1994 season and appears destined for stardom. Ricky Ledee, who signed on as a pro at 17, matured and developed physically to become a good hitter, quick base runner and speedy, knowledgeable outfielder. The Yankees consider him a bright prospect. The 1994 club also showcased some young athletes with major league potential. This club was victimized by an atrocious early season schedule which caused one player to comment, "The only home I know right now is the team bus."

The O-Yanks never recovered from the poor start and never really looked like a contender. But pitcher Matt Drews, whose record of 7-6 was no indication of his promise, never stopped trying. A big kid at 6'7" and 225 pounds, Drews has a strong fast ball and a good mind to go with it.

"He has learned so much since the beginning of the season," Dominguez said. "He is learning how to be a pitcher and not just a thrower. And he's found out what it takes to be successful."

Drews was liked by the Oneonta fans and the feeling was mutual. After the season was over, he ran an ad in the Daily Star thanking the fans for their support.

Jason Jarvis, Dave Meyer and Ray Ricken also appeared to have promise during short stays in Damaschke Field.

Among position players with potential, Yankee officials liked late signees Brian Buchanan and Carlos Yedo while Fernando Seguignol, who was here for the entire season, put up solid numbers. He played in 73 games, hit .290 and led the club in hits, runs, doubles and triples.

And so, 28 seasons have come and gone during the New York Yankee working agreement with the Oneonta baseball team. The 1994 season came to a close with the announcement the New York club had agreed to another year at Damaschke Field in 1995.

The mediocre 1993 and 1994 seasons had already been forgotten as Sam Nader and Company turned to the challenges of a new season. Ahead was a busy winter of preparation and an equally busy spring of setting the stage for the return of the O-Yanks to the winners' circle.

'FILBERTS'

There is no question statistics are an important part of the baseball scene even though some question their importance. Scouts, coaches, managers and owners peruse them constantly in their efforts to ferret out the best talent; although many deny it, players keep a close check on them in judging their progress toward the big money.

And the real fans quote them as they would the Scriptures in the never-ending argument over the abilities of various players.

We believe no book about baseball would be complete with listing statistical information and we, have, therefore, included the facts and figures on the Oneonta Red Sox and the Oneonta Yankees since 1940.

Because of incomplete record keeping during the years of World War II, we have not included the Red Sox in the all time record department and did not include Sox "graduates" in the big league list for feat of missing a name. However, the fact that Austin Knickerbocker, Frank Malzone, Sammy White and Dick Fowler made The Show cannot be overlooked.

What follows is the statistical look at every year of organized based in Oneonta since the 1940's and a list of the leaders in the hitting an pitching department for the Oneonta Yankees.

Here's hoping the *"Figure Filberts"* (otherwise known as fanatical stat lovers) enjoy it.

'SHOW'

A host of players, coaches and managers have appeared in an Oneonta uniform on their way to or from The Show...the major leagues. We recognize them here and apologize to those we inadvertently missed.

Adkins, Steve
Allenson, Gary
Alston, Del
Ausmus, Brad
Azocar, Oscar
Beattie, Jim
Bergman, Dave
Berry, Ken
Bevington, Terry
Kammeyer, Bob
Bergman, Dave
Bradley, Scott
Brett, Ken
Butterfield, Brian
Canseco, Ozzie
Case. George
Chapin, Darrin
Christiansen, Clay
Christopher, Mike
Cloninger, Tony
Cook, Andy
Cooper, Don
Corsi, Jim
Davidson, Bobby
Dayett, Brian
DeMola, Don
Deshaies, Jim
Destrade, Orestes
Diedel, Jim
Dineen, Kerry
Draper, Mike
Eenhorn, Robert
Eiland, Dave
Espino, Juan
Evers, Troy
Ferraro, Mike
Filer, Tom
Filson, Pete
Fischlin, Mike
Frey, Steve
Fulton, Bill
Garcia, Damasco

Geronimo, Cesar
Gowell, Larry
Greer, Ken
Heath, Mike
Hudler, Rex
Hutton, Mark
Imes, Rodney
Johnson, Jeff
Jones, Daryl
Kaufman, Curt
Kelly, Pat
Kelly, Roberto
Klutts, Mickey
Landestoy, Raphael
Layana, Tim
Leiter, Al
Leyden, Mitch
Leyritz, Jim
Lezcano, Carlos
Maas, Kevin
Majeski, Hank
Martinez, Tippy
Mata, Victor
Mattingly, Don
McGaffigan, Andy
McGee, Willie
Medich, George
Meyer, Russ (Monk)
Militello, Sam
Milner, Brian
Morris, Hal
Murray, Larry
Napoleon, Ed
Nielsen, Jerry
Niemann, Randy
Nieves, Juan
Obando, Sherman
Olwin, Ed
Otis, Amos
Pagan, Dave
Pagliarulo, Mike

Pagliarulo, Mike
Pasqua, Dan
Heath, Mike
Patterson, Gil
Patterson, Ken
Polinsky, Bob
Ramos, Domingo
Ramos, John
Reed, Darren
Rodriguez, Edwin
Rosenberg, Steve
Santana, Rafael
Scheid, Rich
Seminara, Frank
Showalter, Buck
Smith, Keith
Snow, J.T.
Stankiewicz, Andy
Tabler, Pat
Tewksbury, Bob
Timberlake, Gary
Tolliver, Freddie
Torres, Rusty
Turner, Shane
Upshaw, Willie
Verdi, Frank
Villaman, Rafael
Walker, Jerry
Ward, Turner
Welsh, Chris
Werly, Jamie
Werth, Dennis
Wever, Stefan
Whitfield, Terry
Wilborn, Ted
Wilkins, Dean
Williams, Bernie
Williams, Gerald
Winters, Matt

Bold-type: O-Yank Pennant Winning Managers

BATS

AVERAGE

Kerry Dineen	.362	1973
Don Mattingly	.352	1979
Dave Bergman	.343	1974

RUNS BATTED IN

Brian Dayett	63	1978
Dennis Werth	61	1974
Chuck Lelas	59	1967

HOME RUNS

Darren Mandel	13	1984
Reuben Rivera	13	1993
Chuck Lelas	12	1967
Nick DelVecchio	12	1992

TRIPLES

Terry Whitfield	11	1972
Darryl Jones	11	1972
Matt Winters	11	1978
Kerry Dineen	10	1973

DOUBLES

Dennis Werth	23	1974
Sherman Obando	23	1989
Brian Dayett	20	1978
Tate Seefried	19	1991
Tim Flannelly	19	1991

HITS

Steve Coulson	95	1973
Kevin Jordan	92	1990
Kerry Dineen	88	1973
Pat Patterson	88	1974

TOTAL BASES

Brian Dayett	140	1978
Sherman Obando	133	1989
Kevin Jordan	131	1990
Dennis Werth	127	1974

RUNS

Terry Whitfield	65	1972
Ted Wilborn	63	1978
Marv Thompson	62	1974

STOLEN BASES

Larry Murray	59	1972
Ted Wilborn	57	1978
Rich Barnwell	39	1989

ARMS

WINS

Neal Mersch	11-0	1973
Fred Anyzeski	10-1	1974
Troy Evers	10-1	1985
Fred Toliver	10-2	1979

ERA

Dody Rather	0.31	1985
Mike DeJean	0.44	1992
Art Canestro	1.05	1989
Neal Mersch	1.18	1985
Troy Evers	1.18	1985

UNDEFEATED

Neal Mersch	11-0	1973
Scott Larsen	9-0	1972
Dean Wilkins	9-0	1986
Bill Olsen	8-0	1969
Dody Rather	8-0	1985

SHUTOUTS

Greg Diehl	5	1974
Chris Welsh	4	1977
Mark Mendez	4	1980
Ken Patterson	4	1986

COMPLETE GAMES

Bob Majzcan	12	1973
Chris Welsh	12	1977
Bob Artemenko	10	1972
Neal Mersch	10	1973
Paul Semall	10	1977

INNINGS PITCHED

Bob Majzcan	115	1973
Neal Mersch	114	1973
Ken Greer	112	1988
Chris Welsh	112	1977

SAVES

Mike Gardella	19	1989
Bo Siberz	16	1990
Mike DeJean	16	1992
Ben Short	14	1991
Darren Chapin	12	1984

STRIKEOUTS

Jim DeShaies	137	1982
Chris Welsh	125	1977
Sam Militello	118	1990

STANDINGS

1966

First Half

	W	L	Pct.	GB
Auburn	44	20	.688	—
Oneonta	32	27	.542	9½
Batavia	30	27	.526	10½
Jamestown	31	29	.517	11
Binghamton	25	35	.417	17
Geneva	18	42	.300	24

Second Half

	W	L	Pct.	GB
Binghamton	42	23	.646	—
Jamestown	39	26	.600	3
Auburn	36	29	.554	6
Oneonta	33	32	.508	9
Batavia	28	36	.438	13½
Geneva	16	48	.250	25½

1967

First year of short season

	W	L	Pct.	GB
Auburn	52	26	.667	—
Batavia	41	36	.532	9½
Oneonta	40	39	.506	12½
Jamestown	39	41	.506	14
Geneva	37	42	.468	14½
Erie	26	51	.338	15½

No playoffs.

1968

	W	L	Pct.	GB
Auburn	49	27	.645	—
Oneonta	43	34	.558	6½
Williamsport	40	35	.533	8½
Newark	38	36	.514	10
Batavia	37	38	.493	11½
Geneva	37	39	.487	12
Jamestown	31	44	.413	17½
Corning	27	49	.335	22

Oneonta *over Newark and Auburn over Williamsport in one game playoff.* **Oneonta** *beat Auburn to win title.*

1969

	W	L	Pct.	GB
Oneonta	51	26	.662	—
Batavia	42	33	.560	8
Newark	42	34	.553	8½
Williamsport	39	36	.520	11
Jamestown	33	41	.446	16½
Auburn	31	42	.425	18
Geneva	27	46	.370	22
Corning	27	49	.355	23½

No playoffs 1969 thru 1976.

1970

Auburn	43	26	.623	—
Oneonta	41	28	.594	2
Batavia	37	32	.536	6
Newark	36	33	.522	7
Geneva	33	35	.485	9½
Jamestown	30	40	.429	13½
Niagara Falls	28	40	.412	14½
Williamsport	28	42	.400	15½

1971

Oneonta	45	23	.662	—
Auburn	42	28	.600	4
Niagara Falls	37	33	.529	9
Newark	35	35	.500	11
Geneva	34	36	.486	12
Williamsport	30	39	.435	15½
Batavia	30	40	.429	16
Jamestown	25	44	.362	20½

1972

Niagara Falls	48	22	.646	—
Oneonta	45	25	.643	3
Jamestown	42	28	.600	6
Auburn	39	30	.565	8½
Geneva	30	40	.429	13
Batavia	29	40	.420	18½
Newark	23	46	.333	24½
Williamsport	22	47	.319	25½

1973

Auburn	46	23	.667	—
Oneonta	44	26	.629	2½
Jamestown	41	28	.594	5
Geneva	39	29	.574	6½
Batavia	33	36	.478	13
Elmira	32	37	.464	14
Niagara Falls	27	43	.386	19½
Newark	15	55	.214	31½

1974

Oneonta	53	16	.768	—
Auburn	34	32	.515	17½
Elmira	34	35	.493	19
Niagara Falls	33	36	.478	20
Newark	30	36	.455	21½
Batavia	20	49	.190	33

1975

Newark	47	20	.701	—
Elmira	38	30	.559	9½
Oneonta	35	34	.507	13
Auburn	31	37	.456	16½
Niagara Falls	29	40	.420	19
Batavia	24	43	.358	23

1976

Elmira	50	20	.714	—
Newark	46	24	.657	4
Niagara Falls	35	34	.507	14½
Batavia	30	40	.429	20
Auburn	24	45	.348	25½
Oneonta	24	46	.343	26

1977 *Eastern Division*

Oneonta	47	23	.671	—
Utica	43	28	.606	4½
Elmira	33	36	.478	13½
Little Falls	32	29	.451	15½
Auburn	17	53	.243	30

Western Division

Batavia	42	28	.600	—
Newark	43	29	.597	1
Jamestown	35	32	.522	5½
Geneva	31	40	.437	11½
Niagara Falls	27	42	.391	14½

Oneonta won Governor's Cup playoff over Batavia two to one.

1978 *Yawkey Division*

Oneonta	51	19	.729	—
Utica	37	34	.521	14½
Auburn	32	40	.444	20
Little Falls	29	42	.408	22½
Elmira	21	48	.304	29½

Wrigley Division

Geneva	51	20	.718	—
Jamestown	44	28	.611	7½
Batavia	34	38	.472	17½
Niagara Falls	30	40	.429	20½
Newark	26	46	.361	25½

Geneva won Governor's Cup two games to none over **Oneonta.**

1979 *Yawkey Division*

Oneonta	42	26	.618	—
Elmira	34	35	.493	8½
Little Falls	31	39	.443	12
Utica	25	41	.379	16
Auburn	22	45	.328	19½

Wrigley Division

Geneva	50	19	.725	—
Jamestown	43	27	.614	7½
Batavia	37	34	.521	14
Newark	32	39	.451	19
Niagara Falls	30	41	.423	21

Oneonta *won Governor's Cup two games to none over Geneva.*

1980 — *Eastern Division*

Oneonta	49	25	.662	—
Little Falls	40	33	.548	8½
Elmira	39	35	.527	10
Utica	27	44	.380	20½

Western Division

Geneva	48	26	.649	—
Batavia	31	42	.425	16½
Jamestown	29	42	.408	17½
Auburn	29	45	.392	19

Oneonta *beat Geneva two games to one to win Governor's Cup.*

1981 — *Eastern Division*

Oneonta	48	25	.658	—
Utica	39	31	.557	7½
Little Falls	31	39	.443	15½
Elmira	25	48	.342	23½

Western Division

Jamestown	48	26	.649	—
Erie	44	30	.595	4
Geneva	41	34	.547	7½
Batavia	16	59	.213	32½

Oneonta *beat Jamestown two games to one to win Governor's Cup.*

1982 — *Eastern Division*

Oneonta	43	33	.566	—
Utica	41	34	.547	1½
Little Falls	38	38	.500	5
Auburn	35	39	.473	7
Elmira	34	40	.459	8

Western Division

Niagara Falls	42	34	.533	—
Jamestown	36	38	.486	5
Geneva	36	39	.480	5½
Erie	35	38	.479	5½
Batavia	33	40	.452	7½

Niagara Falls beat **Oneonta** *two games to one for title.*

1983		Eastern Division		
Utica	48	26	.649	—
Little Falls	48	27	.640	½
Auburn	43	31	.581	5
Elmira	38	36	.514	10
Oneonta	32	44	.421	17
Watertown	21	55	.276	28
		Western Division		
Newark	48	26	.649	—
Jamestown	38	36	.514	10
Erie	37	38	.493	11½
Geneva	33	40	.452	14½
Batavia	32	43	.427	16½
Niagara Falls	29	45	.392	19

1984		Eastern Division		
Little Falls	44	31	.587	--
Watertown	39	35	.527	4½
Auburn	38	38	.500	6½
Elmira	35	38	.479	8
Utica	31	44	.413	13
Oneonta	29	45	.392	14½
		Western Division		
Newark	46	28	.622	--
Erie	43	31	.581	3
Batavia	41	35	.539	6
Geneva	38	36	.514	8
Niagara Falls	35	40	.467	11½
Jamestown	28	46	.378	18

1985		Northern Division		
Oneonta	55	23	.705	--
Utica	35	41	.461	19
Little Falls	34	41	.453	19½
Watertown	22	54	.289	32
		Central Division		
Auburn	47	31	.603	--
Geneva	45	33	.577	2
Newark	41	36	.532	3½
Elmira	28	49	.364	18½
		Southern Division		
Jamestown	45	33	.577	--
Erie	44	34	.564	1
Niagara Falls	34	43	.442	10½
Batavia	33	45	.423	12

Auburn beat Jamestown and **Oneonta** *topped Geneva in one-game semi-finals.* **Oneonta** *beat Auburn two games to none for the title.*

1986	*Yawkey Division*			
˙**Oneonta**	59	18	.766	--
Little Falls	36	40	.474	22½
Watertown	30	48	.385	29½
Utica	26	52	.333	33½
	McNamara Division			
Auburn	44	32	.579	--
Newark	41	37	.526	4
Elmira	39	36	.520	4½
Geneva	40	38	.513	5
	Wrigley Division			
St. Catharines	48	28	.632	--
Erie	37	40	.481	11½
Batavia	30	45	.400	17½
Jamestown	30	46	.395	18

Newark beat **Oneonta**; *St. Catharines beat Auburn in one game semi-finals. St. Catharines beat Newark, two games to none.* ˙**Oneonta** *set league records for wins (59) and for division win margin (22½ games).*

1987	*Eastern Division*			
Watertown	44	32	.579	--
Oneonta	41	34	.547	2½
Auburn	39	36	.520	4½
Little Falls	38	36	.514	5
Utica	31	43	.419	12
Elmira	26	50	.342	18
	Western Division			
Geneva	48	28	.632	--
Jamestown	44	33	.571	4½
Newark	42	32	.568	5
St. Catharines	41	36	.532	7½
Erie	36	39	.480	11½
Batavia	23	54	.299	25½

1988	*Eastern Division*			
Oneonta	48	28	.632	--
Utica	47	29	.618	1
Auburn	42	33	.560	5½
Little Falls	39	36	.520	8½
Watertown	35	39	.473	12
Elmira	28	48	.368	20
	Western Division			
Jamestown	47	29	.618	--
Erie	46	31	.597	1½
Hamilton	36	39	.480	10½
Batavia	31	44	.413	15½
St. Catharines	27	46	.370	18½
Geneva	27	51	.346	21

Oneonta *beat Jamestown, two games to none to win title.*

1989 *Eastern Division*

	W	L	Pct	GB
Pittsfield	53	23	.697	--
Oneonta	48	27	.640	4½
Watertown	47	30	.610	6½
Utica	39	39	.500	15
Geneva	36	39	.480	16½
Auburn	35	42	.455	18½
Elmira	30	46	.395	23

Western Division

	W	L	Pct	GB
Jamestown	44	32	.579	--
Niagara Falls	43	33	.566	1
Batavia	37	39	.487	7
Welland	32	44	.421	12
Hamilton	32	44	.421	12
St. Catharines	31	45	.408	13
Erie	25	49	.338	18

1990 *McNamara East*

	W	L	Pct	GB
Oneonta	52	26	.667	--
Watertown	43	34	.558	8½
Pittsfield	43	34	.558	8½
Utica	31	47	.397	21

McNamara West

	W	L	Pct	GB
Geneva	51	26	.662	--
Batavia	41	35	.539	9½
Elmira	32	45	.416	19
Auburn	31	46	.403	20

Stedler Division

	W	L	Pct	GB
Erie	44	33	.571	--
Jamestown	41	36	.532	3
Welland	36	42	.462	8½
Niagara Falls	35	42	.455	9
Hamilton	30	46	.395	13½
St. Catharines	29	47	.382	14½

Oneonta *beat Erie two games to one to win crown.*

1991 *McNamara East*

	W	L	Pct	GB
Pittsfield	51	26	.663	--
Oneonta	42	35	.546	9
Utica	39	37	.512	11½
Watertown	26	53	.338	25

McNamara West

	W	L	Pct	GB
Elmira	47	30	.610	--
Auburn	38	39	.494	9
Batavia	38	40	.487	9½
Geneva	35	43	.449	12½

Stedler Division

	W	L	Pct	GB
Jamestown	51	27	.654	--
Erie	37	41	.474	14
Niagara Falls	36	42	.462	15
Hamilton	35	42	.455	15½
St. Catharines	35	42	.455	15½
Welland	30	47	.390	20½

1992   *McNamara Division*
Utica	42	32	.568	--
Pittsfield	37	37	.500	5
Oneonta	37	38	.493	5½
Watertown	37	39	.487	6

Pinckney Division
Geneva	41	34	.547	--
Batavia	36	34	.514	2½
Auburn	32	40	.444	7½
Elmira	30	44	.405	10½

Stedler Division
Hamilton	56	20	.737	--
Erie	40	37	.519	16½
Niagara Falls	39	39	.500	18
Jamestown	34	43	.441	22½
St. Catharines	33	42	.440	22½
Welland	31	46	.403	25½

1993   *McNamara Division*
Pittsfield	40	35	.533	--
Utica	38	38	.500	2½
Glens Falls	37	40	.481	4
Oneonta	36	40	.474	4½

Pinckney Division
Watertown	46	32	.590	--
Geneva	43	34	.558	2½
Elmira	31	44	.413	13½
Auburn	30	46	.395	15

Stedler Division
St. Catharines	49	29	.628	--
Niagara Falls	47	31	.603	2
Batavia	38	39	.494	10½
Erie	36	41	.468	12½
Welland	35	42	.455	13½
Jamestown	31	46	.403	17½

1994   *Pinckney Division*
Watertown	48	26	.649	--
Auburn	45	31	.592	4
Utica	35	37	.486	12
Elmira	30	43	.411	17½
Oneonta	30	45	.400	18½
Williamsport	26	49	.347	22½

McNamara Division

New Jersey	43	32	.573	--
Vermont	42	33	.560	1
Hudson Valley	37	37	.500	5½
Pittsfield	37	38	.493	6

Stedler Division

Jamestown	42	32	.573	--
Batavia	40	34	.541	2
St. Catharines	35	39	.473	7
Welland	30	44	.405	12

1940

RED SOX: CAN-AM LEAGUE
MANAGER LEE RILEY: WON 62 LOST 63

HITTING	AVG.	AB	H	2B	3B	HR	RBI	BB	SO
Andy Botlock	.129	62	8	3	1	0	4	7	9
Bill Burke	.182	11	2	0	0	0	0	0	4
Tom Fine	.259	54	14	4	2	0	11	1	13
Dick Fowler	.257	109	28	2	2	1	20	9	14
Chick Genovese	.311	309	69	20	7	5	37	66	27
Ralph Hammond	.268	71	19	2	3	1	15	3	19
Jud Harmon	.083	36	3	0	0	0	1	6	12
Eaton Jones	.264	371	98	13	11	0	35	40	43
John Mayhew	.215	65	14	2	2	0	7	5	6
Woody McDonald	.236	106	25	2	1	0	8	12	16
Ed Metro	.180	61	11	0	2	0	3	5	12
Tom O'Donnell	.289	308	89	12	6	1	44	50	23
Frank Perkowski	.346	468	162	34	12	7	104	22	21
Pete Radell	.306	434	133	25	7	3	65	29	31
Lee Riley	.340	394	134	21	10	14	87	84	26
Tony Sabol	.276	156	43	8	2	1	21	9	9
Stan Shargey	.248	287	71	7	2	3	36	25	57
Al Tarlecki	.316	455	144	24	10	3	76	46	39
Tom Torello	.150	80	12	1	2	0	1	14	14
Leon Trumbore	.200	180	36	3	2	1	14	9	24
Paul Veach	.103	39	4	0	0	0	0	1	8
Jim Whaley	.258	240	62	8	3	0	9	27	30
Ed Williams	.222	45	10	1	1	0	6	7	3
Joe Zagami	.317	268	85	10	12	8	54	41	41

PITCHING	W-L	ERA	IP	H	BB	SO
Tom Fine	8-5	3.92	117	94	66	116
Dick Fowler	16-10	3.57	209	231	64	105
Ralph Hammond	9-10	6.08	151	162	102	80
Jud Harmon	9-4	4.16	106	132	41	42
Ed Metro	8-12	4.25	178	179	71	104
Frank Perkowski	1-8	5.86	63	93	22	21
Leon Trumbore	8-9	5.12	188	244	54	68
Paul Veach	3-2	5.97	104	131	61	56

Seven pitchers threw less than 35 innings.

1941

RED SOX: CAN-AM LEAGUE
MANAGER RED BARNES: WON 78 LOST 46

HITTING	AVG.	AB	H	AB	3B	HR	RBI	BB	SO
Red Barnes	.371	318	118	20	10	4	77	95	14
Ken Chapman	.261	487	127	26	13	5	52	88	87
Tom Fine	.225	102	23	2	1	0	6	14	19
Chick Genovese	.367	485	178	37	19	14	97	96	20
A. Knickerbocker	.406	488	202	45	10	12	135	48	26
Carlen Kooker	.167	18	3	1	0	0	3	0	5
Marion Lewis	.227	22	5	3	0	0	3	5	4
Lloyd Makes	.217	23	5	1	0	0	1	1	4
Dan Martucello	.286	7	2	1	0	0	1	1	2
Ed McGah	.329	425	140	31	10	11	82	58	78
Jim McGuire	.250	60	15	3	2	0	8	5	21
Don Moore	.211	19	4	0	1	0	4	2	3
Emil Nascak	.223	184	41	1	2	0	20	18	23
Emmet O'Neil	.219	32	7	3	0	0	2	2	9
Bob Pash	.242	132	32	1	0	1	21	9	22
Mike Prouch	.063	16	1	0	0	0	0	2	1
Earl Rapp	.278	144	40	3	5	0	17	15	24
Tony Sabol	.310	509	15	36	9	3	98	46	44
Charles Swart	.143	7	1	0	0	0	0	1	3
Ralph Waite	.245	94	23	1	3	1	14	4	21
Harold White	.250	76	19	3	2	1	7	15	23
Bill Wolfe	.120	25	3	0	0	0	1	3	2
Jim Young	.050	20	1	0	0	0	0	3	7
Joe Zagami	.308	474	146	17	16	4	103	83	56
Mike Zaher	.250	100	25	6	3	0	12	9	5

PITCHING	W-L	ERA	IP	H	BB	SO
Dave Blewster	1-2	5.63	16	15	16	12
Tommy Fine	22-9	3.83	214	183	128	185
Carlen Kooker	2-4	5.56	34	34	23	20
Lloyd Makes	2-4	5.07	64	91	23	40
Jim McGuire	9-9	4.65	147	142	66	60
Emmet O'Neil	4-3	3.65	69	52	46	75
Mike Prouch	1-3	6.80	41	47	33	12
Tony Sabol	0-0	45.00	1	6	1	0
Walt Slog	0-0	13.00	9	17	5	4
Ralph Waite	15-5	4.94	204	234	89	111
G. VanDeWalker	0-0	0.00	0	0	4	1
Hal White	19-6	3.70	207	177	110	152
Jim Young	3-3	4.36	62	77	9	24

1942

RED SOX: CAN-AM LEAGUE
MANAGER RED BARNES: WON 68 LOST 56

HITTING	AVG.	AB	H	2B	3B	HR	RBI	BB	SO
Red Barnes	.284	261	74	17	5	0	42	40	12
Homer Chapman									
Ken Chapman	.317	445	141	32	6	8	64	73	68
Bob Crues									
Hudson Davis									
Vance Dinges	.338	302	102	17	11	2	68	33	17
Fred Everett	.306	49	15	0	0	1	8	9	5
Mike Fedunick									
Tom Fine	.294	293	86	10	6	0	42	27	52
Joe Grogan									
Ray Henningsen	.316	395	125	16	7	6	37	73	22
Moe King									
Wally Kuloweic									
Jack McCarthy									
Emil Nascak									
Jim Robison	.288	441	127	19	15	4	91	36	82
C. Stevenson									
Lee Wortman									
Joe Zagami	.341	276	94	23	4	10	62	37	29

PITCHING	W-L	ERA	IP	H	BB	SO
Jack Byers						
Ollie Byers						
Ben Cizek						
Steve Fallon	9-0	1.94	79	60	17	79
Tom Fine	13-8	2.78	181	162	74	173
Jim McGuire						
John McGuire						
Frank Mussell	5-2	3.40	74	77	10	34
S. Partenheimer	13-4	3.40	150	121	71	159
Claude Phillips						
Bob Ruff						
John Ryan						
Paul Schott	8-4	3.41	95	96	28	23
Ralph Waite						

(Statistics from 1942 are incomplete as records were kept to a minimum by wartime restrictions on paper usage.)

1946

Red Sox: Can-Am League
Manager Red Marion: Won 68 Lost 54

HITTING	AVG.	AB	H	2B	3B	HR	RBI	BB	SO
John Boryk	.263	468	123	15	9	1	68	59	54
Roy Boyd	.233	146	34	10	1	2	29	11	27
Jim Cloran	.231	13	3	0	0	0	4	1	6
Ted DeGuercio	.310	422	131	21	7	5	73	63	75
Frank DeGregorio	.248	423	105	8	2	0	37	34	44
John Folger	.253	154	39	5	1	0	22	19	15
Don Griffin	.335	188	63	6	4	0	30	13	24
John Hernandez	.302	361	109	17	11	5	63	52	61
Dave Honan	.188	48	9	0	0	4	4	3	11
Bill Hornsby	.215	79	17	3	0	0	4	13	6
Vern Lehrmann	.261	69	18	1	0	0	6	3	8
Dick Littlefield	.211	19	4	0	0	0	1	7	8
Red Marion	.360	372	134	22	4	1	62	91	38
Ralph Mullin	.271	85	23	4	0	1	12	12	8
Bob Nelson	.227	119	27	3	0	0	11	27	27
Ed Nietopski	.248	149	37	4	0	0	16	11	17
Dick Phillips	.263	19	5	0	1	0	2	2	3
Harry Pilarski	.134	67	9	2	1	0	2	7	20
Mel Reeves	.286	308	88	13	11	3	51	54	55
Don Reidle	.094	32	3	0	0	0	4	3	9
Charles Riddle	.281	32	9	0	0	0	6	3	6
Jim Sheekey	.148	54	8	2	0	0	4	6	10
Frank Sturm	.233	203	47	8	1	0	17	31	46
Jim Trainor	.333	33	11	1	0	0	8	6	9
Joe Wall	.214	42	9	2	0	0	4	10	9

PITCHING	W-L	ERA	IP	H	BB	SO
Dave Honan	9-6	3.16	134	117	77	64
Bill Jost	5-3	3.77	62	45	46	21
Vern Lehrmann	15-4	3.28	158	149	90	63
Dick Littlefield	3-7	5.45	66	53	67	42
Harry Pilarski	13-13	2.97	212	179	97	159
Jim Ryan	3-6	4.66	85	78	52	51
Jim Sheekey	11-6	3.95	148	158	68	42
Jim Trainor	4-6	3.73	94	95	58	34

Don Failing, Armand Falcioni, Ralph Graziano, Harry Johnson and Don Roode pitched less than 45 innings—records not kept.

1947

Red Sox: Can-Am League
Manager Red Marion: Won 70 Lost 67

HITTING	AVG.	AB	H	2B	3B	HR	RBI	BB	SO
Fred Bortolotti	.284	486	138	15	12	9	76	76	55
Frk. DiGregorio	.257	490	126	13	4	0	39	46	23
Mike Durock	.242	223	54	12	1	1	29	32	21
Dan Gabrell	.245	102	25	3	1	0	10	8	6
Ed Halsch	.259	317	82	13	4	0	35	30	38
Bill Hays	.333	15	5	0	0	0	3	1	3
Roger Higgins	.214	42	9	2	0	0	3	2	7
Vern Lehrmann	.242	66	16	1	0	0	4	4	8
Dale Long	.311	331	103	13	5	6	60	18	22
Red Marion	.268	138	37	0	1	0	19	39	15
Don McArthur	.125	32	4	0	0	0	1	6	4
Geo. McCafferty	.130	23	3	0	0	0	0	1	9
Bob McLean	.219	96	21	3	2	1	12	12	22
Irv Medlinger	.250	96	24	6	0	0	2	3	10
Carl Mevrn	.094	42	4	0	0	0	2	1	10
Joe Nelson	.241	87	21	3	2	1	8	10	10
Steve Nemeth	.252	107	27	4	2	0	17	7	7
Jack Norton	.203	59	12	1	0	0	4	5	11
Jim O'Connor	.231	529	122	16	4	0	34	68	66
Julio Ondani	.244	246	60	6	4	2	22	40	47
Chas. Riddle	.272	235	64	9	4	1	38	42	21
Allen Richter	.256	86	22	3	2	1	17	5	5
Steve Salata	.312	321	100	17	12	2	39	42	28
Jim Sheekey	.114	44	5	1	1	0	1	4	15
LeRoy Smith	.250	28	7	0	0	0	0	3	5
Bob VanEman	.327	410	134	18	7	4	55	34	65
Art Visconti	.265	189	50	11	4	0	30	47	22
Bernie Winters	.178	45	8	1	0	0	1	2	10

PITCHING	W-L	ERA	IP	H	BB	SO
Roger Higgins	10-6	3.45	128	140	38	62
Vern Lehrmann	6-10	3.54	127	130	74	41
Geo. McCafferty	8-4	3.84	75	77	40	43
Irv. Medlinger	14-13	2.04	234	190	97	182
Carl Mevrn	6-4	3.23	106	100	51	54
Jack Norton	10-10	2.86	173	135	55	114
LeRoy Smith	5-4	2.16	79	66	42	45
Jim Sheekey	7-7	3.98	122	116	73	51

1948

RED SOX: CAN-AM LEAGUE
MANAGER RED MARION: WON 72 LOST 65

HITTING	AVG.	AB	H	2B	3B	HR	RBI	BB	SO
Steve Andreski	.261	479	125	14	13	3	68	59	52
Frank Azzarello	.091	22	2	0	0	0	0	2	3
Lou Blackmore	.091	11	1	0	0	0	0	5	6
Bob Brake	.253	99	25	5	3	1	6	13	20
Cal Burlingame	.337	406	137	15	16	3	62	33	53
Andy Cullen	.252	318	80	14	6	0	38	46	46
Tom DeNoville	.244	156	38	6	4	4	27	12	23
Mike Durock	.249	503	125	25	9	5	74	71	88
Tony Ferrara	.315	111	35	3	1	0	22	13	18
Ed Flanagan	.045	22	1	1	0	0	1	2	7
Joe Gallina	.279	526	147	13	11	3	59	60	70
Dick Games	.223	224	50	9	1	1	26	42	32
Cameron Jury	.256	336	86	18	7	3	60	49	64
Al Lawlor	.300	110	33	4	1	0	19	15	20
Charlie LeBrun	.273	77	21	1	1	0	4	7	25
Julio Ondani	.252	119	30	5	0	1	13	16	23
Clarence Parker	.214	215	46	6	2	1	37	27	51
Paul Perry	.188	16	3	0	0	0	0	2	9
Ed Piano	.183	323	59	8	0	0	33	97	96
Joe Reedy	.349	43	15	2	0	0	8	5	3
Steve Salata	.302	86	26	2	4	2	19	15	13
LeRoy Smith	.325	191	62	9	9	1	28	10	14
Chuck Smozanitz	.222	54	12	0	1	0	6	13	7
George Uhaze	.000	10	0	0	0	0	0	0	2

PITCHING	W-L	ERA	IP	H	BB	SO
Lou Blackmore	2-3	4.70	46	33	62	45
Bob Brake	20-12	2.81	259	239	102	176
Ed Flanagan	3-5	4.23	66	83	23	36
Chas LeBrun	19-11	2.54	219	189	80	161
Paul Perry	1-6	4.06	51	53	44	49
Joe Reedy	5-4	5.14	84	75	74	66
LeRoy Smith	8-4	4.34	116	97	63	69
Chuck Smozanitz	7-8	6.02	142	140	126	118

1949

RED SOX: CAN-AM LEAGUE
MANAGER EDDIE POPOWSKI: WON 75 LOST 62

HITTING	AVG.	AB	H	2B	3B	HR	RBI	BB	SO
John Ahern	.061	49	3	0	0	0	2	4	23
Allen Baker	.143	28	4	1	0	0	3	4	12
Ray Breton	.333	31	7	2	0	0	3	0	6
Ralph Decender	.291	55	16	4	0	0	8	2	12
Ivan Delock	.222	72	16	0	0	0	7	10	13
Joe DeMaestri	.277	506	140	22	14	4	14	43	51
Tom DeNoville	.239	284	68	8	4	1	17	21	20
Fred Folkes	.200	80	16	2	4	0	7	17	16
Joe Fromuth	.194	108	21	2	0	2	11	12	13
Tom Griglak	.294	17	5	2	0	0	1	2	4
Tom Herrin	.244	86	21	1	2	0	5	5	17
Frank Malzone	.329	541	178	26	26	5	92	76	47
Joe Moody	.275	501	138	27	15	11	94	103	121
Julio Ondani	.286	517	148	22	11	9	77	93	89
Bob Pray	.135	74	10	1	1	0	6	10	14
Tom Radcliff	.167	42	7	0	0	0	4	7	22
Max Ross	.250	76	19	4	2	1	17	16	11
Bob Ross	.230	87	20	4	0	0	8	9	12
Steve Salata	.307	335	103	14	5	9	52	58	35
LeRoy Smith	.278	472	131	12	19	10	81	38	68
Bill Smodic	.185	92	17	3	0	0	6	12	12
Jake Stirn	.254	410	104	14	4	8	62	83	106
Sammy White	.256	121	31	5	2	2	21	4	15

PITCHING	W-L	ERA	IP	H	BB	SO
John Ahern	11-8	2.60	163	146	57	140
Ray Breton	1-1	4.79	47	52	19	22
Ivan Delock	12-13	4.21	199	206	107	103
Carl Gustason	3-5	4.25	53	52	35	20
Tom Herrin	16-10	4.00	216	207	132	125
Bob Pray	15-11	2.93	218	192	131	112
Tom Radcliff	10-4	3.68	120	125	46	45

1950

Red Sox: Can-Am League
Manager Ed Popowski: Won 86 Lost 52

HITTING	AVG.	AB	H	2B	3B	HR	RBI	BB	SO
Frank Arcoleo	.287	411	118	13	2	0	40	73	12
Ken Aspromonte	.213	61	13	2	1	0	18	7	12
Bob Baumler	.252	123	31	7	2	5	27	17	30
Hal Buckwalter	.327	505	165	27	7	2	77	46	44
Charles Cadario	.300	320	96	12	6	4	56	49	53
John Campbell	.174	23	4	1	0	0	2	2	3
Jim DiFrederico	.160	25	4	1	0	0	0	4	13
Joe Delock	.208	77	16	3	2	0	8	21	7
Larry DiPippo	.351	37	13	2	1	1	10	11	4
Joe Detoia	.297	489	145	14	11	2	97	115	54
Jake Donaldson	.231	255	59	11	3	2	36	30	16
Herb Drew	.103	29	3	3	0	0	1	3	14
Vince Furfaro	.261	295	77	11	4	5	53	58	57
John Gilbert	.188	69	13	0	1	0	8	4	27
Ed Irons	.435	46	20	2	0	0	11	3	4
Jack Kaiser	.375	72	27	5	2	2	14	18	10
George Lyon	.212	165	35	8	0	0	24	30	28
Bill McMahon	.140	43	6	1	0	0	5	1	10
Herb Rossman	.303	459	139	14	10	1	67	82	17
Neil Smith	.191	47	9	1	0	0	2	10	13
Bob Smith	.082	49	4	0	0	0	3	6	20
Bill Smodic	.262	431	113	30	10	9	77	51	42
Arnie Spence	.260	419	109	11	21	14	80	143	115
Jim Sweeney	.109	46	5	0	0	0	5	4	19
John Wall	.069	29	2	1	0	0	0	7	10

PITCHING	W-L	ERA	IP	H	BB	SO
John Campbell	5-3	4.11	70	71	39	31
Jim DiFrederico	4-3	5.91	70	81	49	32
Herb Drew	6-4	3.15	97	97	44	54
John Gilbert	17-6	2.81	189	195	55	87
Bill McMahon	10-4	3.24	125	123	68	80
Neil Smith	9-7	4.17	149	177	57	60
Bob Smith	13-5	3.65	138	130	88	96
Jim Sweeney	12-5	3.71	143	102	151	134
John Wall	6-4	3.00	90	84	82	50

1951

Red Sox: Can-Am League
Manager Owen Sheetz: Won 83 Lost 34

HITTING	AVG.	AB	H	2B	3B	HR	RBI	BB	SO
Bob Atwood	.293	358	105	20	4	0	45	24	26
Paul Aylward	.247	77	19	1	0	0	7	2	23
Ed Bryan	.270	100	27	6	1	3	29	16	7
Jim DiFrederico	.263	38	10	2	2	1	4	2	7
Frank Gavel	.357	14	5	0	0	0	1	1	4
Chuck Gersten	.214	42	9	1	1	0	7	11	14
Art Getgen	.244	422	103	15	12	4	68	85	67
Bob Guttila	.289	405	117	17	1	0	44	107	31
Bill Kahler	.249	233	58	8	0	3	40	25	24
Rich Karl	.301	452	136	18	5	1	40	94	19
Gene Haering	.292	113	33	4	1	3	23	25	6
Bob McNabb	.222	27	6	0	0	0	1	3	3
John Minarcin	.284	412	117	13	7	6	111	73	14
Ken Paschal	.225	71	16	2	0	0	14	8	9
Ron Root	.230	61	14	1	3	0	8	10	17
Joe Ross	.139	65	9	1	0	0	8	13	15
Bernie Satchick	.077	13	1	0	0	0	2	0	4
Charley Schuck	.220	59	13	1	0	0	9	14	10
Arnie Spence	.302	334	101	16	11	13	75	98	77
George Uhaze	.086	58	5	0	0	0	8	13	15
Art West	.274	190	52	4	2	0	19	24	17
Genero Zizza	.292	212	62	13	5	1	40	94	19

PITCHING	W-L	ERA	IP	H	BB	SO
Paul Aylward	20-4	2.45	191	158	113	91
Jim DiFrederico	5-4	3.56	101	80	80	52
Frank Gavel	3-2	5.60	45	32	59	27
Art Gersten	11-6	3.22	134	143	65	59
Bob McNabb	5-3	3.20	76	58	58	46
Joe Ross	18-6	2.80	199	174	118	81
George Uhaze*	16-3	1.64	165	141	57	88

*—Pitched seven inning no-hitter against Pittsfield
August 4. Final score, 7-0.

1967

O-Yanks: NY-P League
Mananger Frank Verdi: Won 40 Lost 39

HITTING	AVG.	AB	H	2B	3B	HR	RBI	BB	SO
Jerry Albin	.306	49	15	2	0	1	8	11	8
Jim Alvey	.243	115	28	1	2	1	8	16	20
Paul Branca	.065	62	4	1	0	0	1	10	37
Bob Carson	.358	179	64	9	6	4	35	24	31
Ron Cook	.159	44	7	1	1	1	8	5	15
Gle. Cunningham	.157	115	18	3	1	0	13	10	18
Roger Dutton	.287	108	31	4	3	2	18	24	17
Terry Echan	.311	219	68	9	3	0	21	35	27
Cesar Geronimo	.100	10	1	0	0	0	1	1	5
Dave Gunderman	.244	41	10	2	1	0	4	4	13
Archie Haley	.176	34	6	2	0	0	4	5	1
Harry Hewitt	.220	59	13	2	0	0	3	3	10
Chuck Lelas*	.272	235	64	4	3	12	59	50	70
Steve Mezich	.206	170	35	7	3	2	26	15	44
Walt Peto	.243	272	66	3	1	0	13	43	16
John Theisen	.173	81	14	3	0	0	3	9	28
Rusty Torres	.231	13	3	0	0	0	0	10	3
Gary Vanaman	.187	123	23	1	2	1	11	23	43
Gary Washington	.284	261	74	10	2	6	56	42	38
Gerry Wickman	.320	25	8	0	1	0	1	5	7
Dave Wolfe	.222	81	18	1	2	1	6	12	26

set club homer record; hit two grand slams.

PITCHING	W-L	ERA	IP	H	BB	SO
Carl Black	6-2	3.39	69	60	29	51
Mike Clark	2-3	3.29	41	32	25	32
Ron Cook	0-0	9.00	2	4	2	0
Craig Fellows	1-4	9.41	22	25	26	12
Bill Fisher	1-4	3.41	37	33	43	20
Bill Goble	6-6	4.15	65	68	4	52
Larry Gowell	3-2	3.21	56	53	37	43
Joe Hindelang	4-5	4.38	78	77	39	38
Ken Johnson	6-2	1.59	79	59	18	75
Steve Mezich	0-0	0.00	2	1	1	1
Denis Murray	0-0	1.29	14	11	3	8
Miguel Rua	0-0	0.00	2	1	2	2
Allan Simmons	2-4	4.29	42	44	20	34
Gary Timberlake	4-2	4.63	70	57	43	68
Gerry Wickman	5-4	3.82	73	71	28	66

1968

O-Yanks: NY-P League
Manager Jerry Walker: Won 43 Lost 34

HITTING	AVG.	AB	H	2B	3B	HR	RBI	BB	SO
Bruce Bateman	.214	56	12	1	0	0	4	8	11
Dan Bohannon	.276	163	45	8	2	2	17	16	14
Andy Bottin	.150	127	19	4	1	3	20	17	36
Doug D'Addario	.368	19	7	1	1	1	4	1	3
Jim Diedel	.322	121	39	3	2	0	12	14	28
Pat Denning	.259	81	21	5	0	1	15	3	9
Ray DeRiggi	.286	28	8	1	1	1	11	2	1
George Ferguson	.281	121	34	6	0	3	12	13	17
Bob Hefflinger	.211	194	41	4	0	1	15	10	33
Dave Kent	.282	188	53	11	3	3	31	21	43
Rich Koslick	.226	133	30	5	0	1	6	12	49
Jeff Mason	.265	162	43	4	2	1	13	18	33
Bob McDaniel	.286	224	64	10	3	1	28	39	47
Steve Mezich	.256	78	20	2	0	0	10	12	19
Tom O'Connor	.429	42	18	2	2	1	11	9	4
Walt Peto	.252	214	45	7	3	1	21	43	25
Evelio Ramos	.273	200	57	16	2	1	19	18	38
P. Rannenberger	.245	106	26	6	2	3	10	26	25

PITCHING	W-L	ERA	IP	H	BB	SO
Bruce Baudier	0-0	1.80	10	10	8	7
Wayne Crowder	0-0	27.00	3	5	11	5
Ray DeRiggi	6-4	2.74	69	65	17	57
Joel Dorsey	1-1	4.68	81	70	18	25
Bob Elliott	6-4	3.00	81	70	44	66
Stan Evenhaus	5-4	3.15	80	77	25	52
Craig Fellows	1-2	4.91	33	40	18	28
Les Gibbens	4-1	3.72	29	36	10	19
Larry Gowell	0-5	4.50	60	61	28	65
Doug Hansen	8-3	1.67	88	66	19	86
Ken Lange	7-2	0.82	44	27	15	44
Gerry Morse	0-2	6.43	18	12	9	16
Bill Olsen	2-2	2.32	31	25	3	35
Dan Schirrippa	0-0	4.85	13	13	13	7
Larry Womack	3-4	3.21	70	64	26	53

1969

O-YANKS: NY-P LEAGUE
MANAGER GEORGE CASE: WON 51 LOST 26

HITTING	AVG.	AB	H	2B	3B	HR	RBI	BB	SO
Paul Barretta	.296	277	82	16	4	0	30	29	14
Bruce Bateman	.158	19	3	0	1	0	1	5	4
Julius Bender	.301	143	43	9	1	1	21	25	19
Dan Bohannon	.254	193	49	6	0	1	23	21	16
Pat Brown	.333	15	5	5	0	0	2	2	2
Doug D'Addario	.225	129	29	3	1	2	14	34	41
Jim Diedel	.320	225	72	11	4	4	45	34	43
Billy Gardner	.293	273	80	9	3	2	38	35	24
Rich Koslick	.216	37	8	0	0	0	5	5	8
Richie Kriz	.254	181	46	6	2	1	22	23	29
Chuck Lelas	.237	215	51	9	2	4	33	37	48
Jeff Mason	.325	160	52	8	2	1	20	24	14
Papo Mora	.217	60	13	4	0	0	12	4	18
Don Palmer	.262	42	11	11	0	1	9	3	8
Walt Peto	.000	1	0	0	0	0	0	1	0
Jeff Turner	.190	79	15	4	1	0	11	6	6
Ed Waters	.291	292	85	12	4	3	36	42	22
13 pitchers hit	.203								

PITCHING	W-L	ERA	IP	H	BB	SO
Win Chadwick	5-1	2.49	65	59	46	58
Brian Cogan	5-1	2.94	49	40	16	34
Ron Collier	3-3	5.37	52	55	31	40
Wayne Crowder	6-3	4.35	62	67	23	46
Mike Fowler	5-3	2.75	72	65	12	52
Paul Fricchione	1-2	3.50	18	22	6	16
G. Manderbach	3-1	2.08	39	32	23	41
Steve McMullen	3-1	5.28	29	46	9	19
Mike Mullen	5-3	4.78	64	75	22	67
Bill Olsen	8-0	1.23	73	50	11	87
Dick Pogonelski	1-1	4.24	17	18	7	17
Dave Reid	0-3	31.50	4	9	14	4
Dante Schirrippa	6-4	2.60	97	91	28	66

1970

O-Yanks: NY-P League
Manager George Case: Won 41 Lost 28 Tied 1

HITTING	AVG.	AB	H	2B	3B	HR	RBI	BB	SO
John Bakis	.260	246	64	13	4	4	38	29	73
George Beattie	.179	56	10	2	0	0	3	3	16
Irv Homs	.313	150	47	3	2	1	26	9	18
Ricky Kriz	.286	91	26	3	0	0	13	13	20
Tom Matheson	.190	42	8	2	0	0	6	5	9
Papo Mora	.290	91	27	4	2	3	19	5	21
Angel Muniz	.389	157	61	6	5	0	31	8	8
Bob Nielsen	.229	140	32	3	1	0	19	5	13
Tom O'Connor	.277	253	70	6	9	7	50	37	51
Marion Prince	.204	201	41	7	1	1	23	48	37
Mike Punko	.296	125	37	4	2	3	17	33	33
Beau Robinson	.319	119	38	6	2	5	18	16	18
John Shaw	.291	127	37	2	4	0	9	16	10
Ed Waters	.259	278	72	8	2	0	29	27	30
13 pitchers hit	.156								

PITCHING	W-L	ERA	IP	H	BB	SO
Clark Babbit	4-1	3.43	42	47	15	20
Chris Barker	2-4	4.50	44	49	27	27
Tom Couples	4-1	4.04	49	52	18	34
Dan Dalonzo	4-2	3.21	56	54	29	50
Tom Hannibal	3-1	4.03	38	30	34	38
Dave Hazelip	5-2	3.00	57	60	21	49
Robin Hippi	4-4	3.74	65	53	38	74
Jerry Johnson	2-5	4.17	69	69	21	62
George Medich	3-1	1.45	31	16	14	32
Dave Pagan	4-3	2.95	58	54	11	56
Steve Snyder	2-3	6.60	30	39	18	26
Al Tetrault	3-1	3.91	23	25	6	16
Terry Vargason	1-0	6.23	19	16	6	15

Saves: Johnson 3; Snyder 3; Babbitt, Barker and Couples one each.

1971

O-Yanks: NY-P League

Manager George Case: Won 45 Lost 23 Tied 1

HITTING	AVG.	AB	H	2B	3B	HR	RBI	BB	SO
Roger Adams	.302	268	81	10	2	0	26	51	54
Rich Bianchi	.250	60	15	4	1	2	11	12	22
Andy Bottin	.190	142	27	2	3	3	23	32	62
Val Falcone	.188	117	22	3	1	1	12	26	32
Joel Hall	.254	15	15	2	1	2	10	12	16
Irv Homs	.250	24	6	0	1	0	4	2	7
Phil Honeycutt	.230	204	47	4	1	1	30	34	43
Ed Jayjack	.182	33	6	1	0	0	5	5	12
Gene Moser	.188	197	37	4	2	4	19	34	27
Tom O'Connor	.286	199	57	9	1	7	39	30	35
Randy Robbins	.273	161	44	2	2	1	27	19	14
Carlos Rodriguez	.185	65	12	0	0	0	6	8	18
Bob Schiffner	.252	131	33	3	2	2	21	26	17
Billy Stearns	.220	132	29	4	2	0	13	18	13
Phil Still	.239	234	56	8	6	6	32	48	69

12 pitchers hit .261

PITCHING	W-L	ERA	IP	H	BB	SO
Jerry Anderson	0-0	0.00	.3	0	3	0
Rob Arnold	5-3	2.59	94	78	33	66
Clark Babbitt	6-1	1.25	36	36	11	23
Joe Blake	5-4	3.19	96	91	25	82
Bruce Campbell	3-0	3.14	43	41	14	24
Don DeMola	4-4	2.91	68	59	36	60
Chuck Hopkins	3-1	3.52	23	24	7	12
Steve Janosik	2-0	4.33	27	29	22	14
Bill Kostrba	1-2	7.29	21	25	16	17
Dave Lawson	7-4	2.84	92	79	40	97
Bert Raschke	6-3	4.74	76	85	28	67
Billy Sheets	3-1	1.96	23	14	14	31

Saves: Babbitt 5; Sheets 3; Blake, Campbell, Hopkins one each.
Raschke pitched seven inning no hit-no run game August 11, winning 5-0 over Newark.

1972

O-YANKS: NY-P LEAGUE
MANAGER GEORGE CASE: WON 45 LOST 25

HITTING	AVG.	AB	H	2B	3B	HR	RBI	BB	SO
Roger Adams	.288	153	44	10	1	0	77	27	21
Joe Barkauskas	.256	30	10	0	1	1	4	5	9
Jim Cooper	.279	140	39	5	0	1	23	32	24
Phil Honeycutt	.317	145	46	6	3	1	27	27	20
Daryl Jones	.300	203	61	12	11	4	55	13	13
Larry Murray*	.244	234	57	10	3	5	42	66	73
Gary Owens	.302	149	45	5	2	0	18	22	21
Terry Quinn	.252	107	27	3	1	0	7	14	25
Scott Rahl	.228	114	26	4	2	2	15	10	29
Ron Spann	.214	140	30	3	3	3	14	30	60
Brian Stone	.134	82	11	2	1	1	5	13	40
Larry Walker	.259	116	30	5	2	2	17	11	20
Tim Waner	.231	147	34	3	2	2	15	18	22
Terry Whitfield	.273	256	70	6	11	7	47	57	65
John Yeglinski	.429	7	3	0	0	1	3	0	0
12 pitchers hit	.163								

Stole club record 59 bases

PITCHING	W-L	ERA	IP	H	BB	SO
Bob Artemenko	7-4	1.52	95	63	17	75
Kevin Carr	5-2	3.14	63	66	26	35
Arnie Costell	1-1	4.50	10	3	27	17
Caleb Glover	8-5	4.04	89	81	43	96
Jeff Hall	2-4	5.35	37	40	20	36
Bob Kammeyer	6-3	2.25	76	74	27	58
Bill Kostrba	2-3	4.15	39	24	24	34
Scott Larson	9-0	2.64	75	65	16	51
Tippy Martinez	1-0	2.00	9	3	10	9
Bob Niekamp	4-1	3.24	50	46	26	45
Frank Souchock	0-0	6.23	13	19	2	13
Dick Wallberg	0-2	5.63	16	19	10	7

Saves: Artemenko 2; Carr, Hall, Martinez, Niekamp, Wallberg one each.

1973

O-YANKS: NY-P LEAGUE

MANAGER HANK MAJESKI: WON 44 LOST 26

HITTING	AVG.	AB	H	2B	3B	HR	RBI	BB	SO
Del Alston	.321	246	79	13	3	4	34	40	34
Randy Braxton	.254	209	53	6	4	0	21	17	47
Bob Bruno	.083	12	1	1	0	0	0	1	3
Steve Colson	.347	274	95	9	5	3	41	31	29
Kerry Dineen	.352	250	88	11	10	1	46	31	21
Tim Grice	.283	230	65	8	1	3	42	27	24
Mickey Klutts	.319	135	43	7	5	2	22	12	15
Paul Lancaster	.241	29	7	1	0	1	4	2	10
Jon Lunde	.147	34	5	3	0	0	4	5	15
Ray Ventura	.293	229	67	8	1	1	44	16	21
Bob Wasilak	.235	34	8	2	1	0	5	6	7
Craig White	.303	244	74	17	7	3	41	22	42
Bob Wilson	.246	281	69	10	4	4	43	36	63
11 pitchers hit	.181.								

Pitcher Bob Majczan hit .313 with three home runs.

PITCHING	W-L	ERA	IP	H	BB	SO
Don Anderson	0-0	14.40	5	7	5	8
Rich Anderson	3-5	4.60	45	45	23	56
Gary Blevens	4-2	3.43	63	69	28	39
Arnie Costell	1-4	4.85	39	23	42	41
Caleb Glover	5-3	3.58	83	86	27	61
Bob Majczan	9-4	2.58	115	95	38	108
Neal Mersch*	11-0	1.18	114	89	23	104
Jim Otto	0-0	13.50	2	3	3	2
Bob Polinsky	8-3	2.55	99	102	34	99
Tony Ponticelli	0-2	7.00	9	14	9	2
Dick Smith	3-3	2.88	50	39	25	64

Saves: Arnie Costell, Dick Smith two each; Rich Anderson one.
*club record for victories

1974

O-YANKS: NY-P LEAGUE
MANAGER MIKE FERRARO: WON 53 LOST 16

HITTING	AVG.	AB	H	2B	3B	HR	RBI	BB	SO
Dave Bergman	.348	201	70	6	7	10	48	62	29
Randy Braxton	.252	115	29	2	1	0	10	14	11
Bruce Carter	.245	253	62	7	6	2	30	58	77
Sheldon Gill	.256	125	32	5	0	0	16	13	9
Mike Heath	.282	234	66	6	3	3	34	28	34
Steve Lindsey	.278	18	5	0	0	0	3	3	1
Kevin McNichol	.242	157	38	7	1	1	18	43	42
Rich Meltz	.268	205	55	9	4	8	41	28	65
Don Moore	.195	123	24	3	0	1	13	13	12
Pat Peterson	.330	267	88	16	4	2	53	30	33
Pete Schmidt	.239	113	27	4	0	0	13	34	15
Marv Thompson	.304	217	66	10	4	1	38	65	27
Dennis Werth	.336	238	80	23	6	4	61	38	47

PITCHING	W-L	ERA	IP	H	BB	SO
Fred Anyzeski	10-1	1.61	106	92	37	78
Jim Bierman	3-2	3.42	50	35	22	48
Scott Delgatti	9-1	2.44	85	75	43	70
Greg Diehl	8-2	1.76	87	60	15	73
Rick Fleshman	8-5	3.50	90	74	29	74
Bob Shoff	5-2	4.25	55	59	41	39
Dick Smith	2-0	2.52	25	18	24	18
Lou Turco	3-1	3.00	54	49	16	30
Dave Wright	3-4	3.92	39	33	20	36

Saves: Dave Wright five, Jim Bierman, Lou Turco four each.
Greg Diehl pitched a perfect game July 7 as Oneonta beat Newark, 9-0. He faced only 27 batters.

1975

O-Yanks: NY-P League
Manager Mike Ferraro: Won 35 Lost 34

HITTING	AVG.	AB	H	2B	3B	HR	RBI	BB	SO
Jose Alvarez	.155	187	29	3	2	11	17	56	30
Jim Bendick	.250	132	33	3	2	3	31	17	11
Terry Bevington	.264	193	51	11	1	2	23	23	25
Nate Chapman	.270	237	64	2	6	1	23	24	29
Orlando Cruz	.224	174	39	4	0	1	16	9	34
Juan Espino	.229	157	36	5	5	2	23	26	61
Mike Fischlin	.230	135	31	4	3	0	6	15	26
Damaso Garcia	.268	157	42	4	2	0	17	20	37
Joe Kwasny	.500	2	1	0	0	0	1	1	1
Benny Lloyd	.214	182	39	4	1	0	13	20	56
Beban Luis	.239	159	38	3	5	2	16	10	36
Jim McDonald	.284	261	74	11	3	2	37	27	30
Domingo Ramos	.235	166	39	4	1	0	21	34	30
Bob Smith	.277	166	46	4	1	1	22	27	21
Willie Upshaw	.088	91	8	1	0	0	4	15	19

PITCHING	W-L	ERA	IP	H	BB	SO
Jose Alcantara	6-3	2.96	73	79	23	57
Jim Beattie	2-0	1.88	24	15	7	22
Marty Caffrey	3-3	1.45	62	60	21	40
Steve Card	0-1	18.00	3	4	8	2
Enr. Francisco	0-0	4.76	17	18	11	5
Jerry Houston	1-2	6.84	25	23	24	22
Joe Kwasny	4-6	2.90	87	90	26	41
Leonce Laurent	3-5	6.65	46	50	40	21
Sabah Mendez	0-0	1.13	16	11	1	6
Randy Niemann	3-3	2.45	55	53	20	23
Gil Patterson	8-4	1.95	106	79	33	97
Rafael Santana	0-2	4.09	22	20	15	6
Joe Trotter	1-3	4.13	24	24	14	27
Dave Wright	4-2	2.57	35	27	16	31

Saves: Caffrey 4; Wright 2; Houston, Trotter one each

1976

O-YANKS: NY-P LEAGUE
MANAGER ED NAPOLEON: WON 24 LOST 46

HITTING	AVG.	AB	H	2B	3B	HR	RBI	BB	SO
Rodrigo Bellony	.278	126	35	5	2	0	13	39	24
Terry Bevington	.000	3	0	0	0	0	0	0	1
John Crawford	.232	181	42	4	1	2	25	41	63
F. Dorville	.152	164	25	3	2	2	15	13	73
Pete Eshelman	.287	167	48	6	2	4	30	28	16
Bernardo Estevez	.253	198	50	3	1	0	11	47	22
Mike Fischlin	.255	55	14	3	0	0	5	8	6
Don Hogestyn	.305	131	40	9	3	2	23	29	27
Benny Lloyd	.210	224	47	5	4	2	25	32	48
Benny Perez	.325	80	26	4	0	0	8	8	6
Mark Plantery	.178	90	16	1	0	0	4	13	26
Jesus Sandoval	.193	83	16	2	1	0	7	17	35
Garry Smith*	.391	169	66	13	6	4	34	10	18
Pat Tabler	.231	238	55	3	0	1	20	27	35
Mark Thiel	.263	152	40	6	0	4	27	42	9
Luis Thomas	.133	30	4	0	1	0	4	2	11
Darnell Walters	.320	75	24	2	3	2	10	12	19
Ted Wilborn	.188	85	16	3	0	0	4	7	26

league batting champion

PITCHING	W-L	ERA	IP	H	BB	SO
Fred Atkins	0-0	3.60	5	0	8	4
Raf. Carmarena	1-0	4.15	26	28	16	14
Scott Delgatti	3-5	3.73	70	65	43	56
Pete Eshelman	1-2	8.10	20	23	23	14
Don Fisk	4-6	3.56	81	79	61	62
Gerry Gaube	2-5	3.54	28	26	22	23
Leonce Laurent	0-2	8.10	10	9	11	3
Dave Lombardi	1-1	5.54	13	12	12	9
Neil Palmer	0-1	5.40	10	12	15	9
Calvin Rigger	5-4	3.87	79	73	48	57
Julio Robles	2-7	4.30	90	105	49	43
Rafael Santana	3-5	4.41	51	58	21	22
Mark Softy	2-7	4.50	82	86	38	59
Ron Williamson	0-1	13.50	8	9	15	6

Saves: Gaube 3; Delgatti, Eshelman, Lombardi, Santana one each.

1977

O-YANKS: NY-P LEAGUE
MANAGER ART MAZMANIAN: WON 47 LOST 23

HITTING	AVG.	AB	H	2B	3B	HR	RBI	BB	SO
Ken Baker	.311	235	73	12	3	3	35	32	19
Rodrigo Bellony	.267	86	23	3	1	2	10	12	4
Tom Bonfield	.256	133	34	5	2	0	24	18	18
Mark Burlingame	.143	21	3	0	1	0	11	4	5
Rex Farrior	.256	82	21	1	0	0	9	14	17
Dwayne Grey	.324	182	59	5	1	0	26	14	12
Joe Guarasco	.331	133	44	5	1	0	23	19	11
Ron Hess	.263	144	30	3	0	0	10	32	14
Gene Laguna	.357	28	10	2	1	1	7	12	9
Benny Lloyd	.247	198	49	12	7	3	33	29	46
Pedro Labaton	.071	14	1	1	0	0	0	0	6
Willie McGee	.236	225	53	4	3	2	22	13	65
Ed Mickelson	.214	28	6	1	1	0	4	5	7
Dan Moroff	.256	78	20	2	0	0	7	22	19
Kevin Murphy	.235	85	20	2	1	1	15	25	13
Luis Ortiz	.195	41	8	2	0	0	3	5	17
Rafael Santana	.261	157	41	5	0	0	23	19	19
Dan Schmitz	.282	216	61	6	5	1	25	67	19
Aurin Soto	.268	56	15	1	0	0	7	12	10

PITCHING	W-L	ERA	IP	H	BB	SO
Scott Asbaugh	0-0	4.50	10	11	0	5
Byron Ballard	6-2	2.97	88	77	40	47
Bob Fishback	0-1	1.38	13	5	3	6
Leonce Laurent	0-1	2.77	13	10	18	8
Mike McLeod	9-2	3.09	96	73	35	54
Alan Nesbitt	1-2	3.00	15	19	6	13
Stan Saleski	4-1	1.88	26	12	26	12
Paul Semall	8-4	2.46	106	79	49	100
Paul Steets	4-1	2.03	31	16	14	25
Chris Welch	8-5	2.49	112	77	54	125
Jamie Werly	7-3	2.80	74	47	45	91
Jim Wilhelm	0-1	2.25	4	7	1	1

Saves: Steets four; Asbauch, and Laurent one each.

1978

O-YANKS: NY-P LEAGUE
MANAGER ART MAZMANIAN: WON 51 LOST 19

HITTING	AVG.	AB	H	2B	3B	HR	RBI	BB	SO
Brian Dayett	.309	256	79	20	4	11	63	43	61
Roberto Dennis	.333	21	7	1	0	0	1	2	3
Rex Farrior	.216	148	32	6	1	0	13	42	21
John Franks	.500	2	1	0	0	1	2	0	0
Dave Garcia	.234	137	32	3	3	0	18	23	23
Alvin Hall	.222	18	4	1	0	0	0	3	4
Rex Hudler	.281	221	62	5	5	0	24	21	29
Peter Khoury	.274	226	62	15	4	4	36	25	23
Victor Mata	.228	57	13	0	0	3	3	3	11
Dan Moroff	.262	122	32	5	2	2	21	22	35
Har. Nakano	.000	9	0	0	0	0	0	4	5
Dan Plante	.293	181	53	4	3	3	31	25	32
Claude Sammons	.328	186	61	12	6	1	39	73	37
Julio Santana	.125	16	2	0	0	0	1	4	3
Dan Shanahan	.357	14	5	1	1	1	3	2	3
Aurin Soto	.212	85	18	0	2	3	17	21	15
Fugio Tamura	.000	11	0	0	0	0	3	6	2
Rafal Villaman	.240	129	31	4	1	1	14	11	26
Ted Wilborn	.309	220	68	5	2	5	29	45	30
Mike Wilhite	.211	19	4	0	0	1	3	0	6
Matt Winters	.261	203	53	7	11	2	36	36	36

PITCHING	W-L	ERA	IP	H	BB	SO
Rich Carlucci	6-1	2.90	59	52	19	44
Don Cooper	1-2	3.60	20	18	10	22
Tom Filer	2-3	1.67	43	30	14	34
Bob Fishback	4-2	3.89	44	50	15	26
John Franks	8-1	2.82	83	64	54	59
Henry Herrera	0-0	3.00	3	3	7	5
Dan Ledduke	6-0	3.16	75	42	27	47
Andy McGaffigan	0-1	4.50	12	14	9	13
Mark Moore	4-2	1.76	46	37	25	42
Alan Nebitt	2-1	4.38	37	35	22	15
Matt Olli	2-0	5.14	28	36	19	23
Bian Ryder	5-3	3.55	66	43	63	71
Karl Steffen	6-2	2.51	68	46	24	85
Jeff Taylor	6-2	2.19	70	61	31	53

1979

O-YANKS: NY-P LEAGUE
MANAGER ART MAZMANIAN: WON 42 LOST 26

HITTING	AVG.	AB	H	2B	3B	HR	RBI	BB	SO
Hector Angulo	.000	9	0	0	0	0	0	0	5
Dave Buffamoyer	.226	164	37	8	2	1	22	24	27
Brian Butterfield	.218	179	39	1	1	0	13	24	27
Todd Demeter	.253	198	50	3	3	8	38	52	67
Roberto Dennis	.273	99	27	1	2	0	11	5	14
M.Echstenkemper	.258	186	38	15	2	8	39	30	33
Jose Encarnecion	.000	1	0	0	0	0	0	1	1
Dave Garcia	.292	65	19	4	0	0	7	17	8
Dan Girata	.177	147	26	6	1	2	19	23	27
Victor Mata	.268	224	60	6	1	2	23	23	31
Don Mattingly	.349	166	58	10	2	3	31	30	6
Adolfo Mercedes	.152	46	7	0	1	0	6	3	12
Vidal Payano	.118	17	2	0	0	0	2	6	7
E. Rodriguez	.208	24	5	0	0	0	3	7	10
Rich Santarone	.159	44	7	1	0	0	3	5	12
Keith Smith	.244	119	29	0	0	0	9	33	30
Glenn Swires	.283	247	70	14	6	6	41	28	28
Matt Winters	.282	188	53	6	2	10	38	56	42

PITCHING	W-L	ERA	IP	H	BB	SO
Ed Andersen	4-3	2.22	65	62	23	39
A. Ervey	3-2	2.33	54	46	24	50
John Franks	5-2	6.21	58	67	44	37
Paul Gnacinski	1-1	2.81	16	5	14	20
Kevin Irott	0-0	4.24	29	24	30	21
Curt Kaufman	4-1	0.90	30	10	16	50
John Nurthen	1-2	3.23	39	34	23	29
John Seneca	3-3	4.14	50	43	22	36
Karl Steffan	5-7	4.85	89	100	46	80
Freddie Tolliver	10-2	2.10	77	46	66	71
Stefan Wever	6-2	1.77	66	43	36	70

Saves: Kaufman 9; Ervey 3; Andersen, Nurthen 2; Pete Filson, Gnacinski, Irott one each. Filson and Greg Copeland pitched less than an inning and were not involved in a decision.

1980

O-YANKS: NY-P LEAGUE
MANAGER ART MAZMANIAN: WON 49 LOST 25

HITTING	AVG.	AB	H	2B	3B	HR	RBI	BB	SO
Dave Bailey	.264	246	65	9	2	1	32	35	34
Dave Banes	.219	137	30	7	2	2	17	12	38
Scott Benedict	.107	28	3	0	0	0	2	7	7
Brad Bennett	.255	188	48	8	2	1	23	41	30
Rick Despaux	.274	157	43	6	1	5	18	17	37
Randy Filkins	.227	181	41	3	3	7	34	45	47
Jim Gross	.148	61	9	0	2	0	6	14	7
Bob Helsom	.263	171	45	8	2	3	29	37	37
Doug Latrenta	.294	218	64	9	4	2	25	52	27
Dave Littlefield	.176	17	3	0	0	1	2	2	4
Randy McDaniel	.231	173	40	4	0	0	12	25	27
Kevin O'Brien	.198	101	20	3	0	1	13	25	15
Jeff Reynolds	.283	265	75	14	3	7	56	32	62
Kevin Shannon	.230	152	35	5	0	0	26	56	23
Keith Smith	.244	193	47	2	0	0	11	25	46

PITCHING	W-L	ERA	IP	H	BB	SO
Sheldon Andrews	6-3	3.33	81	69	38	89
Jim Campbell	1-2	4.33	27	20	19	21
Mark Cartwright	1-3	3.50	54	43	29	38
Clay Christiansen	4-3	2.54	92	89	24	62
George DeMaria	0-2	5.54	13	12	11	9
Al Ervey	5-0	3.00	42	36	14	25
Herb Fauland	4-2	2.86	44	34	19	46
Luis Figueroa	0-0	3.00	3	4	1	1
Mike Foster	3-0	2.12	51	38	19	41
Larry Kuhn	5-1	1.50	36	26	21	29
Marty Mason	1-0	1.80	5	4	2	7
Mark Mendez	9-3	2.50	101	85	50	72
Ed Olwine	2-1	1.00	9	8	6	8
Kelly Scott	4-4	2.70	40	30	12	34
Joe Stefani	0-1	2.86	44	40	21	36

Saves: Fauland 9; Kuhn 3; Olwine 2; Campbell, Mason, Stefani one each.

1981

O-YANKS: NY-P LEAGUE

MANAGER ART MAZMANIAN: WON 48 LOST 25

HITTING	AVG.	AB	H	2B	3B	HR	RBI	BB	SO
Jesus Alcala	.114	35	4	0	0	0	1	3	7
Pat Bone	.246	65	11	5	0	2	6	7	32
Scott Bradley	.308	276	85	17	4	4	54	22	15
Jim D'Aloia	.250	152	38	7	0	2	25	18	12
Ed Darling	.228	79	18	3	0	0	9	14	24
Roberto Dennis	.322	202	65	12	1	3	29	7	23
Rick Despaux	.255	98	25	5	3	3	16	19	10
John Hughes	.309	178	55	11	1	8	38	40	33
Greg Jewett	.278	18	5	1	0	0	4	1	9
Gary Kempton	.207	111	23	1	1	4	10	13	33
Derwin McNealy	.273	187	51	6	3	5	27	27	43
Bruce Morrison	.143	28	4	0	0	0	1	3	8
Dan O'Regan	.296	186	55	16	7	4	32	32	50
Mike Pagliarulo	.216	245	53	9	4	2	28	38	47
Mike Reddish	.167	6	1	0	0	0	1	1	3
Steve Renfroe	.251	167	42	9	3	4	26	12	39
Edwin Rodriguez	.308	146	45	5	3	0	19	21	22
Steve Scafa	.229	131	30	4	3	0	12	53	32
Keith Smith	.200	50	10	1	0	0	3	14	11

PITCHING	W-L	ERA	IP	H	BB	SO
Bob Brooks	5-3	2.37	56	53	14	15
George DeMaria	0-0	9.00	11	18	11	7
Rick Despaux	0-0	14.40	5	4	10	5
Don DeWitt	2-3	4.40	43	40	22	18
C. Hernandez	4-2	4.50	50	46	56	53
Henry Herrara	0-0	0.00	2	2	3	2
Mike Livesey	0-0	15.75	3	7	5	4
Larry Mikesell	6-2	3.68	71	68	37	53
Dave Niemic	0-0	3.75	12	13	5	6
Kevin Quirk	7-2	2.57	42	30	24	31
Mark Shiflett	1-4	4.15	52	45	35	55
Dave Szmczak	6-2	2.76	87	73	40	44
Bob Tewksbury	7-3	3.40	89	85	37	62
Gary Wex	5-1	2.39	49	36	24	41
Stan Williams Jr.	5-3	3.56	48	43	20	37

Saves: Szmczak 2; DeWitt, Hernandez, Mikesell, Shiflett one each.

1982

O-Yanks: NY-P League
Manager Ken Berry: Won 43 Lost 33

HITTING	AVG.	AB	H	2B	3B	HR	RBI	BB	SO
Pete Adams	.282	103	29	4	1	2	17	9	28
Jsus Alcala	.297	229	68	9	5	1	28	27	37
Orestes Destrade	.232	194	45	12	1	4	30	38	56
John Elway	.318	151	48	6	2	4	25	28	25
Mike Fennell	.246	203	50	7	4	6	33	53	56
Jim Ferguson	.305	118	36	9	3	2	17	14	21
Dan Gasparino	.212	66	14	3	1	1	5	11	17
Mike Gatlin	.246	61	9	2	0	0	7	6	10
Don Giordano	.254	59	15	3	0	1	8	10	14
Brent Gjesdal	.269	201	54	7	3	2	30	38	50
Johnny Hawkins	.248	137	34	3	0	2	21	18	28
Howard Maynor	.259	27	7	3	0	1	7	3	12
Pedro Medina	.266	214	57	6	1	1	32	10	43
Dan O'Regan	.149	114	17	2	1	2	10	23	38
Dan Pasqua	.294	17	5	1	0	2	4	2	3
Jim Riggs	.309	272	84	16	2	6	44	35	32
Bill Ruffner	.193	171	33	4	2	3	22	19	53
Tony Russell	.281	121	34	5	2	2	15	12	22
Rob Woodcock	.173	52	9	0	0	0	6	12	10
Ron Wright	.294	17	5	1	0	0	2	2	6

PITCHING	W-L	ERA	IP	H	BB	SO
Boyce Bailey	0-1	16.88	2	5	3	4
Kirk Bailey	3-0	3.92	39	34	19	42
Tim Birtsas	1-1	3.86	16	19	17	24
Pat Bone	0-2	9.74	20	28	20	18
John Bryant	0-1	11.12	5	7	9	4
Tim Byron	3-5	4.84	57	53	34	37
Steve Compagno	0-0	7.71	2	2	2	4
Jim Corsi	0-0	10.80	3	5	2	6
Jim Deshaies	6-5	3.32	108	93	40	137
Paul Doty	7-3	2.68	107	97	42	92
Trent Ferrin	5-5	3.86	74	73	20	48
Randy Graham	6-0	3.06	35	33	15	74
Ed Lindsey	0-0	27.00	1	1	1	2
Stacy Morgan	2-5	5.56	43	49	18	33
Dick Seidel	1-1	5.14	7	7	4	11
Chuck Tomaselli	7-4	2.88	109	98	40	111
Randy White	2-0	2.59	31	27	14	34

1983

O-Yanks: NY-P League
Manager Bill Livesey: Won 32 Lost 44

HITTING	AVG.	AB	H	2B	3B	HR	RBI	BB	SO
Doug Carpenter	.250	8	2	1	0	1	3	8	3
Mark Chestna	.000	15	0	0	0	0	0	2	9
H. Cunningham	.192	78	15	1	0	1	8	10	31
Bill Englehart	.258	163	42	9	1	4	19	32	37
Dave Frederick	.217	143	31	3	1	6	17	17	51
Greg Funk	.265	34	9	3	0	0	7	9	4
Luis Jiminez	.000	3	0	0	0	0	0	0	2
Stan Johnson	.238	21	5	0	1	0	1	3	7
Alan Jones	.234	239	56	11	2	4	32	32	41
Roberto Kelly	.216	167	36	1	2	2	17	12	20
Richard Lewallen	.282	259	73	13	2	2	37	22	38
John Lopez	.000	2	0	0	0	0	0	0	2
Mitch Lyden	.148	128	19	1	0	0	7	12	36
Freddy Machuca	.209	43	9	3	1	0	5	7	9
Rich Mattocks	.271	258	70	7	3	2	26	42	46
Rich Molnar	.208	24	5	0	0	1	1	4	5
Steve O'Donnell	.385	13	5	0	0	0	0	2	1
Steve Peruso	.269	104	28	3	1	5	22	11	22
Marcelino Pitti	.150	40	6	0	1	0	2	1	14
Josa Rivera	.254	185	47	8	1	8	26	14	54
Bill Ruffner	.189	106	20	2	0	2	9	14	51
Mike Simmons	.226	84	19	1	0	0	8	12	17
Jeff Smith	.257	74	19	2	0	1	11	14	33
Van Starnes	.194	36	7	2	0	0	6	7	13
Scott Todd	.156	32	5	0	1	0	4	5	13
Spud Washington	.156	32	5	0	0	0	1	2	10
Jeff Wiley	.250	4	1	0	0	0	0	0	1
Brad Winkler	.252	155	39	9	2	2	16	21	40

PITCHING	W-L	ERA	IP	H	BB	SO
Tim Byron	1-2	5.85	31	40	17	24
Jim Corsi	3-6	4.25	59	76	21	47
Fernando Davis	2-0	5.57	21	22	9	11
Bob Devlin	2-2	2.38	41	28	18	40
Steve Fingerlow	0-0	6.10	38	49	17	45
Joe Fletcher	2-2	5.57	32	32	26	8
Steve Frey	4-6	2.74	72	47	35	86
Bill Fulton	4-7	3.74	84	73	35	77
Terry Gammage	0-0	4.05	6	7	8	1
Joel Hall	0-1	8.22	7	8	14	5
John Hudson	0-0	27.00	2	8	3	0

1983 Continued...

PITCHING	W-L	ERA	IP	H	BB	SO
Daryl Humphrey	0-2	7.65	20	29	13	11
Larry Lewis	1-0	5.40	15	16	12	13
Stacy Morgan	3-0	3.57	22	19	6	22
Dave Niemic	1-0	4.50	2	0	5	1
Ken Rebiejo	4-4	3.59	67	76	31	67
Bill Ruffner	0-0	13.50	1	0	4	1
Tony Sarno	4-8	5.71	69	66	35	61
Mike Simmons	0-0	9.00	1	2	0	0
Dave Smalley	0-1	6.23	8	8	5	10
Clayton Stidham	1-2	7.27	17	24	11	13
Chas. Westgard	0-1	12.00	3	4	1	0
Tim Williams	0-0	2.00	4	3	1	2
Mike York	0-0	8.18	11	19	8	3

Bill Fulton pitched no-hit, no-run game, 9 innings, against Geneva, July 25th. Geneva pitcher also had a no-hitter going into the ninth. Final score: Oneonta 1 Geneva 0.

Saves: Frey 9; Devlin, Morgan, Smalley, Williams one each.

1984

O-YANKS: NY-P LEAGUE
MANAGER BILL LIVESEY: WON 29 LOST 45

HITTING	AVG.	AB	H	2B	3B	HR	RBI
Kevin Blake	.080	25	2	0	0	0	0
Ike Bradley	.200	85	17	3	0	1	13
Scott Carter	.241	141	34	0	1	3	15
Gary Cathcart	.238	286	68	9	1	3	26
Alex Christy	.195	41	8	1	1	1	6
H. Cunningham	.234	47	11	0	0	0	6
Keith Foley	.211	57	12	1	0	1	4
Randy Foyt	.257	218	56	5	5	3	21
Jeff Franks	.243	173	42	7	0	4	27
Jeff King	.233	129	30	6	0	2	13
Phil Lane	.291	244	71	19	1	8	43
Chris Loschasvo	.199	151	30	1	0	0	15
Darren Mandel	.239	222	53	5	0	13*	40
Chris Maynard	.274	197	54	2	1	0	15
Gordon Meyer	.276	58	14	0	1	0	8
Jeff Ott	.195	41	8	4	0	0	3
Marcelino Pitti	.375	8	3	0	0	1	3
Dody Rather	.000	1	0	0	0	0	0
Darren Reed	.230	113	36	7	0	2	9
Tom Woleslagel	.264	178	47	10	1	0	20

*Darren Mandel set club record of 13 home runs, hitting four in his first four games. O-Yank BB and SO records incomplete for year.

PITCHING	W-L	ERA	IP	H	BB	SO
Ossie Canseco	1-6	3.53	43	44	21	40
Dennis Chastain	4-4	4.70	67	75	30	45
Bob Davidson	2-5	3.45	28	27	11	26
Fernando Davis	0-1	0.00	1	7	0	3
Mark De Latorre	0-3	7.13	35	44	17	32
Pat Dougherty	5-2	2.86	56	54	23	64
Dan Greenleaf	1-3	3.86	46	49	16	34
Matt Harrison	4-6	3.05	91	83	31	62
Al Leiter	3-2	3.63	57	52	26	48
Jeff Ott	0-0	3.86	2	6	3	0
Jeff Preis	3-4	2.48	65	50	27	41
Dody Rather	0-4	5.92	38	34	35	59
Ken Rebiejo	1-1	2.29	35	27	21	40
Tony Sarno	4-3	3.00	57	48	39	46
Jim Stinett	1-1	6.55	11	11	6	16

Saves: Davidson 10, De Latorre 3, Dougherty, Greenleaf one each.

1985

O-YANKS: NY-P LEAGUE
MANAGER BUCK SHOWALTER: WON 55 LOST 23

HITTING	AVG.	AB	H	2B	3B	HR	RBI	BB	SO
Art Calvert	.312	77	24	2	0	3	14	7	22
Todd Ezold	.216	88	19	5	0	0	12	9	28
Tom Giles	.220	118	26	6	2	1	19	14	28
Bob Green	.260	150	39	9	3	3	26	23	47
Ted Higgins	1.000	1	1	0	0	1	1	0	0
Greg Iavarone	.315	54	17	1	0	2	9	18	17
Harvey Lee	.249	169	42	7	1	3	22	25	41
C. Lombardozzi	.246	207	51	9	2	2	25	57	55
Jason Maas	.286	234	67	7	2	1	23	51	42
Matt Mainini	.260	196	51	7	1	3	23	52	46
Tod Marston	.202	109	22	2	2	2	15	15	28
Johnnie Pleicones	.222	144	32	2	1	0	16	11	17
Bob Sepanek	.275	211	58	13	5	5	43	23	37
Scott Shaw	.293	276	81	8	6	4	37	23	54
Ed Stanko	.162	37	6	1	0	0	3	13	14
Shane Turner	.246	228	56	7	3	0	26	35	44
Corey Viltz	.246	224	55	11	1	0	25	38	65

PITCHING	W-L	ERA	IP	H	BB	SO
Oscar Azocar	0-2	4.86	16	21	9	13
Rick Balabon	5-2	1.74	72	50	39	68
Chris Carroll	1-0	0.37	24	13	10	21
Mike Christopher	8-1	1.46	80	58	22	84
Bob Davidson	1-2	2.50	36	28	13	44
Pat Dougherty	6-2	1.96	73	53	30	62
Troy Evers	10-1	1.18	99	69	25	85
Todd Ezold	0-0	3.00	3	2	2	2
Scott Gay	0-1	1.80	5	3	1	6
Al Leiter	3-2	2.37	38	27	25	34
Garrett O'Connor	0-0	9.00	6	5	3	5
Ken Patterson	2-2	4.84	22	23	14	21
Dody Rather	8-0	0.31	58	22	16	88
Aris Tirado	2-3	1.99	45	20	15	68
Ricky Torres	1-2	4.50	16	17	10	13
Kevin Trudeau	8-3	1.64	71	42	24	75
Chuck Yaeger	0-0	0.00	1	0	0	2

Saves: Davidson 5; Carroll, Tirado 3 each; Gay, Trudeau, one each. Rather pitched no-hit, no-run game July 24; Troy Evers threw no-hit, no-run game in playoff against Geneva Sept. 5.

1986

O-Yanks: NY-P League

Manager Buck Showalter: Won 59 Lost 18*

(59-18 a league record)*

HITTING	AVG.	AB	H	2B	3B	HR	RBI	BB	SO
Don Arendas	.153	19	3	0	0	0	2	3	2
Dave Banks	.143	35	5	1	0	1	4	4	11
Tim Becker	.226	257	58	5	2	0	29	22	17
Luc Berube	.242	165	40	8	0	4	25	28	21
Lou Blanco	.161	62	10	2	0	0	6	7	11
Art Calvert	.254	142	36	7	4	3	23	14	26
Fred Carter	.385	65	25	5	1	1	16	2	12
Casey Close	.245	233	57	15	4	3	33	23	40
Kevin Crofton	.124	113	14	5	0	0	5	15	41
Hector Guzman	.179	67	12	1	0	1	5	3	21
Yanko Hauradou	.340	94	32	10	1	0	17	6	11
Chris Howard	.087	23	2	0	0	0	4	5	4
Ralph Kraus	.281	224	63	6	6	0	31	27	38
Jose Laboy	.211	166	35	7	1	2	19	11	35
Rob Lambert	.255	110	28	1	0	1	8	10	28
Jim Leyritz	.363	91	33	3	1	4	15	5	10
Kevin Maas	.356	101	36	10	0	0	18	7	9
Hal Morris	.378	127	48	9	2	3	30	18	15
John Ramos	.500	8	4	2	1	0	1	2	1
Andy Stankiewicz	.296	216	64	8	3	0	17	38	41
Turner Ward	.281	221	62	4	1	1	19	31	39

PITCHING	W-L	ERA	IP	H	BB	SO
Steve Adkins	8-2	1.69	80	59	36	74
Oscar Azocar	2-0	2.86	22	27	9	19
Rick Balabon	4-3	3.48	51	39	36	43
Chris Byrnes	4-1	1.80	45	39	13	29
Tim Layana	2-0	2.37	19	10	5	24
Mark Marris	1-1	1.71	21	10	13	14
Ken Patterson	9-3	1.35	100	66	45	102
Dana Ridenour	4-2	1.56	34	21	11	47
Mark Rose	0-0	0.56	16	9	7	17
Steve Rosenberg	0-0	1.00	9	4	2	10
Ron (Jerry) Rub	3-2	2.12	46	25	21	48
Todd Ryan	0-0	5.14	7	8	11	3
Rich Scheid	9-3	2.23	93	62	32	100
Bill Voeltz	4-1	1.77	35	21	7	24
Dean Wilkins	9-0	3.13	33	64	24	30

1987

O-Yanks: NY-P League
Manager Gary Allenson: Won 41 Lost 34

HITTING	AVG.	AB	H	2B	3B	HR	RBI	BB	SO
Luc Berube	.302	255	77	14	3	7	52	47	41
Tim Bishop	.205	190	39	4	0	3	23	15	33
Bobby Dickerson	.278	18	5	1	0	1	4	2	1
Ray Didder	.185	27	5	2	0	0	2	6	9
Rod Erhard	.250	104	26	6	2	2	19	18	36
Steve Erickson	.174	109	19	0	0	0	11	23	20
Rey Fernandz	.067	15	1	0	0	0	0	0	6
Tony Gwinn	.183	93	17	6	0	0	11	10	29
Freddie Hailey	.252	222	56	3	2	1	24	27	36
Lew Hill	.282	39	11	0	2	0	0	3	16
Robert Hunter	.200	5	1	0	0	0	0	2	2
Dean Kelly	.246	224	55	9	2	3	27	32	31
Mark Mitchell	.344	154	53	4	0	0	11	12	20
Julio Ramon	.267	15	4	2	0	0	0	2	3
Dan Roman	.291	206	60	8	3	0	32	17	35
Darrell Tingle	.209	239	50	10	1	0	22	29	64
Dave Turgeon	.281	178	50	6	1	1	23	13	23
Hector Vargas	.279	43	12	4	1	0	7	2	6
Tom Weeks	.307	238	73	13	2	6	57	41	32
Bernie Williams	.344	93	32	4	0	0	15	10	14
Gerald Williams	.365	115	42	6	2	2	29	16	18

PITCHING	W-L	ERA	IP	H	BB	SO
Chris Byrnes	1-0	5.59	29	38	11	23
Darrin Chapin	1-1	0.68	40	31	17	26
Royal Clayton	0-1	2.25	4	4	2	3
Bill DaCosta	1-3	5.60	27	37	16	12
Dave Eiland	4-0	1.84	29	20	3	16
Luis Faccio	1-1	2.93	40	39	14	41
Randy Foster	6-2	2.26	75	68	28	74
Sean Gargin	1-0	3.71	26	36	14	25
Todd Gedaminski	0-2	5.59	9	13	11	5
Doug Gogolewski	2-7	6.63	81	73	51	62
Rodney Imes	4-0	0.33	27	16	5	10
Jay Makemson	2-1	3.49	28	24	18	15
Mark Marris	2-1	3.79	38	25	29	40
Ed Martel	1-0	3.00	3	2	3	2
Anth. Morrison	4-6	3.57	85	60	57	79
Tom Popplewell	4-6	5.10	65	79	38	54
Bill Voeltz	6-3	3.70	58	62	18	44

Saves: Chapin 12; Marris 4; Makemson 2; Byrnes, Faccio, Foster, Imes one each.

1988

O-Yanks: NY-P League
Manager Gary Allenson: Won 48 Lost 28

HITTING	AVG.	AB	H	2B	3B	HR	RBI	BB	SO
Brad Ausmus	.250	4	1	0	0	0	0	0	2
Jason Bridges	.225	249	36	10	3	3	32	43	53
Bob DeJardin	.295	288	85	8	4	1	27	33	47
Rod Ehrhard	.243	243	59	14	7	3	29	42	72
Herb Erhardt	.203	226	54	12	0	3	30	24	46
Rey Fernandez	.278	198	55	9	4	3	41	8	44
Bob Hunter	.269	108	29	5	1	1	12	23	24
Pat Kelly	.329	280	92	11	6	2	34	16	45
Jay Knoblauh	.173	133	23	3	2	0	9	20	33
Jeff Livesey	.222	126	28	3	1	2	9	17	30
Mark Martin	.278	18	5	0	0	0	3	1	2
Skip Nelloms	.273	205	56	8	3	2	30	25	33
John Seeberger	.333	90	30	5	1	0	14	12	19
Miguel Torres	.262	189	49	7	1	0	24	22	26
Hector Vargas	.259	143	37	5	2	0	16	13	23
Bob Zeihen	.273	99	27	5	4	0	15	24	9
Mark Zeratsky	.077	13	1	0	0	0	1	0	4

PITCHING	W-L	ERA	IP	H	BB	SO
Todd Brill	4-0	2.72	36	39	10	27
Craig Brink	0-1	4.13	24	25	5	12
John Broxton	1-1	1.69	16	11	4	18
Jorge Candalaria	3-0	0.93	10	9	12	23
Art Canestro	2-1	2.43	40	32	16	44
Andy Cook	8-4	3.62	102	116	21	65
Mike Draper	2-1	0.84	10	10	3	16
Ken Greer	5-5	2.40	112	109	18	60
Jeff Hoffman	0-0	3.55	12	15	9	10
Jeff Johnson	6-1	2.98	87	67	39	91
Jay Makemson	4-1	3.38	45	44	27	40
Ed Martel	2-2	3.02	41	53	8	24
Jerry Nielsen	6-2	0.71	38	27	18	35
Bruce Prybylinski	1-2	1.17	23	11	7	27
Frank Seminara	4-7	4.37	78	86	33	60

Saves: Prybylinski 8; Broxton 4; Draper 3; Canestro, Seminara one each.

1989

O-YANKS: NY-P LEAGUE
MANAGER BRIAN BUTTERFIELD: WON 48 LOST 27

HITTING	AVG.	AB	H	2B	3B	HR	RBI	BB	SO
Brad Ausmus	.261	165	43	6	0	1	18	22	27
Rich Barnwell	.289	256	74	17	5	2	29	33	57
Russ Davis	.288	236	68	7	5	7	42	19	44
Todd Devereaux	.364	11	4	0	0	0	1	0	1
Enr. Hernandez	.223	94	21	4	0	2	7	15	21
Jose Herrera	.207	29	6	0	0	0	1	1	7
Lew Hill	.213	164	35	5	3	4	24	14	59
Dave Howell	.257	206	53	7	3	2	24	27	33
Orlando Miller	.291	213	62	5	2	1	5	6	37
Sherman Obando	.312	276	86	23	3	6	45	16	45
Paul Oster	.299	197	59	12	2	2	29	16	26
Joe Ross	.156	32	5	1	0	0	2	5	2
J.T. Snow	.292	274	80	18	2	8	51	29	35
D. Strickland	.353	17	6	0	0	0	7	15	3
Aaron VanScoyoc	.237	224	53	7	0	1	17	20	26
Jose Vasquez	.235	115	27	1	2	0	9	18	17

PITCHING	W-L	ERA	IP	H	BB	SO
John Brubaker	5-2	3.20	39	37	12	21
Art Canestro	7-2	1.05	77	51	20	61
Scott Chase	0-2	3.97	34	42	21	18
Mike Gardella	2-0	1.67	37	23	15	66
David Howell	0-0	9.00	2	3	1	1
Mark Hutton	6-2	4.07	66	70	24	62
Ken Juarbe	7-3	2.82	73	60	26	73
Todd Malone	3-5	6.45	51	78	29	49
Jim Moody	4-3	1.40	64	46	17	81
Joel Petlick	1-0	9.00	2	1	2	1
Ricky Rhodes	2-3	4.70	53	46	35	52
Frank Seminara	7-2	2.06	70	51	18	70
Larry Stanford	4-3	3.83	80	75	30	60

Saves: Gardella 19; Moody 4; Chase 2; Malone 1.

1990

O-Yanks: NY-P League
Manager Trey Hillman: Won 52 Lost 26

HITTING	AVG.	AB	H	2B	3B	HR	RBI	BB	SO
Juan Blackwell	.263	19	5	1	0	0	2	1	7
Jovino Carvajal	.287	171	49	3	1	0	18	7	37
Bob Deller	.243	169	41	7	1	1	22	42	33
Doug Demetre	.204	49	10	2	0	1	12	15	15
Robert Eenhoorn	.268	220	59	9	3	2	18	18	29
Luis Gallardo	.284	141	40	7	1	4	25	9	34
Mike Hankins	.271	166	45	4	0	0	18	30	27
Kevin Jordan	.333	276	92	13	7	4	54	23	31
Richard Lantrip	.183	229	42	5	4	3	33	48	81
Jalal Leach	.288	257	74	7	1	2	18	37	52
Adin Lohry	.197	137	27	1	2	0	14	20	27
Scott Romano	.242	178	43	8	2	1	19	30	38
Ricky Strickland	.245	200	49	5	1	2	18	39	41
Brian Turner	.247	227	56	13	1	0	24	36	49

PITCHING	W-L	ERA	IP	H	BB	SO
Matt Dunbar	1-4	4.15	30	32	24	24
Brian Faw	0-0	9.00	3	6	2	0
Ron Frazier	6-2	2.46	80	67	33	67
Mike Hankins	1-0	0.00	3	1	0	3
Darren Hodges	6-3	1.67	86	81	24	85
Todd Malone	3-0	1.95	27	15	14	37
Sam Militello	8-2	1.22	88	53	24	119
Pat Morphy	3-5	3.02	59	56	26	56
Kirt Ojala	7-2	2.16	79	75	43	87
Cesar Perez	2-2	3.14	28	21	17	32
Steve Perry	6-1	4.64	42	38	38	42
Rafael Quirico	6-3	3.21	87	69	39	69
Greg Siberz	3-2	3.32	40	27	22	48

Saves: Siberz 16; Perez 2; Perry 1

1991

O-YANKS: NY-P LEAGUE
MANAGER JACK GILLIS: WON 42 LOST 35

HITTING	AVG.	AB	H	2B	3B	HR	RBI	BB	SO
Andy Albrecht	.208	192	40	6	4	2	16	40	42
Steve Anderson	.351	114	40	3	3	1	19	19	21
Dennis Burbank	.111	9	1	0	0	0	0	2	6
Roger Burnett	.276	232	64	6	2	4	28	17	39
Bill Coleman	.143	7	1	0	0	1	2	1	3
Tim Flannelly	.272	268	73	19	3	6	46	19	41
Scott Garagozzo	.500	2	1	0	0	0	0	1	0
Mark Hubbard	.237	278	66	13	1	1	26	51	71
Bert Inman	1.000	1	1	0	0	0	0	0	0
Steve Livesey	.143	119	17	2	0	3	15	6	43
Jeff Motuzas	.286	7	2	0	0	0	0	0	2
Lyle Mouton	.309	272	84	11	2	7	41	31	38
Steve Phillips	.260	215	56	12	7	6	43	46	67
Jorge Posada	.235	217	51	5	5	4	33	51	51
Tate Seefried	.246	264	65	19	0	7	51	32	65
Shane Spencer	.245	53	13	2	1	0	3	10	9
Tom Wilson	.243	243	59	12	2	4	42	34	72

PITCHING	W-L	ERA	IP	H	BB	SO
Dennis Burbank	4-2	4.14	50	62	11	32
Bill Coleman	2-3	2.91	52	44	30	36
Andy Croghan	5-4	5.63	78	92	28	54
Whitney Floren	0-0	4.82	9	5	13	8
Keith Garagazzo	4-2	4.40	75	66	62	55
Scott Gully	3-3	4.53	43	46	14	38
Bert Inman	5-3	4.08	90	75	41	42
Frank Laviano	5-3	4.65	62	56	31	31
Joe Long	0-1	12.00	3	9	1	1
Steve Munda	1-1	3.90	38	32	15	14
Andy Pettitte	2-2	2.18	33	33	16	32
Sandi Santiago	2-1	3.38	10	9	5	5
Ben Short	2-4	3.79	35	41	11	44
Grant Sullivan	6-6	4.29	94	92	38	45
John Thibert	1-0	27.00	3	9	6	2

Saves: Short 14; Gully 4; Burbank, Coleman, Santiago one each.

1992

O-YANKS: NY-P LEAGUE
MANAGER JACK GILLIS: WON 37 LOST 38

HITTING	AVG.	AB	H	2B	3B	HR	RBI	BB	SO
A. Cumberbatch	.179	28	5	0	0	0	1	5	7
Glenn Delafield	.292	24	7	0	1	0	2	2	4
Nick Delvecchio	.274	241	66	12	1	12	35	35	76
Scott Epps	.167	36	6	1	0	0	1	6	6
Carlton Fleming	.182	11	2	0	0	0	2	1	2
Kraig Hawkins	.220	227	50	1	0	0	18	26	67
Robert Hinds	.288	264	76	8	2	0	11	34	51
Eric Knowles	.179	196	35	6	2	1	22	29	66
B. Kozeniewski	.267	285	76	18	3	0	36	18	45
Donnie Leshnock	.222	212	47	8	0	1	17	26	58
Robert D. Long	.255	153	39	9	1	0	15	24	31
Matt Luke	.247	271	67	11	7	2	34	19	32
Gordon Sanchez	.143	14	2	0	0	0	1	2	3
Derek Shelton	.382	68	26	40	0	13	1	3	15
Ray Suplee	.224	232	52	11	2	2	28	23	62
Jason Wuerch	.174	23	4	0	0	0	3	4	6
Ernest Yaroshuk	.238	185	44	8	0	2	24	21	18

PITCHING	W-L	ERA	IP	H	BB	SO
Jeff Antolick	4-2	2.13	71	60	31	68
Tibor Brown	0-0	3.75	12	8	15	10
Mike Buddie	1-4	3.88	67	69	34	87
Jeff Cinderich	0-1	9.82	3	6	1	3
Mike DeJean	0-0	0.44	20	12	3	20
Howard Ferguson	2-0	3.29	27	20	16	29
Shane Ferguson	0-0	5.40	3	6	1	4
Bert Inman	6-5	2.52	93	69	28	81
Ryan Karp	6-4	4.09	70	66	30	58
Bruce Pool	3-6	2.84	44	46	3	43
Sandi Santiago	1-2	5.18	24	31	13	27
John Sutherland	3-0	1.15	15	58	2	16
John Thibert	0-4	3.60	50	43	19	48
Bill Underwood	3-6	2.70	60	43	19	72
Kent Wallace	8-4	2.55	81	76	11	55

Saves: DeJean 16; Pool 2; Santiago, Thibert one each.

1993

O-YANKS: NY-P LEAGUE
MANAGER KEN DOMINGUEZ: WON 36 LOST 40

HITTING	AVG.	AB	H	2B	3B	HR	RBI	BB	SO
Steve Aldridge	.313	112	35	5	1	0	12	12	18
Kurt Bierek	.234	274	64	6	6	5	64	19	49
A. Cumberbatch	.289	142	41	3	6	0	18	33	28
Elston Hansen	.272	239	65	16	3	7	32	35	46
Ricky Ledee	.255	192	49	7	6	8	20	25	46
Brian Lewis	.208	72	15	2	1	1	4	11	17
Brian McLamb	.227	194	44	7	2	0	18	19	61
Silverio Navas	.270	189	51	5	2	0	15	14	30
Dave Renteria	.233	129	30	7	0	0	16	14	25
Ruben Rivera	.276	199	55	7	6	13	47	32	66
Mike Schmitz	.180	245	44	7	3	2	32	17	65
Steve Smith	.196	116	23	5	1	1	10	15	33
Jaime Torres	.260	104	27	6	0	1	8	9	9
Rob Trimble	.219	160	35	3	1	0	12	9	36
Jason Wuerch	.103	39	4	0	0	0	2	7	10
Ernie Yaroshuk	.300	100	30	3	5	2	18	12	13

PITCHING	W-L	ERA	IP	H	BB	SO
Shawn Alazaus	2-1	0.98	37	23	21	37
C.Cumberland	4-4	3.34	69	109	28	62
Al Drumheller	3-1	5.04	30	28	11	28
Mike Gordon	0-3	6.91	14	13	11	15
Ken Heberling	2-1	0.99	27	20	8	27
Mike Jerzembeck	8-4	2.68	77	70	26	76
B. Kozeniewski	2-1	4.86	37	45	17	21
Frank Langford	4-5	3.34	64	60	22	61
Donnie Leshnock	0-5	5.21	19	23	8	12
Jim Musselwhite	1-1	2.25	20	15	8	18
Jason Rathbun	2-0	2.67	30	27	15	26
Greg Resz	3-0	3.76	26	18	16	16
Scott Standish	2-3	4.35	49	58	22	45
Jim Thomforde	2-7	5.14	75	73	34	64
Joe Wharton	0-1	1.45	19	13	5	30
Clint Whitworth	1-2	7.07	36	48	17	20

Saves: Resz 9; Alazaus 6; Wharton 4; Kozeniewski, Standish one each.

1994

O-YANKS: NY-P LEAGUE
MANAGER KEN DOMINGUEZ: WON 30 LOST 45

HITTING	AVG.	AB	H	2B	3B	HR	RBI	BB	SO
Carlos Yedo	.336	122	41	11	2	4	22	17	34
Ryan Beeney	.301	103	31	5	1	1	7	12	19
Mike Mitchell	.298	104	31	7	0	2	12	10	9
Derek Dukart	.296	233	69	8	0	0	33	19	36
F. Seguignol	.290	266	77	14	9	2	32	16	61
Sloan Smith	.246	138	34	5	5	0	17	25	41
Cody Samuel	.228	101	23	4	0	1	17	7	20
Derek Shumpert	.226	239	54	6	1	0	22	26	86
Brian Buchanan	.223	175	39	8	2	4	26	24	53
Marcus Gipner	.213	136	29	4	1	0	11	22	32
Brian McLamb	.183	262	48	10	2	1	20	12	59
Julio Garcia	.136	22	3	0	0	0	1	8	7
Tray Nelson	.125	40	5	1	0	0	2	7	17
Jason Troilo	.125	16	2	1	0	0	1	4	3

PITCHING	W-L	ERA	IP	H	BB	SO
Casey Mittauer	3-2	1.63	39	34	13	31
Jeremy Benson	0-1	1.97	32	23	13	36
Matt Drews	7-6	2.10	90	76	19	69
Jason Jarvis	4-2	2.38	64	39	17	78
Dave Meyer	3-4	2.90	50	45	17	30
Ray Ricken	2-3	3.58	50	45	17	55
Chris Corn	1-1	3.73	50	49	19	49
Steve Shoemaker	3-5	4.30	59	63	27	45
Berry	1-2	4.56	24	22	7	27
Rafael Madina	3-7	4.66	73	67	35	58
Shelby	1-3	4.79	26	35	7	14
Brown	2-1	5.14	21	20	12	21
Dwayne Edgar	0-3	10.53	14	21	20	10

Saves: Mittauer 4; Benson 3; Jarvis, Brown 2 each; Corn, Berry, Edgar one each.

Index

BOB

Bob Whittemore has covered sports in Central New York for more than a half century. He has been involved with the Oneonta Yankees since the beginning, spending 22 of those years as official scorer, at one point scoring 448 consecutive games.

Whittemore broke into sportswriting with the *Utica Daily Press* in 1938 covering his own Ilion High School football team which, he recalls, failed to score a point the entire season.

Since then, he has covered the full spectrum of scholastic and collegiate sports for The *Daily Star* in Oneonta, the *Binghamton Press*, WENE radio in Endicott, WDOS in Oneonta, WLFH in Little Falls, WBNG TV in Binghamton and OKTV, local cable in Oneonta.

Whittemore spent several years on the news side, having served as editor of the old *Endicott Daily Bulletin*, The *Norwich Evening Sun* and the *Oswego Palladium-Times.*

He has earned several awards for writing and for layout and was honored by the Oneonta Yankees in 1973 for his contribution to the club. He also has been honored by Oneonta High School, Hartwick College and Oneonta State University for his coverage of their athletic teams.

He twice left the news and sports fields to work in the New York State Legislature as a legislative assistant to Senator Edwyn E. Mason and later as executive assistant to Assemblyman Ray T. Chesbro of Oswego.

Whittemore and his wife Betty are the parents of two boys and two girls, grandparents to six and great-grandparents to one.

Baseball Town is Whittemore's second book. His first book, *All We Had Was Us*, was the story of a local amateur baseball team. The sellout book was published in 1992.

He has always worked closely with managers and players of the Oneonta Yankees, becoming a personal friend of many. Current New York Yankee Manager Buck Showalter says, "I'm pleased to know Bob as a close friend and as a man who loves baseball as I do. I also recall him as a writer and broadcaster who got his quotes right."